Praise for Griffith Review

'*Griffith Review* continues as the lodestar for what we can expect in excellent Australian writing.'

Melissa Lucashenko, award-winning author

'In just over two decades, *Griffith Review* has mounted guard over Australian letters in a way that no other publication – established or new – has been able to replicate. In a world where critics and commentators too often talk across each other, its focused, topic-based approach has cleared a space for genuine engagement, recalling us to the (retreating) ideal of a living intellectual culture.' Richard King, writer and critic

'*Griffith Review* is the sound of Australian democracy and culture thinking out loud.' Geordie Williamson, *The Australian*

'*Griffith Review* is my quarterly literary feast. I have discovered many new favourite writers and ideas between its covers.'

Sharlene Allsopp, author

'[*Griffith Review*] traverses genre and form, culture and continent… in what is a vibrant and impressive cross-section of modern Australian writing.' *Good Reading*

'…informative, thought-provoking and well-crafted.'

The Saturday Paper

'It turned out that the only place we could write the truth that was in our hearts was in literary journals like *Griffith Review*, that everywhere else, we were stifled into silence – but here a poem, an essay, a story that said what was painful to admit.' Yumna Kassab, author

'This quarterly magazine is a reminder of the breadth and talent of Australian writers. Verdict: literary treat.' *Herald Sun*

'This is commentary of a high order. The prose is unfailingly polished; the knowledge and expertise of the writers impressive.'

Roy Williams, *Sydney Morning Herald*

SIR SAMUEL GRIFFITH was one of Australia's notable early achievers. He occupied positions of authority during some of the most momentous events in the history of Queensland: the frontier wars, the 'blackbirding' trade of people from Melanesia, the shearers' strike and Federation. At times he challenged power, at others he used it – he was a complex yet pragmatic man of words, a man of his times. Not all his decisions have stood the test of time. Sir Samuel was twice the premier of Queensland, its chief justice and author of its criminal code, remembered most for his pivotal role in drafting the Constitution adopted at Federation, and as the new nation's first chief justice.

Griffith died in 1920 and is now most likely to be remembered by his namesakes: an electorate, a society, a suburb and a university. In 1971, ninety-six years after he first proposed establishing a university in Brisbane, Griffith University, the city's second, was created. Griffith's commitment to public debate and ideas, his delight in words and art, and his attachment to active citizenship are recognised by this publication that bears his name.

Like Sir Samuel Griffith, *Griffith Review* is iconoclastic and non-partisan, with a sceptical eye and a pragmatically reforming heart. Always ready to debate ideas. Personal, political and unpredictable, it informs and provokes Australia's best conversations.

During Griffith's lifetime, and while he was in positions of power, the First Nations of Queensland resisted invasion. Sir Samuel made it possible for some Aboriginal people to testify in court when charges were brought against settlers. The First Australians survived, but at a terrible cost. In the twenty-first century, the need for a thorough and lasting settlement is urgent, one that respects and honours the rights, history and culture of the descendants of those who were dispossessed.

Griffith Review staff acknowledge and pay particular respect to the traditional custodians of the lands on which their office is located, the Jagera and Turrbal people in South-East Queensland.

GriffithReview85

Status Anxiety

Edited by Carody Culver

GriffithReview85

INTRODUCTION

NON-FICTION

IN CONVERSATION

FICTION

POETRY

PICTURE GALLERY

Pierre Châtel-Innocenti
Work from ReMix 2021
Digital media
Courtesy of the artist

Griffith Review gratefully acknowledges the support and generosity of our founding patron, the late Margaret Mittelheuser AM and the ongoing support of Dr Cathryn Mittelheuser AM.

GriffithReview85 2024
Griffith Review is published four times a year by Griffith University.

Publisher	Scott Harrison
Editor	Carody Culver
General Manager	Katie Woods
Managing Editor	John Tague
Senior Editor	Margot Lloyd
Business Co-ordinator	Esha Buch
Typesetting	Midland Typesetters
Printing	Ligare Book Printers
Distribution	NewSouth Books/ADS

ISBNs
Book: 978-1-922212-98-6
PDF: 978-1-922212-99-3
Epub: 978-1-923213-00-5

ISSN 1448-2924

GRIFFITH REVIEW
South Bank Campus, Griffith University
PO Box 3370, South Brisbane QLD 4101 Australia
Ph +617 3735 3071 Fax +617 3735 3272
griffithreview@griffith.edu.au griffithreview.com

SUBSCRIPTIONS: See griffithreview.com

FEEDBACK AND COMMENT griffithreview@griffith.edu.au

INTRODUCTION

Joker in the pack

Playing the status game

Carody Culver

THINKING ABOUT STATUS reminds me of that faintly threatening riddle about the future: *I am always in front of you, but you will never see me.* Status itself is a little like a riddle: a code to be cracked, a hand in which you can't see all the cards. Unless you're Batman, however, the stakes for solving riddles tend to be comfortingly low, whereas the pressures of deciphering status can occupy a far more consequential role in our lives (it's all fun and games until somebody loses their cultural capital). It's also easiest to define status according to what it isn't: gender, race, class, job, accent or postcode, although all these elements circulate in its DNA.

This shapeshifting quality is surely why status today increasingly seems the wrong way around, or like the punchline to a bad joke: the well-off dress down (but at high prices), the political right is winning the working-class vote, the left is charged with intellectual and cultural elitism, buying a one-bedroom flat is a sign of intergenerational wealth, and having zero free time is now a curious way to win prestige – the rich and important are idle no more. Then there are the insidious ways in which status, like an invisible yet insistent hand at the small of your back, pushes you into or away from particular social and professional circles where seemingly innocent questions – about what you do, where you're *really* from and where you went to school – cast looming shadow puppets of double meaning.

Status isn't always negative, of course. Accrue the right kind, and its gifts can be manifold. Would it be any easier to parse if we could say the quiet parts out loud – if we could just ask and answer the question so memorably put by the Spice Girls back in 1996: *who do you think you are?*

THIS EDITION OF *Griffith Review* is unlikely to resolve your status anxiety, if you're so afflicted. But its essays, short fiction, conversations, poems and visual art seek to make status and its attendant frustrations, iniquities and (occasional) pleasures a little more visible. It surveys the ways in which status plays out socially, environmentally and institutionally: the end of mass politics (and what might come next), the inversion of class markers, the existential and practical consequences of climate inaction, the problems plaguing the tertiary sector, the medical industry's specialisation conundrum, and what Australia's short-lived obsession with a nineteenth-century bush poet can tell us about today's literary infrastructure (a lot). It also gets personal, laying bare the emotional tripwires of family relationships, the anxieties of identity markers, and what it really feels like to have someone write a hatchet-job review of your first novel (not great).

Thank you, once again, to the Copyright Agency Cultural Fund for their generous support of *Griffith Review*'s Emerging Voices competition. We're thrilled to be publishing Alex Cothren's 'The Juansons', one of the winning 2023 stories, in *Status Anxiety*. Thanks also to Arts Queensland for their generous support of two essays in this edition, Bebe Oliver's 'Birthmarks' and Beau Windon's 'Drowning in a puddle', through the Queensland Arts Showcase Program.

What fresh, and freshly confounding, guises will status adopt in the coming years? It's anyone's guess – we can't see the future, even though it's always in front of us. I suspect the best we can hope for is that we'll still be here; that some tech bro in designer leisurewear won't have decided to colonise Mars en route to hacking his own immortality; and that we'll have discovered some kinder, less confusing ways to figure out where we fit in all the actual and imagined hierarchies that populate our lives.

Those are my wishes, anyway. And I like to think they matter. Because, well…don't you know who I am?

June 2024

NON-FICTION

Into the void

Democracy and the death of mass politics

Shahar Hameiri

THERE REALLY SHOULD be a German word for it – maybe there is: when you know something should shock you, but it just doesn't anymore. You've become desensitised. In politics, this feeling has become increasingly familiar. Over the past few years, all that was thought solid has melted into air – hot air in most cases.

The first sign of serious political climate change arrived in June 2016 when a majority of Britons voted for Brexit, giving the proverbial two-fingered salute to almost the entire British political class. This was a huge surprise from which British politics is arguably yet to recover. But when later that year in the US presidential elections Donald Trump, a boorish, self-aggrandising businessman with a penchant for lying, defeated Hillary Clinton, doyenne of the American political establishment, the shockwave that rippled through newsrooms and political-science departments could have triggered seismometers. Hardly anyone predicted the outcome, but there it was. Decades of political convention were upended.

Voters in Western liberal democracies had become used to seeing elections as akin to a choice between two brands of skimmed milk on the supermarket shelf. The labels looked a bit different, but the contents were pretty much the same and not very tasty. It seemed that many American voters wanted something very different, perhaps even to burn the supermarket down.

A maelstrom of commentary and soul-searching followed Trump's surprise win. Outside the US, in other Western liberal democracies, most pundits and political experts reacted with horror and disbelief, but there was also a palpable sense of smugness. *This couldn't happen here*, they thought. His success must have had something to do with flaws peculiar to the American character and political system. America was losing its mind, but politics as we know it would continue elsewhere. Germany, under the leadership of Angela Merkel, was widely proclaimed the new 'leader of the free world', at least until the US sorted itself out.

Fast forward to the present, and it is clear the malaise – and the tilt to hard-right parties – is not confined to the US, or indeed to Trump. At the time of writing, most polls put support for Germany's Alternative für Deutschland in second place overall, ahead of the ruling Social Democrats. In France, Marine Le Pen looks within striking distance of the presidency. Her party, National Rally, is also polling better than President Macron's Renaissance party. In the Netherlands, Geert Wilders' Party for Freedom received the biggest share of the vote in the 2023 parliamentary elections. In Spain, Vox is the third-biggest political party. In Portugal, Chega, established in 2019, won nearly a fifth of the votes and quadrupled its seats in the 2024 legislative election. In Italy, Giorgia Meloni, whose party descended from the post-fascist National Alliance, has been prime minister since 2022. Then there's the democratic backsliding afflicting many of Eastern and Central Europe's newer, post-communist democracies such as Hungary, Slovakia and Poland. Brexit Britain looks like an island of political stability by comparison, with its enduring two-party duopoly and a centrist from central casting, Keir Starmer, favoured to become prime minister after this year's election.

Trump, meanwhile, is still here. He refused to recognise the outcome of the 2020 presidential election, encouraged supporters to storm the Capitol in January 2021 and is facing numerous criminal charges. And yet if Trump triumphs over President Joe Biden in November 2024, few will be truly shocked. Even if they feel like they should be.

While Australia has not yet succumbed to these extremes, many of us are uncomfortably aware of what's unfolding overseas. The far right in its various guises has become a core feature of politics in many Western liberal democracies and it seems to be here to stay. Politicians like Wilders or Le Pen have been around for years, usually in the political wilderness. Anti-immigration and nativist sentiments are nothing new. So why are these ideas, and the politicians espousing them, finding so much purchase now?

One oft-heard explanation points to the impact of a polarised public sphere due to the rise of the internet and social media. Designed to keep people engaged, the algorithms used by social media platforms and popular search engines push users further and further into an angry echo chamber where more extreme versions of their preferred ideas are readily available. This is surely part of the story, but it is confusing the symptom for the disease. Amplifying the impact of online polarisation is the disintegration of society in most Western liberal democracies into an amorphous, disorganised amalgam of atomised individuals whose sole connection to politics is a periodic invitation to cast a vote. Our democratic institutions and traditions took their current form in the era of mass politics, in which major political parties were rooted in, and represented the interests of, mass movements in society. As mass politics slowly withered, democracies became increasingly dysfunctional.

MASS POLITICS WAS a product of the two great revolutions of the 'long nineteenth century' from 1789 to 1914 that, according to the British historian Eric Hobsbawm, gave us the modern world: the French Revolution, from whence came our conception of nationalism and popular sovereignty, and the Industrial Revolution, which catalysed the expansion of capitalism. The former established the idea that political institutions should represent the wishes of the whole nation, not only the sovereign or a small number of aristocrats. The latter, meanwhile, created the material conditions for the emergence of new classes and class consciousness that ultimately contributed to democratising politics. Mass movements on the left, which emerged during the nineteenth century in the new heartlands of industrial capitalism in the North Atlantic, fought to expand political and socio-economic rights and, at a deeper level, make workers history's subjects, not just its objects. By organising and acting collectively, otherwise disempowered individuals could articulate and pursue their interests against more powerful forces.

The process of democratisation was far from straightforward, however. Workers and their social and political movements faced frequent repression as old and new elites battled to uphold more exclusive political systems. After the Russian Revolution of 1917, which led to the establishment of the world's first socialist regime, and against the backdrop of mass unemployment due to the Great Depression, some governments sought a political compromise with workers to prevent further radicalisation. President Roosevelt's New Deal was a notable example, harnessing government spending to alleviate the worst of the economic crisis, though not without stiff resistance in Congress. At the more extreme end, fascist regimes came to power in Italy and Germany on the back of support from the petite and not-so-petite bourgeoisie to curtail the organised left's growing power by force.

After the war, a compromise between the owners of capital and workers spread throughout the West, encouraged by the society-wide mobilisation of World War II and by efforts to prevent the emergence of socialist regimes in the context of the expanding Cold War. By the mid-twentieth century, the political systems of most liberal democracies consolidated around the core social cleavage of industrial society – a party representing labour on the centre left and a party representing capital and the middle class on the centre right. Those parties were typically rooted in society's mass movements and drew their legitimacy from their claim to represent their collective interests in government. The state was also reconfigured to uphold the postwar social compact, whereby organised labour agreed to refrain from pursuing radical alternatives to capitalism, while capital agreed to share the gains more widely with workers. New capacities and institutions were created in Western liberal democracies, significantly expanding the state's reach and ambition: Keynesian macro-economic management tools designed to maintain full employment; extensive health, education and social-welfare systems to provide a strong safety net; and corporatist institutions, such as wage-arbitration mechanisms, that allowed for the direct involvement of organised societal interests in policymaking.

The period from 1945 to 1975 is often called the 'golden age' of capitalism. The French call it 'Les Trente Glorieuses' – the glorious thirty. Across the West, this was, overall, a time of largely uninterrupted rapid economic growth and vast productivity gains. Happily, the benefits of economic development were shared relatively equitably, creating the affluent consumer societies most of us were born into.

It wasn't to last. In the 1970s, economic crisis hit Western liberal democracies, combining high inflation with economic stagnation and rising unemployment – captured by the ugly neologism 'stagflation'. Industrial conflict returned with a vengeance as powerful unions fought for higher wages to match rising prices and to prevent mass lay-offs. An economic crisis thus turned into a social and political crisis too.

What caused this? Across the spectrum, political leaders believed that the problem was a state that was too responsive to demands from society. This sentiment was pithily summarised in a high-profile report released in 1975 by the Trilateral Commission, a non-governmental organisation convened by financier David Rockefeller to encourage dialogue among elites from North America, Europe and Japan. The authors of the report – titled *The Crisis of Democracy* – complained:

> The democratic idea that government should be responsive to the people creates the expectation that government should meet the needs and correct the evils affecting particular groups in society… it becomes difficult if not impossible for democratic governments to curtail spending, increase taxes, and control prices and wages.

This was a major turning point. For decades after the end of World War II, governments in Western liberal democracies were in the business of promising progress and a better life to their societies. Now, to paraphrase American political scientist Fritz Bartel, politics became about breaking promises. If societies had come to possess unrealistic expectations of government and the capitalist economy, one solution was to tell people to expect less. This is what is often referred to as 'neoliberalism', an ideology that extolls the virtues of the mythical free market. The tune had suddenly changed. States had to get out of the way and stop 'distorting' markets with their redistributive policies. Big spending by governments was 'crowding out' the nimble and more efficient private sector. Workers organising to demand better pay and conditions were 'rent-seekers', who were thereby making everybody else poorer. Ordinary people could no longer look to the government to help them but had to learn to look after themselves in the marketplace. The new orthodoxy was summed up in US President Ronald Reagan's quip that the scariest nine words in the English language were 'I'm from the government and I'm here to help.'

NEOLIBERAL IDEOLOGY NOTWITHSTANDING, in reality states rarely shrank. In fact, the share of public spending to GDP for most member states of the Organisation for Economic Co-operation and Development (OECD) – the rich countries' club – has either grown or remained static since the 1980s. Rather, the response to the crisis had a second, and arguably more important, facet: restructuring the state to make it less democratically responsive.

In postwar Western democracies, governments sat atop hierarchical command-and-control structures that gave them enormous power to get things done. The downside, however, was that with great power came great responsibility, at least in the eyes of voters. Facing economic crisis and social and political upheaval, governments of both centre right and centre left set about disavowing their responsibility for addressing society's problems by dismantling the hierarchical structures that gave them the power to act directly upon these problems.

From the 1980s, important areas of policymaking and implementation were gradually handed over to quasi-autonomous, unelected public and private bodies. To give one notable example, central banks in most Western liberal democracies were made independent of government and given control over monetary policy. Whereas governments earlier used monetary-policy tools, such as setting interest rates, to strike a balance between different objectives, like price stability and full employment, independent central banks focused on defeating inflation regardless of how this affected workers or particular industrial sectors. And because elected governments were no longer in charge of monetary policy, there was practically nothing those who were affected negatively by central-bank decisions could do. Central banks' monthly pronouncements on interest rates became almost like the weather – one could try to forecast them, prepare for various possible outcomes or react after the fact, but that was about it.

Having left broad swathes of public policy beyond its remit, government retreated to a regulatory role, co-ordinating, 'steering', coaxing and incentivising a growing multitude of agencies no longer under its direct control. Political leaders could happily claim plausible deniability over policy choices and their outcomes, but this came at a steep cost: the hollowing out of democracy. As many important policy areas were safely locked away in technocratic hands, political competition in most Western liberal democracies converged on a very narrow policy spectrum. With little of substance to fight over, major political parties churned out identikit politicians who spouted endless spin and promoted carbon-copy policies, often presenting minor differences from their rivals as monumentally important. Political participation duly collapsed. Voting rates plummeted in most Western liberal democracies (aside from countries such as Australia, where voting is compulsory). Why vote if nothing much changes whatever the result? Accordingly, trust in democratic institutions plunged.

Political parties themselves also de-democratised, turning their backs on the rank and file, who therefore stopped turning up to branch meetings, causing party membership to decline. The mass party of yore gave way to what the late political scientist Peter Mair called the 'cartel party'. Whereas in the era of mass politics parties in Western liberal democracies were sustained by their members and represented the interests of distinct societal groups, the cartel party has inverted this logic. Political parties are now sustained by the state and therefore represent the state's interests in society. Meanwhile, the mass movements that earlier connected ordinary people to politics withered away as their capacity to advance collective interests faded, creating a void, as Mair described it, between those who govern and those being governed.

The singular achievement of mass politics was allowing otherwise powerless individuals a greater say in how society was ruled. It gave ordinary people the kind of status that hitherto they could hardly imagine. Its withering away, therefore, has allowed those in society whose status has always been higher to assert their interests more fully. Business and the wealthy are no longer forced to make big compromises to accommodate the interests of those below them in the social pecking order. For example, trade and financial liberalisation policies have permitted many companies to shift production, and even some services, offshore to capitalise on lower labour costs, weakening unions' bargaining power considerably. Many lower paid workers have been pushed into insecure, low-paid jobs with poor conditions, a transformation justified by political and economic elites as contributing to greater economic 'efficiency' and labour market 'flexibility'. Owners thus pocket a greater share of the economic pie, while workers' incomes often stagnate or even decline in real terms, causing wealth inequality to rise steeply, as documented by economists such as Thomas Piketty and Branko Milanović. Lower paid workers' grievances can find limited political expression, as traditional labour parties have turned to business-friendly Third Way agendas and reduced unions' influence over policy. Many working-class voters no longer trust 'their' party, refusing to give their support even when well-meaning politicians, such as UK Labour's Jeremy Corbyn, attempt to revive old-school social-democratic politics that are in their interests.

And yet, for a while, democracies seemed to do just fine. Sure, social gaps were growing and trust was eroding, but there were no riots on the streets. Instead, most people turned their backs on politics and retreated into their domestic bubble. This was made possible by the widening availability of credit, mainly as home loans and credit cards, which helped offset declining real wages. In his sobering 2014 book, German political economist Wolfgang Streeck called this 'buying time'. Consumer societies in the West could uphold relatively high living standards by borrowing lots of money. Their governments were also borrowing big to sustain public functions, even as the burden of tax on corporations and the rich was declining. Public and private debt rates have therefore grown exponentially, while the rich have become even richer on interest payments and asset price appreciation. But as Streeck argues, the crisis of democratic capitalism could only be delayed, not avoided. The day of reckoning came when global financial markets seized in September 2008, kicking off the global financial crisis. Governments and central banks used trillions to bail out the financial system, while the costs were borne by society at large.

This outcome should not surprise us given the decay of the movements and institutions that in an earlier era could have advanced an alternative response. In the US, anger erupted on both left (Occupy Wall Street) and right (the Tea Party), as Wall Street quickly thrived again, while Main Street languished. In Europe, the strictures of the Eurozone and fiscal conservatism, especially in Germany, made things even worse. In quick succession, the financial crisis became a sovereign debt crisis, which was then followed by painful budget austerity that caused widespread social harm and resentment.

In the wake of these crises, apathy, disappointment and distrust in public institutions calcified into a fury that would not subside. While politics-as-usual endured in the first half of the 2010s, manifesting in leaders such as Barack Obama, Angela Merkel and David Cameron, the ructions caused by the GFC intensified into an earthquake by the decade's second half. The currents that brought politicians such as Trump to power hence run deep. We are not witnessing a mere blip followed by a return to mean.

However, as Philip Cunliffe, George Hoare, Lee Jones and Peter Ramsay argue in their insightful book on Brexit, *Taking Control* (2023), while populists thrive on the anger and distrust that permeate our atomised society, they are creatures of the void and therefore offer no genuine solutions to the problems that make them seem attractive to voters. The absence of mass movements mediating between individuals and governments provides the space for them to insert themselves as a voice for an amorphous 'people' against the corrupt 'elites'. Not for them the painstaking work of establishing durable organisations and mass parties. Under these circumstances, whether Western liberal democracies can survive is an open question.

WHERE DOES AUSTRALIA feature in this story? In our 2023 book, *The Locked-up Country*, which examines Australia's response to the COVID-19 pandemic, Tom Chodor and I argue that Australia has travelled a very similar path to other Western liberal democracies since the 1970s. Having created a regulatory state, Australian leaders struggled to revive capacities from scratch or implement complex public policies during the pandemic crisis. Therefore, they resorted repeatedly to lockdowns and border closures, blunt measures with harmful social costs and diminishing returns.

And yet, Australia seems immune to many of the ills now plaguing other Western liberal democracies. Its two main parties continue to rotate in and out of office. The Labor government has dared to restore some of the industrial-relations rights workers earlier lost, but is otherwise pursuing a familiar, centrist Third Way agenda. While the Liberal Party has shifted rightwards, especially under the leadership of Peter Dutton, it is nothing like the increasingly unhinged Republican Party. Its Trump-lite antics are also failing to cut through. The only Liberal government in Australia at the time of writing is in Tasmania.

Why does Australia seem to stand apart from most other Western liberal democracies? Tom Chodor and I grappled with this question on the global-politics podcast *Aufhebunga Bunga*. The simplest explanation is that Australia's combination of compulsory and preferential voting privileges the major parties. Indeed, Labor now holds a majority in the lower house despite winning only 32.6 per cent of the primary vote at the last federal election. This answer is unsatisfactory, however. True, the major parties' share of the vote has declined over the years, but no populist insurgents appear to be waiting in the wings. Pauline Hanson's One Nation has been around for decades without making substantial gains. Clive Palmer tried to become Australia's own Trump but won fewer votes than the Legalise Cannabis Party at the 2022 federal election, despite outspending all the other parties combined on political advertising. The most successful newcomers in Australian politics are the so-called Teals, who embody the polar opposite of Trumpist populism. Efforts to import to Australia US-style 'culture wars' around issues such as trans rights, for example, have so far remained a niche pursuit for the small audience of Sky News' *After Dark*.

That so many Western liberal democracies are in a state of profound crisis today suggests, however, that Australian complacency would be foolhardy. Ever the lucky country, Australia has managed to sustain exceptionally high levels of economic growth since the early 1990s on the back of strong demand from Asia for its exports. For example, China's economic-stimulus program, which focused on infrastructure construction, allowed Australia to dodge the GFC and the deep recession that followed. Economic growth has been further buoyed by high rates of immigration creating demand for services, retail and housing; financial liberalisation providing abundant credit to households; and high rates of home ownership increasing household wealth as housing prices have rapidly appreciated.

Australia has also been assisted by its relatively high wages combined with low taxation and social spending (by OECD standards at least), a legacy of its late colonial and post-Federation development model. High wages have helped spread the benefits from economic growth more widely without requiring significant redistribution through the tax system. Australia has thus largely avoided both middle-class resentment for paying high taxes seen to support the undeserving poor, often framed in racial or ethnic terms, and working-class resentment of migrants supposedly taking away locals' jobs, sentiments that drive support for nativists and right-wing populists in other countries.

The problem, however, is that many of Australia's stabilisers are unravelling. The Chinese economy is slowing, amid rising geopolitical tensions that have soured relations between the two countries, hampering growth prospects. While wages are high by world standards, they have remained largely stagnant for a decade and have been battered by rising inflation and interest rates, creating a slow-burning cost-of-living crisis. Rising asset prices were once a boon for the Australian economy, but now high mortgage repayments are stifling consumption, while many are permanently locked out of the housing market. Since the assumption of widespread home ownership underpins Australia's limited welfare state, a more exclusive housing market has a serious impact on social inequality. These circumstances suggest that although Australia's Trump or Le Pen is not yet visible, it shouldn't come as a shock if one emerges in the coming years.

The big question is whether we in Australia have become so desensitised to the political problems afflicting other liberal democracies to not even bother trying to correct our own course before it is too late. The society of the past, which gave us the democratic institutions we used to take for granted, no longer exists and cannot simply be resurrected. This should not dissuade us, however, from fighting to fill the void and rebuild the ties linking society and the state.

May 2024

Shahar Hameiri is Professor of International Politics and Australian Research Council Future Fellow in the School of Political Science and International Studies, University of Queensland. He is co-author, most recently, of *The Locked-Up Country: Learning the Lessons from Australia's COVID-19 Response* (UQP, 2023).

NON-FICTION

Class acts

The changing art of social performance

Diana Reid

THIS PAST YEAR, I saw perhaps the subtlest skewering of contemporary class performance that I've ever witnessed. Oddly, it was buried within an otherwise unsubtle tale. *Saltburn*, by writer/director Emerald Fennell, takes explicit delight in ogling at the richest of the rich. It's an almost immorally beautiful film, which an AI might have plotted had it been given the prompt, 'Rewrite the first third of *Brideshead Revisited* with Tom Ripley as the protagonist.'

The film follows Oliver, who aspires to befriend and eventually *become* Felix, the most aristocratic classmate in their year at Oxford. And we can understand why. Oliver's obsession with Felix's privilege mirrors the audience's: Felix is impossibly charismatic (he is portrayed by Australian heart-throb Jacob Elordi), and his family home, where Oliver stays for the summer, is achingly grand. All this desire and longing turns to desperation, however, when Felix suddenly decides to do something nice for poor Oliver. And Oliver *is* poor. Or at least, that's what he's led Felix to believe by providing a backstory that includes just enough detail (a dead father) and just enough sordid allusion (addiction, housing estates and a fractured relationship with his mother) to hint at a life of abuse and deprivation.

Felix drives Oliver to his mother's house in the hope of staging a reconciliation. It's a well-meaning act – if not also immature and misguided – which ends the boys' friendship, because it reveals that Oliver has lied to Felix.

The dead father is alive and very nice, and the abusive mother has made her beloved prodigal his favourite spaghetti to celebrate his return.

I said before that Oliver is a modern Tom Ripley, the sociopathic protagonist in Patricia Highsmith's crime novels. Ripley ascends the social ladder in the 1960s by pretending to be someone he's not and killing anyone who threatens to expose his lies. Oliver does the same. Except, seventy years on, the lies you need to tell have changed. In fact, they have inverted. Where Ripley donned a Princeton jacket and styled himself as wealthy, Oliver plays poor.

How many times, in fiction and in life, has a character lied about their wealth to increase their social status? We've seen every iteration, from the delusional tragic (Blanche DuBois) to the ruthless con artist (Anna Delvey) to the innocent opportunist (Cinderella). But I still can't think of a fake-it-till-you-make-it story that echoes Oliver's. Let alone one so deeply culturally disseminated that it holds the status of a fairytale. In the past, people might have exaggerated their suffering for pity. But in the twenty-first century, here is a character – a conniving schemer – downplaying his fortunes for social *ascension*.

As unique as it is to see such an arc in fiction, Ollie was nonetheless familiar to me. It seemed pop culture had finally caught up with a very real phenomenon: disavowing privilege to consolidate or even increase it. And (spoiler alert!) in art, as in life, it's a ploy that pays off.

IN ANY SOCIETY that aspires to a degree of egalitarianism – that is, anywhere that social mobility is, at least theoretically, possible – social status is both performed and asserted. In rigid hierarchies, by contrast, status functions as birthright: it's articulated by your name; it runs in your veins; it's an immutable fact of your existence.

Under capitalism, perhaps the most conventional mode of asserting status is through the performance of wealth. In the early twentieth century, German sociologist Max Weber identified that Northern European societies had conflated an individual's personal worth with their financial value. This represented the amalgam of two distinct theories: one moral, the other economic. The first was the Protestant idealisation of work ethic – the idea that to work hard was to exhibit virtue. The second was what historian Eli Cook, author of *The Pricing of Progress: Economic Indicators and the Capitalization of American Life*, calls 'the lessons of mainstream neoclassical economics, which suggested, through [the economist] John Bates Clark's theory of marginal productivity, that everyone earns what they in fact produced'. If you accept that what someone has earnt correlates to how hard they worked, it's only logical that a society that prizes work would also afford respect and status to those who have managed to amass wealth.

Needless to say, that basic assumption doesn't hold in societies with entrenched inequality. It certainly doesn't apply in contemporary Australia. A 2023 Australia Institute report notes that 'the bottom 90 per cent of Australians receive just 7 per cent of economic growth per person since 2009, while the top 10 per cent of income earners reap 93 per cent of the benefits'. This gap falls largely along generational lines, as older Australians are more likely to own their homes outright, which means the majority of first homebuyers (more than 60 per cent, according to sociologist Julia Cook) now turn to their parents for financial assistance. In a modern economy for which ascension up the property ladder – and, by extension, the accumulation of wealth – is increasingly dependent on the largesse of older relatives, affluence no longer correlates to hard work. Therefore, its ethical significance is compromised.

While economic inequality is undermining the virtuousness of personal prosperity, mass consumerism fuelled by debt has made displays of wealth more accessible. The RBA reports that household debt has risen at a faster rate and to a higher level in Australia than in most countries. And, as Anthony Lloyd and Mark Horsley point out, higher credit-to-income ratios have the dual effect of destabilising the middle classes and diluting traditional class markers. Put simply, anyone with access to a line of credit can *perform* being wealthy, irrespective of their actual income.

While debt makes such performances possible, the internet makes them more accurate, as the habits of the upper classes are studied and disseminated to a wider audience. *Saltburn*, for example, sparked a TikTok fashion craze called Neo Posh Boy (think rugby jerseys and boat shoes). You don't need to have Felix's estate; any student with an Afterpay account and a smartphone can adopt the appearance of off-duty aristocracy.

On the one hand, such trends are deliciously democratising. I'm reminded of an anecdote in critic John Seabrook's *Nobrow*, a study of mass marketing and the homogenisation of popular culture, in which Seabrook's very dapper (and, it is implied, very wealthy) father is so outraged at Ralph Lauren Polo advertising what he sees as an 'individual' style that belongs to him – a preppie Princeton alumnus – he actually rips the offending ad out of a magazine.

On the other hand, this dilution of coherent class markers makes genuinely wealthy people – as opposed to mimics – more difficult to spot. In *The Atlantic*, Jeffrey Winters explains that unequal societies are usually characterised by political instability; anything that can obfuscate the inequality is stabilising. Therefore, almost paradoxically, the democratisation of class markers can ultimately become a tool to further entrench division.

In contemporary society, then, wealth and status have an uneasy relationship. First, because surface displays of wealth, like fashion, are now an incoherent language for describing someone's actual position. Second, because if you know someone well enough to see beneath the surface trappings, whatever wealth they have will not automatically be considered a virtue when it's just as likely to have come from family money or generational luck as from personal industry. And even if someone *has* personally earnt their wealth, they are liable to be resented for profiting from a system that is strikingly inequitable.

IF WEALTH AND status have bifurcated – if the rich are not necessarily afforded respect – where, then, do we derive social capital?

I can think of no more precise articulation than that offered by Sally Rooney in her 2021 novel *Beautiful World, Where Are You*. In an email to a trusted friend, the protagonist, Eileen, reflecting on online political discourse, writes: 'The only apparent schema is that for every victim group (people born into poor families, women, people of colour) there is an oppressor group (people born into rich families, men, white people). But in this framework, relations between victim and oppressor are not historical so much as theological, in that the victims are transcendently good and the oppressors are personally evil.'

As far as sweeping cultural generalisations go, this one feels apt. We only need to look to social media bios, which typically explicate profiles in terms of demographic factors (age, gender, sexual orientation, race), as if the group to which a person belongs is the most reliable shorthand for the particular human who lives and breathes within it. In such a climate, where virtuousness is situated in victim status, being powerful can, paradoxically, be undermining. *Privileged* is a slur; it's a value judgement about a person's character as much as it is an articulation of their circumstances. Whether from belonging to a demographic majority ('straight white man') or simply from being rich, to be privileged is to be out of touch, irrelevant.

In observing that identity politics shapes much of contemporary moral thinking – especially online – I'm offering a descriptive, not a normative, judgement. It's not necessarily a bad thing – in a society where opportunity is distributed so unevenly, this approach can feel like the only means we have to redistribute social capital. But this redistribution is occurring almost exclusively at the level of public perception. It does not appear to have a trickle-down effect to cultural capital. A good example is the publishing industry, which is often criticised for over-prioritising the representation of racial minorities in deciding who and what to publish. A 2020 *New York Times* report titled 'Just How White Is the Book Industry?' found these concerns to be largely overstated: between 1950 and 2018, 95 per cent of novels published in the US had white authors. While social capital, at least online, seems to accrue to marginalised groups, this doesn't neatly translate into real-world opportunities.

This reconceptualising of social capital has little effect on actual capital, either. The threat of exposure to derision is not reason enough for a powerful minority to throw away their privileges. Even though personal wealth can no longer buy respect, it remains as desirable as ever. Which means that this new relation between wealth and social status – where wealth undermines rather than improves status – affects wealth only at the level of performance. Rather than being cast aside, privileges are now carefully navigated. The modern challenge is to pursue the age-old desire for money without compromising on social standing: to enjoy privileges without having to suffer being called 'privileged'.

ONE MECHANISM FOR reconciling these newly conflicting desires for wealth and status is through political beliefs – specifically, socialism. According to *Generation Left* (a report by the right-wing think tank the Centre for Independent Studies), Generation Z adults are less likely than any previous generation to become conservative as they age. On TikTok, the tag 'Eat the Rich' has over a hundred million views. Democratic congresswoman Alexandria Ocasio-Cortez, the poster girl for making socialism cool again, famously wore a gown imprinted with the words *Tax the Rich* to the 2021 Met Gala (for which tickets cost at least $35,000).

Of course, for wealthy people, who are conscious of the generalised cultural disdain for privilege, announcing your allegiance to socialism can be a means to sidestep criticism. It's a way of saying, 'I might *have* wealth, but I don't endorse the system that gave it to me.' In fact, in many spheres of modern life – especially the arts and media industries – socialist credentials are a status symbol. They endear you to other people; they mark you as serious and morally righteous; they grant you entry into friendship groups and a licence to speak on particular issues.

Just because there are personal gains to be made from declarations of socialism does not mean that every contemporary socialist is disingenuous. Many of the avowed socialists I know are deeply thoughtful, passionate people, whose political commitments are what they see as the only ethical and logical response to a deeply unequal society. But individual motivations aside, the uncomfortable economic reality is that those (yes, very genuine) commitments function as a brand. They add value to an individual's voice; they mark you out as trusted and respectable.

I worry that the radical potential of socialism is diluted when its proponents stand to gain *within* capitalism for the very fact of their commitment to anti-capitalist politics. This is the point at which activism becomes gestural, where political commitments – however earnestly or righteously held – benefit individuals within capitalism rather than groups. Socialism, then, is no longer about collective action. It's about personal branding.

ANOTHER WAY IN which contemporary culture allows people to have and enjoy wealth without having to endure social disapproval is through ironic consumerism.

Social media has made available to us whole new audiences and vectors for class and lifestyle performance. Where previously your political commitments or what books you were reading might have been topics of conversation with close friends at the pub, now they can be projected to hundreds or thousands of followers. Eating at a restaurant is another example; a previously private and intimately social act can now be a place to be *seen*, not by the people you're dining with, or even the other patrons, but by everybody who follows you.

It seems to me that this proliferation of 'lifestyle' posting is a direct – and in some ways, highly logical – response to precarity. It allows young people to accessorise with the trappings of wealth, to engage purely at the level of performance. In a way, it's democratising; we're approaching wealth in an ironic way that divorces it from an actual assertion of superiority. We're not claiming to be richer than anyone else; we're just indulging in an endless slideshow of, as they say online, 'little treats'. Indeed, as with those Ralph Lauren customers who so infuriated the genuinely preppie, by turning the habits of a whole class into tools for personal branding, we dilute their power. Appropriation is distinct from appreciation; it's imitation as mockery, not as flattery.

But in 2024, as the housing and cost-of-living crises continue in Australia, the effect of such appropriation is to flatten and distort ever-calcifying class divides. The uncomfortable reality behind all those pictures of beaches and wine bars is that some of us stand to inherit money and others don't. The haves can still potentially amass wealth in their lifetimes (even if it's a matter of waiting for their parents to die). The have-nots have their small plates. And refusing to talk about money seriously is yet another way of not talking about it at all. Worse, it's a way of not talking about it while giving the appearance of candour.

Looking back, I cringe at the many ways I've personally exploited this distance between the performance of wealth and the cold, intergenerationally unfair reality. Perhaps one of the more subtle (and, therefore, more insidious) ways was at the sentence level – particularly my liberal use of the word *bougie*, an abbreviation of *bourgeoise*, which is essentially used as a synonym for *lush* or *indulgent*. A few years ago, any nice meal I had or holiday I took was *bougie*. I never said it in a confessional, self-identifying way. If I was going for a frank acknowledgement of my good fortune, I would have said *bourgeoise*. *Bougie* is a joke, a trope, a 'bit'. It is to *bourgeoise* what *tradwife* is to *housewife*. As a full-time novelist and freelancer, I am a member of the cultural elite. (That's a horrible sentence to type. But horror is precisely the problem. I might tell myself it's a horror of sounding smug, of making others feel inferior. Really, it's the opposite: a horror of being judged. By not mentioning it, I'm protecting myself, exploiting the gap between who I am and how I'd like to be perceived. I'm lying by omission. I'm being an Oliver!) And my entry into the creative class was the direct result of a lifelong chain of structural advantages. I wrote my debut novel while I was unemployed and living rent-free with my parents, for starters. So who did I think I was, a paradigm example of the bourgeoisie, going around calling my own life 'bougie'?

It seems, in our very reaction to social inequality and financial precarity – frowning upon privilege, performing wealth ironically – we may have found a new way to compound structural disadvantage. Class solidarity is made more elusive when people are being dishonest (with themselves, with others) about the privileges they enjoy.

SO ENDLESS AND ever-complicating is this hall of mirrors that one can pick up a Jane Austen novel and feel almost a perverse longing for the hierarchy it describes. Status, in such a world, is not a matter of self-curation but of common knowledge. The assessments of worth are unsubtle and unambiguous: £10,000 pounds a year versus £500. Yes, Austen's world was elitist and oppressive. But we can see in it, perhaps only because we have lost it, the pleasure in certain constraints. Because these days, our privileged few enjoy the privilege of self-invention, too; they can pass as 'just like everyone else' by performing their privilege as a bit. No Regency-era lord or lady ever had that. (Try saying '10,000 a year' ironically.)

That fatigue accounts, in part, for the popularity of *Saltburn*. It can be refreshing to see characters who are so obscenely, eye-wateringly wealthy that feints and disguises are not an option. But 'popularity' is perhaps misleading. *Saltburn* was one of those rare 'must-see' films that is not so much over-hyped as over-analysed: a film that got under people's skin and had to be talked out. It got under *my* skin; it's deeply uncomfortable to catch yourself delighting in overt displays of wealth – empathising with the very people who, according to contemporary ethics, warrant the most disapproval on account of having the most power. And it was offensive to contemporary sensibilities that Fennell chose to make her villain not the stale aristocracy but the middle-class sociopath in their midst.

But I wonder if there was a deeper discomfort, too. Because, in depicting the wealthy as unapologetic and the middle class as grasping, Fennell said something no less true for being a taboo. She forced us to admit that, although we know personal wealth is wrong and that billionaires are public-policy failures, being really, unethically rich would be…well, fun. We can take Fennell's word for it: she is also the daughter of an Eton-educated millionaire jeweller, Theo Fennell (nickname: 'The King of Bling').

While it's galling that this critique of middle-class covetousness should appear within a film that was explicitly marketed as a critique of the super rich, it does tell us something about class today. Wouldn't we all, given the option, prefer *more* – more money, more status, more power, more praise – rather than less?

The reticence to admit that basic human greed persists, that our desires and our principles might clash, is dangerous. Such self-deceit allows even very genuine egalitarian principles to become tools for entrenching class divides, as people find new ways to disavow privilege so they can reserve more of it for themselves.

If we are genuinely committed to a more egalitarian society, we could start by acknowledging the ways in which we are all equally flawed. We could admit that, sometimes, 'eat the rich' is not so much a revolutionary sentiment as a *vampiric* one.

What we seek to destroy, we wish to become.

Diana Reid is the author of the bestselling novels *Love & Virtue* and *Seeing Other People*. She is also a freelance writer, currently based in London. In 2022 *Love & Virtue* won both the Literary Fiction and the overall Book of the Year categories at the Australian Book Industry Awards. She was also awarded Best Young Australian Novelist by *The Sydney Morning Herald*. Her third novel, *Signs of Damage*, will be published in 2025.

FICTION

New shoes

Michelle See-Tho

THIS IS WHERE I work: the kind of sneaker store that stocks shoes with the names of famous American rappers or athletes. The kind of sneaker store with plywood everywhere and hip-hop and young staff who look like customers except for their fluoro lanyards.

Tomorrow a famous American basketballer will drop his new line of shoes.

At our morning catch-up, Corrine reads out a list of names. It's the staff who have pre-paid for the shoes. I am on the list, and Jules and Ruby are too. Corrine reminds us that this is a 'privilege' for staff.

'Fucken rip,' Danny says, pushing up the sleeves of his hoodie.

Everyone laughs, except Corrine who never laughs.

'If you didn't pay for the shoes, you can't have them. Simple as that,' she says.

'Sucker,' Jules whispers to Ruby, shaking back her thick chocolate-brown hair.

I laugh and she looks at me and I think maybe I wasn't supposed to laugh.

'Can everyone stop talking?' Corrine barks.

I try not to look at Jules as she elbows Ruby.

Afterwards, when everyone gets to be loud again, Corrine says to me, 'Ellie, can you read something for me?'

'Okay. What is it?' I ask.

'Something in Chinese.' She pushes her phone at my face. I can see the characters in a little table on the screen.

'I can't read Chinese,' I say.

'Oh, sorry. What are you, like, Vietnamese then?'

'Oh, no.' I clear my throat. 'I was born in Australia. My parents are Chinese. I just don't know Chinese.'

She stares at me for a moment. When she frowns I can see the greasy make-up clumping in lines around her eyes.

THE SNEAKER STORE is in a shopping centre in a suburb that people know from the news. Jules and Ruby and I walk through the centre on our break. I like it because the paths are wide enough for all three of us, except when it's busy.

But when we get to the hallway to the staff locker room, Jules and Ruby walk together and I have to walk behind them and I can't really hear them properly except for bits like 'she said' and 'oh, is she the one who' and 'and then she vomited in a bin!' and laughter.

'Where was this?' I ask, watching their backs.

Neither of them responds.

In the locker room, Jules says, 'I'll get my wallet, then we can go to the food court.'

I watch her dig around her locker, throwing aside bobby pins, empty chip packets and uni textbooks curling at the corners. Her body makes a perfect S-shape – chest forward, butt backward.

Ruby doesn't look at me and folds her arms over her chest. Her skin is spattered with freckles and she has a nose stud, but it's too big for her face. She leans back on the wall, on a poster with a picture of an open locker that says *Lock it or lose it!* Someone has drawn a balloon penis over it in permanent marker.

I imagine being invited to drinks with Jules and her uni friends. Somewhere dark with collages of photos stuck on the wall, maybe in Brunswick or the city. The kind of place where everyone wears wide-legged jeans and caps with flat peaks. We would all sit in a booth, laughing, drinking out of glasses that I'd have to pick up with two hands. Her uni friends would notice we both had the same shoes on and compliment us. I wouldn't be the one vomiting in a bin – that would be someone else. And Jules and I would tell Ruby about it together.

AFTER THE STORE closes for the day, everyone stays back to stock the shelves with the shoes for the release tomorrow. We wait until late in the evening for the delivery.

Danny is trying to do a TikTok dance he just watched but he keeps moving his feet and arms on the same side when they're supposed to be at opposite sides. Everyone laughs and Jules throws a balled-up pair of the store socks at him.

'Oh, that's rank,' he yells.

'There's more of 'em if you don't stop,' she says.

He sits down on the floor. Jules leans back on the plinth she is sitting on. She looks like someone from a slick TV drama where the teenagers are played by twenty-somethings.

The shutter door rattles. There are two fluoro yellow blobs outside.

'Don't just sit there. Open the door!' Corrine yells.

Danny opens the roller door. Two men in high vis walk in with pallets of shoes.

We unload the pallets. A few boxes are marked with bright-green stickers that say *Staff*.

We stock the shoes on the main shelf and on the podiums at the entrance to the store. We use a guide from the visual-merchandising team at head office. It tells us to display the shoes at forty-five-degree angles. We hang posters from the ceiling. The paper is thick but tightly wound and keeps flicking back at us as we try to hang it up.

It's after nine by the time we're done, and the store looks like the photo sent from head office. My fingers are fuzzy with dust from the stock and I have a small cut on my thumb from a box.

WE GATHER IN the back room to open our packages, surrounded by the smell of plastic garbage bags and old carbon-copy receipt paper.

'It's like Christmas!' Ruby says as Corrine passes the boxes around. They're bright red with little logos of the basketballer doing a famous move.

'Yeah, well, don't get too excited,' Corrine says. 'You can't wear them outside the store until tomorrow. So try them on, make sure they fit, and I'll lock them in here when we leave.' She hands Jules a Sharpie. 'Everyone write your name on the box so you know they're yours.'

I want to take care with mine, but when I see Jules and Ruby shredding their boxes open, I do the same.

Tissue paper rips, boxes thud to the ground.

The shoes look smaller than I'd imagined, but somehow still too big for me. My body shakes as I examine them, trying to absorb every detail. I'm afraid if I look away, they'll disappear. They are mostly white, with arcs of black, slashes of red. I turn the left one over, admiring the stitches: large loops around the base, finer ones on the rest of the shoe. The high tops feel cushiony, the soles tough and sturdy.

I kick off my old sneakers, the ones that were not made by a famous American athlete or rapper. In the new shoes, I walk out to the empty store. The yellow lights are still on. I admire myself in the full-length mirror. The hip-hop music thumps around me, the excited shouts from the back room fall away. I feel like a badass. Maybe I could join Jules on her TV show.

I text my parents to say I'm coming home and head out to the staff car park, where it's empty under the blackened sky. Someone has keyed Dad's car – a tag, an illegible scribble. I drive out past a pile of people and camping chairs.

Last Monday I came in to see police cars surrounding the entrance. Corrine told me there'd been a robbery the night before. 'Probably dumb little shits again,' she said. They'd spray-painted over the CCTV cameras.

There are now posters of the robbers everywhere, but they're all wearing hoodies and the pictures are black and white and blurry. The cameras still aren't fixed.

BEFORE I GO to sleep, I read a hack on the internet to make any shoe look 'laceless': tie a little knot on the end of the laces and push it above your toes in the shoe. I memorise how to do it for tomorrow.

MOST OF THE stores in the centre aren't open yet when I arrive at work, but there's a queue out the front of the shutter door. It's mostly young people; I recognise some boys and girls from my school. There are also older men, like, in their forties.

Jules and Ruby are already in the staff locker room when I come in, laughing at something. They are both holding olive-green coffee cups.

'You ready for a day of selling sneakers to crazy people?' Jules asks me.

'We also have them so we can't say they're crazy,' I say. I laugh but no one else does.

'What?' Jules says.

'Oh, y'know, like, if they're crazy…' I say. 'Um, never mind.'

They both look at me with blank faces and I want to keep my mouth shut forever.

We put on our shoes while the crowd grows beyond the door, taking over the tiled space. I make sure to tie the little knot from the hack first, even though I don't see anyone else doing it. Jules and Ruby just wear theirs flapping about.

The pointy bits at the end, wrapped in plastic, press into my toes. I wriggle a little until I can't feel them.

'Most of these people are here for one thing,' Corrine says to us before she opens the door. 'They just want help with sizing and paying. But let's use this opportunity to give them something extra. Upsell the socks, shoe cleaners and insoles at the counter. And don't forget to sign people up to the mailing list.'

The boys at the front of the line press their faces against the shutter door.

Corrine clicks her fingers at us. 'Oi! Stop looking at them.'

Jules rolls her eyes.

'Remember to keep your eyes out for thieves,' Corrine continues. 'There's always someone who'll try to nick the shoes or something else. So check every bag that is not a handbag.'

The shutter rumbles as fists outside thud on the thick plastic.

'Okay, spread out!' Corrine commands.

We move to different corners of the store. I'm at the front near the podiums. I shift from side to side, not really sure what to do with my hands. I turn to look at Jules, at the back. She has her arms crossed over her chest. Ruby is near her, with a hand on her hip.

Corrine turns the music on, a slow hip-hop beat matched with 'uh...uh' as it builds. She goes over to the door. 'Ready?' she shouts over the noise from outside. She unlocks the shutter door.

People burst in. They run straight past me, some of them bumping me, all of them with determined looks on their faces and arms outstretched. They reach for the shoes, grab them, check the size or shout numbers at us.

There are already new shoes scattered all over the floor. Customers step on them as they ask me for their size.

THROUGHOUT THE DAY I catch myself looking at my own shoes in the mirrors, even with people moving around me. I stare at the shapes, the edges, the laces. I look at how they all come together. I sigh when a customer talks to me and I have to pull my eyes away.

Corrine has organised our lunches so only one of us is away at a time. I don't really want to eat alone but I'm glad that Jules and Ruby can't eat together without me.

When I sit down at the food court for lunch I realise my feet are in pain. I stand up, and the soles feel like beds of nails. The little knot I tied this morning has grown into a shoelace fist that's punching my toe. I try to rearrange my foot as I limp back to work but it doesn't help.

'WHERE HAVE YOU been?' Corrine demands when I reach the store.

'I was eating my–'

'Well, you're late. Hurry up and get behind the register so Danny can go.'

I rush behind the counter, pulling my lanyard over my head.

'Sorry, Danny,' I mumble.

'No worries, mate,' he says with a wink. There is a wad of pink chewing gum showing through his teeth. His breath is sugary fake strawberry.

Corrine opens the register and checks the change inside. 'This is one of our busiest periods,' she says, not looking at me. 'We can't have people being late, mmkay?'

'Yes, Corrine,' I say.

'Don't just say "Yes, Corrine". I need you to come back on time, every time.'

'Okay,' I say, not really sure what she wants from me. 'I'm sorry. It won't happen again.'

She sighs, a low sigh that rumbles in her throat. 'The reg is out of fifties again. I'll go out back and grab some from the safe.' She slams the drawer shut and the desk wobbles.

ALL AFTERNOON, HORDES of people continue to spill in and out of the store, all making a beeline for the shoes by the famous basketballer.

I keep hoping for a lull so I can go to the back and sit down. But as soon as one customer leaves, another enters. I am annoyed at them for not caring about me and my feet.

Everyone else – Jules, Ruby, even Corrine – seems to be fine in the shoes. There's no sign of limping or the hot spiky pain I'm feeling from the polyester ridges scraping my skin. I ball my hands into fists and wish I was like them.

I stand on the squishy mat behind the counter we had to buy to comply with ergonomic standards. If I stay here maybe the aches will go away.

I watch Jules chatting to Ruby. She says something and Ruby laughs so hard she needs to hold on to Jules to stand up. I wonder, if someone punched Ruby in the face, would her nose piercing stab her at the same time?

A group of teenage girls walks in, still wearing their school uniforms and giant backpacks. Two are blonde, one is brunette and the other looks Asian or half Asian. Jules and Ruby bound over to them with too-big smiles, saying 'Hey. How's it going?'

I sigh, leaning my weight into the counter. The pain from scrunching my toes inside the shoes starts to creep up my shins and I wonder if it will take over my whole body.

Jules says something and gestures to the new shoes. The girls laugh and smile at her, the way they might look at a favourite young teacher chatting about their personal life. People always look at Jules like that.

She goes to the back to find another size. The girls keep chatting to Ruby. The maybe half Asian one glances at me watching them and I look down at the hourly sales record. My feet are still hot and throbbing.

A WOMAN, MIDDLE-AGED with dimpled elbows and in a faded, stretched pink T-shirt comes in and walks straight to the counter. On her arm is one of those 25-cent paper bags from the supermarket, clean and boxy.

'Do you work here?' she asks me, but she says it like a busy mum would to a young child.

I want to say, *No, I'm standing behind this counter for fun*, but instead I just grin and say, 'Yes.'

'Can I get some help with a pair of running shoes, please?'

'Oh, we don't really sell those here,' I say.

'What do you mean?'

'These are more like…street sneakers,' I say. 'You could try going to–'

Before I can finish, she groans as if I'm about to suggest she go to another country. 'This is a running-shoe store, isn't it? You have runners *there* and *there*!' She jabs her finger in the direction of some shoes from brands that also make runners.

'Those are, um, casual sneakers,' I say. 'You're not meant to run in–'

'I just want running shoes!' she says. 'Do you know what I mean by *runn-ing* shoes?'

I stare at her.

'Do. You. *Understand*?'

'Yes, but–'

'Can I speak to somebody else, please?' She drums her fingers on the counter.

I nod and go to the back room to find Corrine.

'Um, Corrine,' I mumble.

'What?' She's bent over a calculator and some spreadsheets.

'This woman wants to speak to you. She's looking for running shoes.'

'We don't have any,' she says, still looking at her spreadsheets.

'That's what I told her, but she won't listen to me.'

Corrine sighs and gets up, walks out to the counter. 'Hi, how can I help you?'

The woman dangles a finger at me. 'This person says you don't stock running shoes, which you clearly do.'

'No, we don't,' Corrine says, smiling apologetically. She lists some places the woman can go to, but none of them are hell.

As the woman leaves, she turns around to give me one last look, her eyes narrowed and lip curled. Corrine has already returned to the back room.

AT THE END of my shift I go to the staff locker room to get my bag. I can feel something wet inside my shoe, on the heel. I pull off the shoes and throw them into my locker. A red splotch has appeared on the back of my sock, its spidery lines creeping through the cotton, blood the same colour as the basketballer's silhouette.

I sit on the floor, staring up at the wall.

The poster with the warning about thieves is gone. One corner of it is still stuck to the wall, the oil from the Blu Tack seeping through.

I decide to drive home without shoes. The hard pedals sting my soles.

I pause at an intersection as I leave the centre. The pain comes in little waves in time with the indicator. *Tick. Throb. Tick. Throb.* A ute is approaching, but I think I can make it so I turn. The ute speeds up and blasts its horn at me, then overtakes on my right.

The man driving it, balding, wearing Oakley sunglasses, glares at me as he passes. 'Fucken Asian drivers!' he yells.

I try not to cry because I shouldn't cry about that and also because I won't be able to see the road.

When I get home, my parents are out. I turn on the water in the shower until the bathroom fills with steam. My feet are red and the veins are lumpy. Everything that's sore feels better and worse. I let the water run down my face.

I WEAR MY old shoes to work the next morning.

I park Dad's car in the staff car park and walk in via the locker room. The sky is a burst of white light. My locker door is yawning open when I get to it. The new shoes are gone. I look around the room. Other random lockers are open too. There's no one else here. I start to walk out and step on something. It's a red chewing-gum packet.

I walk to the shopping centre help desk. There's a man there in his security uniform, eating a McMuffin.

'I think there was a robbery last night,' I say. 'Someone stole a pair of shoes out of my locker.'

He stares at me. There is dust from the muffin stuck in his patches of stubble. 'Didya lock it?'

'Um, I thought I did.'

He sighs. 'Ya gotta lock your locker.' He taps the *Lock it or lose it!* poster tacked to a cabinet behind him.

'Sorry,' I say.

He sighs. 'No point sayin' sorry now. Did ya find anything there?'

I show him the chewing-gum packet. 'Just this.'

He hands me a clipboard. 'Fill out one of these forms.'

The pen *thunks* on the clipboard through the paper and my writing comes out kind of wonky. He takes another bite out of his McMuffin and I try not to breathe in the egg's heavy smell.

'I'll let you know if they turn up,' he says when I hand him back the clipboard.

As I walk to the store I think I hear Jules and Ruby's laughs echoing in the centre. But when I get to the shutter door, I'm alone.

Michelle See-Tho's work has appeared in *Kill Your Darlings*, *Meanjin*, *Overland*, *The Big Issue Fiction Edition* and *Nintendo Life*, among others. *Jade and Emerald*, her first novel, won the Penguin Literary Prize. She can be found at michelleseetho.com.au or on Instagram @michelleseetho

Tim Loveday

Aca-lyte

Che Guevara is white and wearing a shirt
with his face on it, mansplaining Derrida or Adorno
a hat like your grandfather used to wear though at least
the man knew something about the great war [2]. This Che
hasn't worked out how to borrow a book from the Baillieu yet
& his diary suggests a paranoid persona not a propensity
toward engines – see, he is trying to build something here
the exact proportions of which were lost with Da Vinci
or was it Dan Brown? Your dog, likewise, is a sommelier
of poop. Can snack twice on an idea of self but never
quite muster a technology. The part of the rewriting
in present tense hasn't become present yet. Present
to self: presence. The sort of gift that keeps giving
you anxiety. Untangle a tongue, but still the memory
of knots. You are me are him, in a sense of difference
though there is nothing deferential about this. We both
hate him, hate you. Just join the environmental society
& hoon a cherry vape with someone just as old & stupid
as you will be. Imagine: dealing with humanity every day.
Imagine: people turn to you, gasp. Imagine: mansplaining
but this time end up with an abanico, a PowerPoint &
a briefcase. Imagine: the classroom gets that much
smaller and becomes an office.

Tim Loveday is the verse editor for Extinction Rebellion's Creative Hub and the director of Curate||Poetry. In 2023 he was awarded the Venie Holmgren Environmental Poetry Prize, came second in the Kyogle Poetry Competition and was shortlisted for the David Harold Tribe Poetry Award. In 2022 he won the Dorothy Porter Award for Poetry. He teaches poetry and performance at RMIT.

NON-FICTION

Dying of exposure

Horrible things famous literary men have said about me

Kate Pullinger

IN 2009 MY sixth novel, *The Mistress of Nothing*, a historical fiction set in Egypt in the 1860s, came out to good reviews. It began to do well. It made it onto one very long longlist, then a shorter longlist, and then onto the shortlist of a prize that, confusingly, doesn't have a longlist. That shortlist, for the Governor General's Award for English-language Fiction, one of Canada's major literary honours, also contained a book of short stories by Alice Munro, who was, as Jennifer Lawrence said of Meryl Streep, a GOAT. As well as that, another master of the short story, Alistair MacLeod, one of my all-time favourite writers, was on the jury. There was no chance I would win but knowing that MacLeod had read my book was its own special reward.

Prior to that, I'd managed to sustain a twenty-year career writing fiction without ever wasting a single moment pondering the winning – and the much more common not-winning – of prizes. The prize cycle, with its longlists and shortlists, its outrages and debates, was not on my radar. I thought, *Oh, that happens over there; it doesn't concern me*. This seems odd now, living as I do in London, the city where literary hype and scandal originated (at least in the English language; I'm sure there's been plenty of bitchiness elsewhere in the world over the centuries). Margaret Atwood once told me that she liked coming to London because the gossip and malice is better here than elsewhere. Like Atwood – and Munro – I'm Canadian (this is where the comparisons stop), though I've lived in London the whole of my adult life. But I'm an immigrant here, a foreigner as the current government likes to call us, which means that I'm an outsider, and this is part of what enables me to think, *Oh, that doesn't apply to me.*

Of course, the ability to remove oneself from the culture is double-edged. While I'm more comfortable on the outside looking in here in the UK, my long years away from Canada mean I'm an outsider there as well. And yes, clearly there is something about this hardly unique arrangement that suits me. I'm happy in my corner, doing my thing.

But, reader, I won. I won the Governor General's Award for English-language Fiction.

(I doubt Alice Munro minded that much – and, of course, four years later she won the Nobel, which I think of now as a kind of consolation prize.)

That win brought me firmly into the heart of literary culture with all the exposure it entails (of course, in Canada people die of exposure). And with the win, that crushing and capricious cycle – pre-publication, publication, reception, the longlists, the shortlists, even the book-sales charts themselves – came roaring into focus. And now the prize cycle haunts me every time I publish.

As does the formal photograph that was taken at the prize ceremony in Rideau Hall in Ottawa, a grand event in a grand location. I took it upon myself to hire a dress, something I've never done before or since, and, given I was in an unfamiliar city, pay a visit to a hairdresser I'd never met. My curly hair was shorter than usual at the time and she styled it absolutely bone-straight, like a silky valance with slits for my ears to poke through. Combined with the off-the-shoulder vintage black gown (a gown!) and the black-and-white satin shawl, I managed to render myself virtually unrecognisable. I don't know what possessed me; perhaps it was because, at the time, the Governor General of Canada was the supremely accomplished and glamorous Michaëlle Jean. Perhaps it was because even though I've never become a British citizen, I've been away from Canada for a very long time.

More than once friends have looked at that photo and asked *Who's that woman winning that prize?* And part of me wants to reply: *I have no idea.*

So, success is not only hard to come by; it is also difficult to own. I want my work to be widely read and discussed, but I also want to hide away. And this leads me to return to the original scene of the crime, one of the reasons why I prefer being alone in my happy corner, why writing itself is so much more fun than being published.

IS IT STILL possible to be a famous book reviewer? I'm not sure – but if it is, James Wood is that thing. When my first novel came out in 1989 – a follow-up to my unusually successful first book from the previous year, a collection of short stories (unusual because Brits don't much like short stories) – he wrote what was his *first-ever* review, about my novel, for *The Guardian* newspaper. This review was an epic stinker, vicious and unrelentingly show-offy, the worst review I've ever received. Wood used my novel to stake his place in the firmament of literary life and managed to drive that stake through my heart at the same time (more on vampires later).

The novel...well, the problem with this story is that the novel probably isn't very good. It has a terrible title. I was trying to write something that I felt reflected the London I knew as a young woman in the 1980s, a world of cheap eateries, anti-Thatcher activism, gay bashing, National Front fascists, homelessness, reggae, post-punk bands and great parties. My mother came to visit me when I was living in an artists' community of squatted houses in Vauxhall, across the Thames from Westminster. Vauxhall is now the home of both MI5 and the brand-new heavily fortified US Embassy, but at the time the architectural highlights included an enormous derelict cold storage building on the riverbank and an abandoned Marmite factory about ten minutes' walk away that we used to raid for furniture. When asked by a friend what my life was like, my mum said, *Imagine the worst place possible, then fill it with your friends all having a wonderful time*. So that's what I was trying to write about. The novel was published as part of a glossy promotional campaign, along with the first novels of Deborah Levy, Geoff Dyer and Rose Boyt. This campaign also provoked a fair amount of derision, including a second nasty take-down from Wood in *Vogue* magazine.

I think, with thirty-five years' worth of hindsight, that part of the reason Wood despised my novel was because I was a young Canadian woman attempting to write about London, a city steeped in centuries of writerly history. What could be more annoying to an ambitious twenty-five-year-old Oxbridge-educated Old Etonian than finding an upstart colonial girl on his patch? (No one since Tony Blair has tried to pretend that Britain is a classless society; in one version of the recent Conservative government's Cabinet there were more men who'd been to Eton than there were women.)

Unlike what the pundits like to claim – no publicity is bad publicity – that review actually did do a fair amount of damage to my life as a young writer. At the time, the cult of the bright young man was much stronger than the corresponding – perhaps non-existent? – cult of the bright young woman. All those blokes who wanted to be Martin Amis, including Amis himself. My editor at Jonathan Cape for those first two books, Frances Coady, moved away from the imprint (Cape had gone from being an independent on Bedford Square to a cog in a series of corporate takeovers during this brief period). David Godwin stepped in, and David Godwin did not like me. When I handed in a draft of my next novel, he invited me to his office and said, *I don't know what kind of a woman you are, but you can't publish this novel.*

The novel in question, a feminist and literary revision of *Dracula*, has a bit of sex in it, and Mr Godwin didn't think nice girls should write about sex. At least, that's what I took away from that meeting, along with the fact that he was sacking me. Plus, he was wearing bobby pins in his hair.

I don't know what kind of a woman you are, but you can't publish this novel.

I did find a publisher for that book, *Where Does Kissing End?*, the first of several novels I've written that tease and play with genre fiction. Unlike my first novel, I'm fond of it still, though I don't know if it is any good – doubtless Godwin would claim it was not. It came out around the same time as Francis Ford Coppola's *Bram Stoker's Dracula* and Christopher Frayling's wonderful survey *Vampyres: Lord Byron to Count Dracula*. It might seem hard to believe now, but vampires were rather neglected back then; there was Anne Rice and Stephen King's *Salem's Lot*, but it was another dozen years before *Twilight* arrived, let alone the current marvel that is *What We Do in the Shadows*. Anyway, I do believe that James Wood's ruthless review informed David Godwin's even more ruthless behaviour. Wood went on to *The New Yorker* and a professorship at Harvard; Godwin became an agent. Despite the best effort of those boys, I continued to write novels while building a parallel – dare I say it? – award-winning career in digital media.

WHY AM I still thinking about this thirty-five years later? That's what writers do, baby: we let things fester because that's where the good stuff comes from (as well as the bad). It's part of the grit, the grist, that keeps us going. The book came out so long ago that the review is not available online, so it doesn't follow me around the internet. It turns out Wood felt a degree of remorse over it as he *brought it up unprompted* in an interview in *The Guardian* in 2018 with a demeaning and untrue story about me weeping my way through my own launch party because of his review; in other words, he raised me from the dead only to kill me once again.

As I write this, I'm about to go back in for another rewrite of a novel that I had convinced myself was finished. You'd think that after publishing eight novels, winning a literary prize or two and establishing myself as Professor of Creative Writing and Digital Media in a university – in other words, after accruing some status – I'd be able to rely on my own judgement over whether a book is ready to submit for publication. But no. Turns out writerly status does not equal editorial wisdom. And this book needs to be strong enough to convince publishers to say yes in an environment where it is much easier to say no. This book needs to be strong enough to make publishers want to invest in its future as well as mine. And in my agent's well-seasoned and somewhat spicy opinion, we're not there yet. The good news is that her verdict suits me because, well, I like writing much more than I like publishing.

Publishing is a weird industry, a retail supply service where every day hundreds – thousands – of brand-new, untested products are launched, each one a little bit different to the last. The long-haul career trajectory of most writers is increasingly difficult to maintain with incomes nosediving, as evidenced by multiple surveys. The road is cluttered with novelists brought down by 'bad track', their new books rejected because of the poor sales of previous titles. But as readers we still need help to discover good books, to figure out what to read next. As book pages, magazines and newspapers shrink or disappear altogether, it's no longer clear what impact book reviewers can have on a career. The endorsement of someone whose work – critical or otherwise – you admire remains important to many writers. That blighted first novel of mine was admired in a review written by Ruth Rendell who was, at the time, the Queen of British Crime Fiction. However, it's taken me six drafts of this essay to remember Rendell's piece; somehow one terrible review obliterated all other opinions.

The moral is...there is no moral. Reviewers sometimes have an agenda when they hate your work; they sometimes have an agenda when they love it. I've had great reviews; I've had terrible reviews. In 2009 I won a prize, and

I've won a couple of others since. I've been ditched by publishers and revived by publishers. I've kept writing. When Martin Amis died last year, a wash of memories came over me from those heady days when publishers paid for lavish launch parties and, for a brief moment, I was a bright young woman who believed the world of reading and writing was open to me, a person of little status who was therefore a person without status anxiety.

Kate Pullinger is a Canadian writer who has been based in the UK since 1982. She has published eight novels, two collections of short stories and several digital-only works, including the smartphone ghost story *Breathe*. Her novel *The Mistress of Nothing* won the Governor General's Award for English-language Fiction in Canada in 2009, and in 2021 she won the Marjorie C Luesebrink Career Achievement Award, given every year by the Electronic Literature Organization. She is Professor of Creative Writing and Digital Media at Bath Spa University.

NON-FICTION

The Gordon cult

The rise and fall of an Australian literary icon

Jeff Sparrow

ON 30 OCTOBER 1932, about 2,000 people gathered to celebrate the unveiling of a monument to Adam Lindsay Gordon at the intersection of Spring and Macarthur Streets in Melbourne. It depicts the poet in riding boots with his sleeves rolled up, clutching, somewhat disconsolately, a book in one hand and a pencil in the other. A passage from the poem 'Ye Wearie Wayfarer' appears on the column's base:

> Two things stand like stone,
> Kindness in another's trouble,
> Courage in your own.

Today, the statue still stands in prime position across from Parliament House – its prominence a reflection of the astonishing fandom evident in the huge crowd at its opening. But when I visited Gordon Reserve on a recent sunny autumn day, I couldn't find anyone who knew who or what the monument honoured.

'A bushranger?' guessed the young office worker eating her lunch. She put down her sushi and squinted at the statue dubiously. 'An explorer?'

Well into the 1930s, a remarkable literary cult revered Gordon's poetry, his life and – perhaps especially – his death. The decline of that faith reveals something important – not just about what Australia reads but, more fundamentally, about why.

I'D STARTED THINKING about Gordon's dizzying rise, and equally calamitous fall, when researching the life of a very different poet. I'm working on a biography of Lesbia Harford, a woman born in 1891 with a damaged heart valve that made strenuous exertion impossible – and pretty much guaranteed her an early death. She studied law at the University of Melbourne (among the first women to do so), debated Robert Menzies about the First World War, campaigned against conscription with the Industrial Workers of the World, and wrote extraordinary love poems to women and to men. Harford's grandfather, I recently learnt, knew Adam Lindsay Gordon in Ballarat and became sufficiently close to the poet to witness his will.

Gordon came from a wealthy Scottish family. His father despaired of the boy's inability to settle into a military career and banished him to Australia. The young Gordon served briefly in the South Australian mounted police but showed more talent as a horse breaker and hurdle rider. After inheriting money, Gordon won a seat in the South Australian parliament but, lacking any interest in politics, soon resigned. He wrote light verses for sporting newspapers (some of which became popular) but his privately issued poetry collections did not sell well, despite praise from writer and editor Marcus Clarke in the *Colonial Monthly*. In Victoria, Gordon frittered away his funds, only to learn he would not receive an estate in Scotland as he had expected. His book *Bush Ballads and Galloping Rhymes* appeared on 23 June 1870; the next day, he walked into the scrub on Brighton Beach and shot himself dead with a rifle.

In October 1870, only months after his suicide, Gordon's admirers erected a monument to the man *The Australasian* hailed as 'our greatest – we almost said our only – national poet'. By 1879, Marcus Clarke could introduce a collection of Gordon's work as containing 'something very like the beginnings of a national school of Australian poetry'.

Gordon's rediscovery received a fillip from, of all people, Oscar Wilde, in an exquisitely bitchy review of an Australian poetry anthology compiled by Douglas Sladen. Wilde regarded with fastidious disdain 'the extraordinary collection of mediocrities whom Mr Sladen has somewhat ruthlessly dragged from their modest and well-merited obscurity'. Yet in Gordon, Wilde declared, Australia had 'found her first fine utterance in song'.

In a subsequent piece Wilde walked back the suggestion that Gordon represented any kind of national achievement, suggesting instead that his flaws illustrated the stultifying effect of Australia on writers of talent. But the reassessment ('Had he stayed at home he would have done much better work') made no difference to the antipodean enthusiasm for Gordon as a poet – and, just as significantly, as a man.

Sladen, for instance, explained that Australians treasured Gordon as 'a magnificent type of manhood, as the Bard of the Bush and the Race-course'. The editor and writer PJ Holdsworth said he was 'distinctly martial and soldierly' and 'never unmanly'; the Adelaide *Herald* declared him 'the poet of manhood and manly sports'. The emphasis on Gordon's personal virility – reinforced by tales of his horseback derring-do – paradoxically allowed, as the scholar Melissa Bellanta notes, his admirers to indulge in a distinctive weepy sentimentality. The famous lines from 'Ye Wearie Wayfarer' advocate a crack-hardy, keep-your-chin-up stoicism. But for readers aware of Gordon's suicide (that is to say, all of them), the passage's reference to personal troubles – and its dismissal of life's 'froth and bubble' – encouraged an overt and emotional identification with the poet's tragic destiny. As early as 1888, Gordon's first biographer, John Howlett Ross, described how 'pilgrim Australians' were making their way to the Brighton cemetery ('a wild and lonely spot') so as 'to stand and weep by the side of the grave of their "poor Gordon"'.

More formal graveside visits began in 1892, promoted by groups such as the Australian Natives' Association, the Lindsay Gordon Lovers' Society and the Adam Lindsay Gordon Pilgrimage Committee. In 1920, *The Age* described an astonishing 8,000 people in attendance, with 'pilgrims, panegyrists and moralists assemb[ling] on the reserve at the main entrance, where addresses and recitations were delivered and one song was sung'.

This lachrymose tendency also attached itself to relics associated, however tangentially, with the poet. When Brighton Council refused to preserve Gordon's rackety old cottage, a local admirer called Cyril Goode personally collected the component elements of the demolished shack, storing its 25,000 individual bricks while waging a long (and ultimately fruitless) campaign for the house's reconstruction.

I recently stumbled on a similar talisman when I walked along New Street, Brighton, and passed the currently closed Marine Hotel, a pub established back in 1856. On its steps, I noticed an iron fence around a long-dead and precariously leaning tree stump, preserved for eternity with a coating of concrete. A plaque read: *Adam Lindsay Gordon, poet and horseman, tethered his horse to this hitching post during his residence in Brighton 1869–1870.*

The commemoration of an old post – like the adulation directed to a pile of bricks – suggests an enthusiasm extending beyond civic memory into something like the mystic realms of religion.

All through the first decades of the twentieth century, Gordon's admirers campaigned for sites at which the poet might be more fully venerated. They erected a cairn in Mt Gambier 'near the spot where the poet took a fearsome jump with his horse, Red Rover'; they convinced the South Australian government to preserve Dingley Dell, another cottage once occupied by Gordon; they improved and adorned the Brighton cemetery pilgrimage grounds.

The greatest local achievement of the so-called 'Gordon Monument Movement' came in 1932, when Victorian Premier Sir Stanley Argyle unveiled Melbourne's long-awaited sculpture of the poet. The artist Paul Montford's efforts did not receive unanimous acclaim: a certain John B Mather (described in the press as 'an artist and old Adelaide identity') complained that the statue showed the poet 'posing', something Mather insisted Gordon would never do, since 'he was too well bred for anything that even remotely savoured of shoddiness and his intellect carried him far beyond the scope of paltry minds'. Nevertheless, a huge crowd still came for speeches by Sir Stanley as well as the President of the Legislative Council, the President of the Senate and sundry other politicians, before 'the Brighton Band played, and Mr GJ Mackay led the singing of hymns'.

Two years later Sladen, armed with testimony from Kipling, Galsworthy, Conan Doyle and other luminaries, succeeded in installing Gordon's bust (labelled *National Poet of Australia*) within Westminster Abbey, making him the only Australian writer then or now so honoured.

THAT WAS ABOUT the point at which the air began to leak from the well-pumped tyres of Gordon's reputation. In a 1973 study, Brian Elliott could write that 'the writer who, fifty years ago, was regarded as without dispute the most vital and representative of Australian poets, has become for contemporary criticism almost a dead weight'. In their 2011 book, *Australian Poetry Since 1788*, Geoffrey Lehmann and Robert Gray discuss Gordon's status like analysts assessing a bearish stock. 'Gordon was overrated as a poet for some years,' they say. 'His reputation faded during the twentieth century.'

We might consider the reasons for such declining enthusiasm entirely obvious. When John Howlett Ross titled his 1888 Gordon biography *The Laureate of the Centaurs*, he, like most critics, took for granted that readers would share Gordon's equestrian enthusiasms. But in more recent times, even an avowed fan such as Elliott expresses a certain weariness at what he calls the 'horsey poems'.

Gordon's attitudes have dated just as much as the *rumpty-tum* rhythms of bush ballads and galloping rhymes. Famously, the poet Henry Kendall lauded Gordon as 'a shining soul with syllables of fire / who sang the first great songs this land can claim'. In the twenty-first century, Kendall's elision of Indigenous culture serves more as an indictment than a recommendation, drawing attention to the racism that underpinned the culture of white settlement.

Yet we're missing something if we dismiss Gordon as simply a product of the colonial era. In many respects, the Gordon craze makes more sense if understood in relation to Australia's modernisation as well as its relationship to the British Empire.

In 1872, Victoria – considerably ahead of comparable regions internationally – made education free, secular and compulsory, an innovation that soon spread across the other states. The new system required an appropriate syllabus, and that in turn entailed literature. In making the case for their man, the Lindsay Gordon Lovers' Society and similar bodies were generating the required canon: as Brigid Magner explains, '[Gordon's] cult following and the events organised by his fans [led] directly to the establishment of the Australian Literature Society, which aimed to promote the recognition and support of local authors.'

The celebration of Gordon – and, for that matter, other local authors – relied upon one of the most up-to-date communications systems anywhere in the world. In 1909, Australia had three times as many newspapers (relative to population) as Britain. Gordon's poetry did not spread through word of mouth in shearing sheds but was distributed by a mass media that also promoted critical essays lauding Gordon and articles about the activities of his admirers. As early as 1916, the craze jumped from print to celluloid, with a five-reel film entitled *The Life's Romance of Adam Lindsay Gordon*, written by WJ Lincoln and GH Barnes, a narrative (featuring actor Hugh McCrae) about the poet's life, interspersed with genuine footage of crowds in Brighton cemetery.

The support for Gordon coincided with a widespread security panic among the political class. By 1900, Australia had become one of the most urbanised countries in the world. The rapid pace of industrialisation fostered considerable unease, much of it centred on concern that stalwart bushmen would degenerate into weedy slum larrikins, too feeble to defend their country against the coloured hordes said to be menacing it. The Crimean War had fanned anxieties about a Russian invasion (only briefly supplanted by fears of an American attack during the US Civil War). The perceived need for British protection led to early enthusiasm for Australian involvement in the Boer War; Japan's victory over Russia in 1905 shook local politicians deeply invested in the European presence in Asia.

The relationship between Gordon, the supposed 'virility' of his work and his status as a national poet makes sense in that context. In a typical piece from 1915, the Reverend JJ Malone asserted Gordon's importance because of his role in 'awakening the effeminate and the indolent to forsake the foetid atmosphere of the city, and dare [the] toil and...adventure' of an outdoor life. This is why the 'horsey poems' mattered. Olive M Carter's 1916 school text *A Course of Lectures on the Poems of Adam Lindsay Gordon and Henry Clarence Kendall* invited students to contemplate snippets of verse like this:

Yet if once we efface the joys of the chase
From the land, and outroot the Stud,
Goodbye to the Anglo-Saxon Race
Farewell to the Norman blood.

Most of Carter's pupils lived in cities. No one who read the poem at the time actually expected – or, indeed, wanted – Sydney schoolboys to rediscover the 'joys of the chase'. Already, by 1915 and 1916, Gordon's horses represented a metaphorical rather than literal alternative to mundane domesticity. In practical terms, the effeminate and the indolent were wanted not at the racetrack so much as the recruiting station – ironically to fight in the industrialised total war that sounded the death knell for equestrian transport.

The Great War cemented Gordon's reputation – that strange blend of phlegmatic forbearance and extravagant sentiment for which he was admired meshing perfectly with the emotional official rhetoric about stern wartime duty. The copyright on his poetry had recently expired, so publishers churned out cheap paperback editions for the front, which were then distributed around the nation by a generation of returning soldiers.

The importance of the war in Gordon's rise brings us closer to an explanation for his subsequent fall.

Before the first formal graveside pilgrimage of 1892, Gordon's boosters had contacted an English woman called Jane Bridges. Bridges had been the object of Gordon's affections before he left for Australia, the inspiration for poems such as 'To My Sister'. That was, of course, some forty years earlier: by 1892, Bridges was a grandmother, long married to someone else. Nevertheless, she obligingly presented the pilgrims with a wreath of wildflowers, which they brought to Australia and laid on Gordon's grave. The Lindsay Gordon Lovers' Society preserved the token in a glass case; it was later displayed in a Melbourne shop window, with individual flowers eventually distributed as relics to members of the Adam Lindsay Gordon Memorial Committee.

All of this took place irrespective of Gordon's 1862 marriage to Margaret Park, who bore him a daughter. Margaret lived until 1919 and so was obliged to endure decades of the Australian literati swooning about her husband's tragic failure to marry someone else.

For Gordon's supporters, Jane mattered and Margaret didn't precisely because of the former's distance and the latter's proximity. If an infatuation with a woman from Worcester had spurred Gordon's departure for the antipodes, he could be presented as an unhappily exiled Englishman rather than an upstart colonial – and, as a result, better represent Australia.

From a modern perspective Gordon makes an odd choice for a national poet, since he wrote only rarely about the country that embraced him. He set many of his popular verses in England and studded the others with the classical references familiar to an English gentleman. Yet before the passage of the 1931 Statute of Westminster – or, more exactly, until similar laws passed through the Australian Parliament in 1942 – Britain retained the legal right to determine foreign relations for the Australian Commonwealth. Accordingly, prior, during and for some time after the Great War, respectable Australian nationalism generally manifested as Empire patriotism. As *Punch* explained in 1914, 'The British Empire is our family circle and we cannot live outside it.'

It was thus quite possible for the rhetoric of nationalism to avoid any mention of the nation at all. When, for instance, war broke out in August 1914, the United Pastoralists' and Grazing Farmers' Association of Queensland moved at their annual meeting to 'intimate…our warmest loyalty to the British Throne and…pledge ourselves to give support to any steps taken to uphold the honour and integrity of our Empire'.

Gordon's reputation swelled in response to, and as an extension of, this sentiment. At the ceremony to mark his inclusion in Westminster Abbey, the archbishop of Canterbury described him as 'the voice of the national life of one of the young nations of the British race'. He was, in other words, the poet of Australia precisely because of his Englishness.

Such a presentation became untenable by the end of the 1930s. In the direst moments of the Second World War, John Curtin delivered the famous speech in which he declared that, despite 'traditional links of kinship with Great Britain', Australia now looked to the US for support. In retrospect, we can understand the comments as marking the beginning of the decline of the Gordon cult. The realignment of the Australian state away from British imperialism (and into the orbit of the new American order) meant that Gordon's unselfconscious Englishness sounded suddenly and irrevocably dated.

You can see the issue in a comparison between Gordon and two writers of a slightly later vintage, Banjo Paterson and Henry Lawson. They, too, wrote rhyming ballads of the horsiest kind; they, too, voiced deeply unpleasant colonial attitudes. Where Gordon expresses a casual bigotry, Henry Lawson (as Humphrey McQueen explains in *A New Britannia*) voices a programmatic racism of an almost proto-fascist kind, centred on an obsession that non-white people seek 'fair girls for their lusts'. Nothing in Gordon's corpus comes close to the viciousness of Lawson's praise for racial pogroms in 'The Cambaroora Star':

> Charlie wrote a stinging leader, calling on his digger mates,
> And he said: 'We think that Chinkies are as bad as syndicates.
> What's the good of holding meetings where you only talk
> and swear?
> Get a move upon the Chinkies when you've got an hour to spare.'

Despite this – and many, many similar passages – Lawson's star remains at least partially visible in the literary sky despite Gordon's near total eclipse. Though I didn't test the theory, I suspect that the lunching office workers I quizzed about the Melbourne monument would have recognised the name 'Henry Lawson' even as 'Adam Lindsay Gordon' made no impression at all. Because Lawson and Paterson lack Gordon's deep association with Britishness, they've retained an association with a national literature, despite the reformulation of national tropes in the context of the US alliance.

TODAY, NO POET of any kind attracts the fervour once associated with Adam Lindsay Gordon. That's what makes the 'Gordon craze' both fascinating and worthy of contemporary consideration.

William Trainor, one of Gordon's earliest enthusiasts, came to identify so much with his literary hero that he purchased a plot in Brighton cemetery to be buried alongside him. To be fair, Trainor had known Gordon personally. Nevertheless, such an extravagant gesture highlights the very different status of poetry today. Most contemporary poets (indeed, most literary authors) receive so little notice for their work that they simply could not imagine a reader voluntarily giving them attention for all eternity.

In *The Great War and Modern Memory*, Paul Fussell identifies the different elements that created the culture of 1914. When war began, classical and English literature still played a central role in traditional education, even as increased literacy and democratic participation fostered a new enthusiasm for 'self-improvement' and study. 'The intersection of these two forces,' Fussell argues, 'the one "aristocratic", the other "democratic", established an atmosphere of public respect for literature unique in modern times.'

Cometh the hour, cometh the man. The poetry of Adam Lindsay Gordon offered manly Anglophile erudition in a popular and memorable style. 'You might,' suggests Olive M Carter to students about the extracts in her Gordon textbook, 'write some of them in your friend's autograph book.' The prompt illustrates how the poetry functioned: Gordon's talent for metre resulted in short phrases ideal for repetition and recitation almost as pre-digital memes.

That moment did not last. Ad-hoc organisations such as the Lindsay Gordon Lovers' Society gave way to more professional bodies. As the institutionalisation of literary culture intensified, the universities took on more of a role in determining the literary canon, especially after the Whitlamite expansion of higher education in the early 1970s. Yet throughout the twentieth century, a writerly preoccupation with national identity remained. The forms of literary nationalism might have changed (with, for instance, the acceptance of multiculturalism), but its aims remained recognisably similar, with poets and other writers valued for somehow articulating an Australian sensibility.

This centrality of literature to nationalism rested on particular ideological and institutional foundations, facilitated by a certain kind of nationalism but, more importantly, sustained by a commitment to the liberal arts as a foundation of a public career. If a degree in literature credentialed young men and women seeking wealth and status, the insistence that poetry determined 'national identity' still made a kind of sense. But higher education doesn't work like that anymore. The road to wealth runs through business school; would-be politicians study law or economics, not poems. Accordingly, debates about the relative status of one poet over another miss the point. 'It has,' says the critic John Guillory, 'proven much easier to quarrel about the content of the curriculum than to confront the implications of a fully emergent professional-managerial class which no longer requires the cultural capital of the old bourgeoisie.'

The redundancy of that cultural capital becomes obvious in the forms that political struggle take. In many important ways, our moment echoes the period in which Gordon's reputation so spectacularly soared. If you squint at today's unstable, multipolar world, you can see, in the war in Europe and the Gaza genocide, a geostrategic situation increasingly reminiscent of August 1914. The decline of American power has fostered familiar symptoms of political morbidity, not least a renewed obsession with masculinity evident in the weird conservative vocabulary about *cucks* and *beta males* and *soy boys*. A belligerent nationalism drives culture wars centred on social media, in video games, in TV programs, in Hollywood movies and pretty much every other aspect of social life. The occasional skirmish flares up within the literary milieu but by and large today's reactionary populists do not consider poetry a major field of operation.

That's a good thing, you might say. Yes, except that the relative tranquillity stems primarily from literature's marginalisation. The culture warriors ignore poetry for the same reason politicians cut funding for writing: the old justification for literature as a means of fostering patriotic cohesion no longer persuades anyone.

I've been thinking about that a lot, because, in writing about Lesbia Harford, I'm discussing a once-obscure poet more widely read today than during her lifetime. The late Les Murray, for instance, described Harford as 'one of the two finest female poets so far seen in Australia' and claimed he couldn't read her poem from August 1915 without choking up. It runs:

Ours was a friendship in secret, my dear,
Stolen from fate.
I must be secret still, show myself calm
Early and late.

'Isn't it sad he was killed!' I must hear
With a smooth face.
'Yes, it is sad.' – Oh, my darling, my own,
My heart of grace.

The last line gets me every time, too.

But when I read Murray discussing 'our poem of World War I', I'm tempted to respond, 'Who's "we", Les?' His 'our' recuperates Harford to a national tradition, in the usual way. Yet she did not write *of* the Great War – she wrote *against* it and against all those who supported it.

Harford considered the conflict an obscenity, so much so as to render poetry itself almost an indulgence. 'I will not rush,' she says, in a different poem, 'with great wings gloriously / Against the sky / While poor men sit in holes, unbeautiful, / Unsouled, and die.'

Murray's imposition of an imaginary national unity distorts the meaning – and, I would argue, the value – of a poetry that instead challenges that unity.

Lesbia Harford and Adam Lindsay Gordon are, of course, very different writers. Yet, with politicians no longer commissioning statutes to poets of any sort, literature increasingly relies on its own structures and institutions, independent of – or indeed opposed to – those of the state. A renewed literary infrastructure today seems much less likely to take shape as a nationalist venture than as a counter-hegemonic project, drawing its energy from movements for social change. And that creates opportunities to value, in new ways, poetry of all kinds, including works now entirely out of fashion.

The cult around Gordon has vanished and will not come back. But if we abandoned the anxieties of nationalism, we might find ways to re-read him, even if against the grain.

I'm no particular fan of nineteenth-century verse, but I think about the famous lines from 'Ye Wearie Wayfarer' a lot. In this world, kindness and courage don't stand like stone. Perhaps, though, we can yet make them.

Jeff Sparrow is a Walkley Award-winning writer, editor and broadcaster. The author of many books, his most recent is *Twelve Rules for Strife*, a collaboration with Sam Wallman, published by Scribe earlier this year.

Grace Yee

how to launch a poem

i) recall democracy is pretty numbers & orange clusters, strategically
bold and critically wet, intemperate type-c photographs;
ii) advance stagger: inkjet-laboured nested griefs & hybrid animals,
radio waves & gaze-detail, yellow tableaux & charlie foxtrot figments,
clusterfucks;
iii) shoot east shoot west, strike a pose, teem prada, preoccupy with
night lights, sex and billboards, sex on billboards, belled skirts & wasted
chaste;
iv) grandscale the food you eat the way you eat the hell you eat,
immaterial bread in a hot-desk-metropolis-cum-umbrage, huff,
shirtfront a superpower;
v) manipulate sewer systems, decompress anomie in cinematic frames,
long exposures, far-flung procrastinations;
vi) tilt abs, beams & lunar grief, levitate laundry lists, fold & stack;
vii) dispense the demerits of your own internal terrain, drain, simulate
the passing of witnesses, chrome, crack seizures, flicker;
viii) suck sea-garbage, disorient the landscape, portrait horizons, harvest
documents, document contemplations, posture downward dog and
driverless;
ix) swing equanimity, aviate the neighbourhood, tourniquet
technologies and all judicial glosses, glow;
x) headlight corridors, tunnel frugal, agitate outages and provisional
liminal pipes, frack cooking cleaning stroking, weed;
xi) foul the sounds of brooks & birds;
xii) keep the glue gun loaded and the bones cool and dense, collate fruit
& unbreakable eggs, texturise melamine, unsheathe by the side of the
road, surveil;

xiii) laminate absurdities, bait ceilings & subfloor spaces, fibrillate the past, box the light there, salt the snow;

no more pre-school baby: my poetic practice requires periodic sips of rescue, resuscitated drift, glycerine cocoons (stanzas of childbearing & rooms of equal conviction), epsom salts & quiet fridays, no jars of *meh* or party gummies, no cystic alienations, no unnatural breath or bigotry or beef, no astringent grave affect, but vanishing on waking, capes

---

Grace Yee's collection *Chinese Fish* won the Victorian Prize for Literature, the Victorian Premier's Literary Award for Poetry, and the Mary and Peter Biggs Award for Poetry at the Ockham New Zealand Book Awards in 2024. Her work has been widely published and anthologised across Australia and internationally, and has been awarded the Peter Steele Poetry Award and the Patricia Hackett Prize. She can be found at graceyeepoet.com

IN CONVERSATION

The great divide

Notes from the '80s

Anna Broinowski and Carody Culver

Before she was a Walkley-winning documentary-maker and author, Anna Broinowski was a precocious seventeen-year-old who believed in Australia's idea of itself as a classless utopia. But when she arrived at the University of Sydney in 1985, she found herself in a strange new world of preppies and punks, an ivory-towered microcosm of the warring factions that defined '80s culture: jacked-up capitalism versus anti-mainstream rebellion. Intent on seeing the 'real' Australia, Anna set out on a madcap hitchhiking adventure that's the subject of her wildly entertaining new memoir, Datsun Angel. *In this conversation, which has been lightly edited and condensed, Anna talks to* Griffith Review *Editor Carody Culver about gender politics, room jackings and an unforgettable journey north.*

CARODY CULVER: *Datsun Angel* has two parts: the first details your experiences as a newly minted freshman at the University of Sydney in the mid-1980s, the second describes a trip you took during the summer of 1987, when you and your uni mate Peisley hit the road and hitched all the way to Darwin and back. What drew you to revisit this time in your life?

ANNA BROINOWSKI: There was a logistical consideration – I'm a freelance filmmaker and writer, and I was casting around for what to do next. I found my diary of the trip when I was cleaning out some boxes. As you read it, it's like a scene from that Robert Crumb documentary about his brother, whose writing gets more indecipherable as he becomes more insane. It's the visual embodiment of my unravelling – the unravelling of everything

I thought I knew as this highly educated but incredibly ignorant teenager, who suddenly found herself navigating the madness and danger of the 1980s outback. It felt both alien and eerily similar to today, and I thought I should do something with it.

The other reason was that my daughter is now the same age I was when I went hitchhiking and at the University of Sydney too. She's also highly adventurous and a risk-taker. Thankfully, she's inherited good manners, which I don't have, from her English father. I wanted to revisit my life back then to understand what she might be going through. The thing that stayed with me from that trip was the deep, insidious, entrenched misogyny I felt almost every day on the road. I also experienced this at uni through the college hazing system, although I wouldn't have called it misogyny at the time. So I wanted to unpack what feminism and being a young woman was like in Australia in the '80s, and whether the challenges and hurdles I'd faced then are still there for my daughter now.

CC: The 1980s was a time of extremes, as you detail in the book: there were big political dick-swingers like Reagan and Thatcher, there was big spending, there were big monocultural forces, everything from Robert Palmer to Super Mario. You write that 'artists chipped at the edges' of this milieu and 'danced to a nihilistic beat'. You were the child of diplomats and grew up largely outside Australia – can you tell me about the culture shock of moving back here in 1985?

AB: I had double culture shock, because even though I was a diplomat brat it never occurred to me that I had status. I didn't even know what status was until I turned up at Sydney Uni!

I grew up mainly in countries very removed from the West: Burma, the Philippines, Iran. I was born in Japan. I was aware that I was privileged; I just didn't understand what the markers of status were, and I had this lingering guilt about being rich compared with children my age in the countries where I went to school, who were living in ghettos on the other side of barbed-wire fences. I went to international schools where all the kids were trustafarians and the future captains of big tech. I was never at any school long enough to fully understand the status codes, and everyone was from different countries so the codes were already diverse. It was only when I came to Sydney and walked into my first law lecture that I discovered there was a rigid set of status codes in '80s urban Australia that I had no idea about. Not only that – there were codes that delineated one subset of students from another. If you wanted to look like you had status (which everyone in the mainstream was chasing in the '80s – it was all about being rich; you couldn't be too thin), it was preppie, it was Sloane, it was Ray Bans, it was Lacoste. That's what everyone was wearing in my law lectures, which I found bizarre because to me that was really boring. And the alternate status symbols I saw on campus, which rigorously delineated the two sections of the undergraduate body, were the opposite: a defiantly poor aesthetic symbolised by early Madonna, with ripped lace and op-shop clothes and torn, scuffed-up boots, army great coats, men in eyeliner, punk. Anything to signify that you were against the system, you were kicking against the pricks, you were out to change the forces of greed for the good.

CC: I love that law lecture scene in the book, where you end up sitting beside a preppie in Ralph Lauren duckbill loafers that you assume he's wearing ironically – but then he asks you which school you went to and you realise, *Oh, there's no irony here*. It's interesting to consider how that compares with today, when many wealthy people want to aestheticise their status downwards.

AB: Yes, stealth wealth, downward mobility. I completely agree. But I also think fashion subcultures have been commodified to the point where they've lost their political meaning. In the '80s, and maybe the early '90s, fashion was a political statement just like art was…and real art wasn't about selling out or succeeding in a mainstream context; it was the opposite. The whole idea was that you didn't want to conform. Anyone who was trying to make money off your art or helping you make money was corrupt or compromised. The last thing you did as an artist or a writer in the '80s was self-publicise – it was so naff, it wasn't done. Street cred was what mattered. And I've been watching, with social media and the internet, this 180-degree shift over the last few decades. My daughter's generation and the millennials, they're the opposite – you put yourself out there, fake it until you make it, flaunt your possessions, celebrate your success. I kind of admire the chutzpah of that. I'm not totally putting it down. It's just completely alien to the way I grew up.

CC: Early on in the book, you observe that 'This strange country I've landed in prides itself on a unique idea of mateship which transcends money and class, but within the university's secluded cloisters there's a vigorously upheld divide between the haves and have-nots'. Did you still believe in that egalitarian ideal of Australia before you started university?

AB: I did, mainly because I hadn't really lived here, apart from a few times as a child in between my parents' posts. My idea of Australia was formed by what I knew of Gough Whitlam's fantastic egalitarian project to make education free for all, and Bob Hawke's cocky attitude towards the Americans when we won the America's Cup, and Midnight Oil's brilliantly angry anti-nuke anthems and the brazen bands on *Countdown* – this kind of rollicking, larrikin celebration of Australian masculinity and pride that was sold to us through the Foster's ads.

When I turned up in 1985 to Sydney…I was profoundly shocked by how class and status were front and centre. I was part of the haves at Wesley College, and the friends that I gravitated towards were part of the have-nots – the public-school kids. The have-nots regarded the haves as wankers and dickheads and didn't want to be part of what they were into and vice versa. For me, the immediate questions were: where do I belong and who do I like? I leant to the people who were anti-mainstream and progressive. But at the same time, the '80s were driven by Reaganomics and Thatcher's call that we're all individuals – there's no such thing as society. This turbocharged the exploitation of resources around the world, the increasing wealth gap, corporations over consumers. The mainstream was extremely right wing. So while I gravitated to the lefties on campus, I was also repulsed by civil-rights activists who were still clinging to these fuzzy '60s flower-power concepts of 'we're all free' and 'love will stop war'. That to me felt ridiculous, and the fashion of the '80s kind of underlined that. If you were a woman, it was about dressing tough: the padded shoulders, the brutal make-up, the sharp, metallic, inorganic shapes. There was a tough individualism young women aspired to that was replacing the collective '70s sisterhood, that huggy-feely stuff our feminist forebears had embraced. And I think we chose this individualism, in retrospect, to our own detriment.

CC: That notion that you had to be a bit brutal in order to survive really comes through when you talk about some of the hazing rituals that went on. How did these rituals shape the social hierarchy on campus? Did they reflect that wider '80s sensibility of rampant individualism?

AB: Look, I think it's important to also say that I really was a wanker when I was seventeen.

CC: Weren't we all?

AB: I was so pretentious. A mouthy intellectual with the EQ of a three-year-old. I knew absolutely nothing, even though I could quote scads of Shakespeare, Joyce, Wilde and so on. I was a virgin, and all I knew about life was what I'd read. I'd devoured anything I could get my hands on about Oxbridge life – everything from *Brideshead Revisited* to Monty Python's crazy undergrad capers. So when I came to Sydney Uni I had this fabulous vision that yes, there would be hazing, yes, there would be iconoclasm and rebellion and regressions and hijinks, and I couldn't wait.

At Wesley College, it was delightful to me that there were all these hallowed rituals: gapping, which was stripping freshers naked and dropping them at The Gap with nothing but a sock, and they had to find their own way home; ponding, which was the least harmful hazing ritual and pretty much happened to all the freshers, which involved being thrown, fully dressed and drunk, into the library atrium pond; and jacking, which was the most ingenious ritual of all. The seniors would pick on the most opinionated and irritating freshers, of which I was definitely one – I actually prided myself on it – and when they were off somewhere, get into their room and radically alter it. My room jacking was clever. I remember coming home from this turgid ferry formal (we had to dance with the third-year engineers who were too drunk to say anything interesting), opening my door to discover that my entire room was empty, looking through the diamond-pane window and seeing its contents laid out perfectly, just as they had been inside my room, on top of the Bosch lecture theatre over the road – complete with my hat stand and poster hanging in thin air, above my wardrobe, bed and desk. And before feeling irritation about 'how do I get it down?', feeling a sense of awe and wonder that the seniors had decided I was worth such energy.

I should qualify this by saying Wesley was the only co-ed college at the time – their hazing rituals were much less extreme than at the single-sex colleges. And in terms of how these rituals fit into the whole dog-eat-dog, we're-all-individuals rat-race of the '80s, there was a prevailing sense that it was power, not civility, that got you to the top, and as a woman you had to be tough and wear a mask. Even the way we danced was aggressive. No matter what the seniors did to us, and there were many rumours of non-consensual sex, we sucked it up. The last thing any of us would have done back then was complain to the higher-ups.

CC: You write that when you're seventeen, you barely identify as a woman, and when someone catcalls you on campus one day, you think, *I don't really understand how my gender is relevant here.* How would you describe your growing awareness of what you might call the status divide between men and women?

AB: I developed very late because I did gymnastics for ten years and that stunted my body. I was as flat as a plank, and the minute I stopped gymnastics and started university, my body changed almost overnight. Suddenly I was walking around in the curvaceous body of a woman, which I had no idea how to be and didn't identify as. My mindset was asexual and non-gendered, in a way. I was able to look at the divisions between men and women at uni and in outback Australia and refuse to be part of it. I saw immediately that the apex predators at Wesley were male and they competed with each other by getting freshette head jobs, getting drunker than the others, being loud and obnoxious and – most importantly – being good at sport. The women were also loud and fantastically opinionated and funny, but unfortunately they weren't given apex-predator roles – they were facilitators, enablers, hecklers, jokesters but not rulers, and that gave me the shits. I thought, *That's not fair*, you know? *Why should this be the case?* I resented being cast as a secondary citizen just because of the way my body suddenly looked. I was also bewildered by it. I didn't understand it...I saw feminism as this worthy, bra-burning, outdated '70s thing. But I also suspected, the more I encountered this implicit othering that I got because of my gender – indeed, that all women got, or anyone who didn't conform to heterosexual male ideals – that I needed to understand what feminism was.

CC: Gender is something you grapple with throughout the book, first at university and then when you and Peisley set out on your hitchhiking adventure. Something terrible happens a short while into this trip: you're kidnapped and assaulted by truckies. Afterwards you carry on travelling, and at the time you don't think of yourself as a victim – but you realise that outside the university as well as inside it you are, as you put it in the book, 'nothing more than my gender'. How did that trip reshape your relationship with gender politics?

AB: Once I got on the road with Peisley I was slapped in the head by an ongoing misogyny and warfare between the sexes in which masculinity was definitely winning. I saw it and experienced it just by walking around in my newly female body. Immediately the assumption was that if I was with Peisley, we were married, and if I corrected people then I was fair game sexually, and any old bastard who was feeling horny would have a go. It's a complex thing, and we didn't have the language for it in the '80s. Words are powerful – if you can label something and amplify it, as the millennials know, you can change the world. We didn't have words for rape culture; we didn't have words for misogyny. The words we had were *patriarchy* and *male chauvinism*. But a chauvinist was an old drunk-uncle type who was handsy at a party. It wasn't seen as this endemic, institutionalised thing, and yet that's what the books I was reading, by de Beauvoir, Friedan, Dworkin, Solanas, Greer, were telling me – that this oppression, casual or overt, is all part of patriarchy. I understood it in theory, but being on the road really highlighted how physically vulnerable I was as a woman, alone or with a guy.

CC: You also discover that Australian egalitarianism is a myth in the outback. When you visit North Bourke in Queensland, you write that 'the aggression dial is turned up to eleven'. It reminded me of that scene from the *Wake in Fright* film adaptation in which the protagonist goes into the town pub and a local offers to buy him a drink; he declines, so the local gets very aggro and insists, 'I'll buy you a bloody drink!' Could you tell me how this realisation of Australia's wider social divide affected you?

AB: I had an intellectual understanding of the outback from Xavier Herbert's *Capricornia* and *Poor Fellow My Country*, and from Patrick White – but no lived experience at all. Herbert talked about inequality, insidious racism, colonialism – and I was completely against the British imperialists and terra nullius lie that had established white Australia.

When we got to Bourke, the other whites wouldn't go near us – they thought we were freeloaders, and obviously filthy lefties because Peisley had a Midnight Oil decal on his guitar. But the Indigenous people, the Greeks, the Germans, basically all the outcasts from Anglo society, immediately joined us in a drinking circle and we passed around warm bottles of port for eight hours. I remember a lovely shy man called Allan, who was Indigenous, his sister or aunty Rosie (it was never clear) and his mother. Our conversation was aggressive, revealing, moving, funny – we had been embraced as fellow outsiders, so that when the cops came past, it was us against them. That comradeship was new to me, and beautiful, but it also highlighted a divide I hadn't been aware of physically or emotionally – the divide between those in power, white men, and everyone else.

I also understood that as a middle-class white person I was more privileged than the people I was drinking with, who did not live in great circumstances. We were desperate to get out of North Bourke but we couldn't – the cops ignored us, the whites ignored us. But Allan and his mother got their weekly dole cheque and used the entire $159.00 of it to shout us a taxi to Cunnamulla – they were visiting their relatives, they said, but what an act of profound generosity and decency. That moment brought home to me a lot of things: guilt that I could get out of Bourke anytime I liked if I called my parents, shame that I relied on the kindness of people who were much less privileged than me, astonishment and wonder at the comradeship I'd discovered. And anger and disappointment that Australia, far from being this egalitarian, progressive utopia, was simply doing what the rest of the Western world was doing, following increasingly unequal, elitist class divisions based on status and wealth.

That was the other thing I was trying to grapple with in this book – whether there's a connection between Australian misogyny, which is about brutally repressing women, and Australian racism, which is about denying what we've done to our First Nations people. How much of that misogyny is connected to white denial and rage and guilt, the need to pretend that 'she'll be right', as long as no one looks too hard at the past? I don't know, it's a big thing, but I was trying to work that out while I was writing.

CC: You close the book by advocating for kindness: 'Cruelty and inequality are everywhere. Humans, whether from the city or the country, need love. In a fracturing world, kindness counts.' How hopeful are you about the future?

AB: I'm both terrified and hopeful. I think we're slow-boiling frogs as far as global warming goes – it is an emergency now, and that terrifies me. As an artist I'm hopeful, or at least invigorated by the problem because it gives me a reason to make films and write books. But we're at a major crossroads, and it started in the '80s. That rapacious, exploit-at-all-costs, profit-before-people attitude that Reagan and Thatcher began – we're now living its end game. We're in a monumental struggle between this billionaire mentality of 'technology has destroyed the world and technology will save us' – in other words, let's just colonise somewhere else, forget Earth, find a Planet B – and the civil, human-centred values that Thatcher and Reagan repressed. The values of community, the values of preserving nature, and the values of our First Nations people, who know this better than anyone: look after the planet and it will look after you.

As a mother I find hope in my daughter's generation, because Gen Z seems switched on to this. As I was writing the book, my daughter resisted my absolutes about men and women – she says it's all more nuanced and complex. She's right, but all revolutions start with absolutes. As someone who came of age in the '80s, I belong to Gen X – the first generation of women to grow up without a map. The second-wave feminists burnt down marriage in the '70s – they said, *Don't be a '50s housewife*. They left it in cinders, but they didn't give us a life raft – so we said, *Okay, we've got no map, we've got no rules; all we know is we don't want to be housewives*. We wanted careers – getting pregnant and having babies was horrifying. The women above us who had successful careers were ruthless loners – that's how they survived – and many treated us with suspicion. The men around us presented sexist hurdles we had to avoid or jump over, daily. It was hard. And then we saw your generation [Gen Y] start to work out how a new map might play out, and all these ingenious identities and ways of being have since evolved, right through to Gen Z and gender fluidity and my daughter's desire for nuance. It all flowed from the rule-free, anarchic '80s. We had no map, but we figured it out.

Anna Broinowski is a Walkley Award-winning filmmaker and author who documents countercultural subjects. Her films include *Aim High in Creation!* (about North Korean cinema), *Forbidden Lie$* (about hoax author Norma Khouri) and *Helen's War* (about nuclear campaigner Dr Helen Caldicott). She is the author of *The Director Is the Commander* (2015) and *Please Explain: The Rise, Fall and Rise Again of Pauline Hanson* (2017). A senior lecturer at the University of Sydney, she researches propaganda film and deepfakes.

FICTION

High life

Jess Ho

'THE BEST SHIFT is me, the bottle crusher and no customers for thirty minutes,' says Joe. He's leaning back in his chair, top three buttons undone with sweat collecting on his upper lip while sinking the off-label beer the restaurant buys in pallets specifically for our knock-offs. He makes the face he always makes, like he's just tasted cat's piss, but he doesn't care because it's free. He goes for another sip. We are allocated two bottles per shift, but no one ever goes in for a second. He wipes the sweat off his face, tries to decipher the foreign language on the label as if learning something new about the beer would change its flavour, and sneers.

We've just finished one of the longest and hardest shifts of the year, and we are too tired to leave the building. It's Christmas Eve, a 35-degree night, and we survived three dinner seatings while being two people down. We also all worked a double, and our staff meal was the butt ends of bread choked down with blood-temperature water while polishing cutlery. Every single person we served was tired, stressed, sick of spending money and not looking forward to seeing their in-laws. They also all wanted dressing on the side, no garlic and everything gluten free, but to also have multiple serves of the pasta of the day. Bah, humbug.

I roll up my sleeve and catch a glimpse of my Apple watch. 'Guys, it's one. Merry Christmas. Shall we celebrate?' I mime the universal sign for a drink.

'Yeah, I'm in. Champagne?' says Graham, one of our oldest staff members. To me, he was born in the kitchen, and despite his slipped disc, high blood pressure and the RSI in both hands, he will be in the kitchen until the day he dies.

'Yeah, why not?' says Kathy, his sous and twenty-five years his junior. Kathy rarely sticks around for a knock-off anymore because, as she keeps reminding us, she is 'saving for a deposit', so her momentary lapse in character makes the rest of us nod in agreement. There are six of us and six glasses of champagne in a bottle. It was meant to be.

Lena, our junior sommelier, grabs the wine list from the waiters' station and begins to thumb through it.

'Blanc de blanc, brut, blanc de noir or rosé,' she says. 'Or we can do a crémant–'

'No,' interrupts Graham. 'No crémant. We're celebrating. Just don't send me broke before the break.' We aren't getting paid for the next three weeks while we're closed.

'Try to keep it under a hundred each?' says Joe.

'A hundred?' asks Kathy. 'Make it fifty, I'm–'

'Saving for a deposit. We know,' the rest of us say in unison.

'Yeah, I'm living week to week,' says Dan, our senior waiter, who always cries poor but somehow comes to work in a new pair of sneakers every week.

'Well, if we factor in our staff discount, we can get a pretty decent bottle,' I say.

'We're still paying 70 per cent, and 70 per cent of 500 – 'cos, like, what's the point if we're gonna drink a bottle we'd order any day of the week – divided by six is tonnes to spend for a 125 mils. That's forty-six cents per mil. Per mil!' As part of the wine team, Lena does a lot of wine study and maths. Usually, the wine team calculates the cost per glass, but Lena always takes it a step too far.

'If I'm dropping sixty bucks on a glass of wine, I want it to be fucking great,' Dan says, turning to me while raising his palms. 'Am I right?'

'Damn straight,' I say, thinking about the table that forked out $600 on two bottles of wine that were five years too young to drink. If they knew their shit, they could have spent fifty less for the vintage produced a year later that's good to drink now. What a waste.

'I can live with spending sixty bucks,' says Kathy.

Lena doesn't give her a chance to change her mind and disappears into the cellar, returning with six Zalto crystal champagne flutes, a bottle of 2014 Bérêche et Fils Mailly Grand Cru champagne and the EFTPOS machine.

'Have we done cash out yet?' she asks.

'It's fine, I'll amend it,' says Dan, 'but bags not polishing the wine glasses.'

I immediately stick my thumb on my forehead and shout out 'Bags not!' at the same time as Kathy and Graham. We all look at Joe, who just shrugs his shoulders to say, *Whatever.*

'So, this is a 100 per cent pinot noir–' begins Lena as she cuts the foil off the neck of the bottle and eases the cork out without a sound.

'Aaaaaap, bap, bap, bap,' Graham silences her. 'You're off the clock now. You've already fetched the wine; we're about to tap a few hours of our lives away to pay for it. Just let us enjoy it.' Typical chef. If we ever told him the diners said this when we started describing his food, he'd lose it.

'But how do you know what you're drinking, or if you're going to like it?' says Lena.

'I have tastebuds, don't I?'

Kathy slides Graham his glass and he takes a gulp. He wiggles his nose and says, 'Not bad, Lena. Not bad. You might just keep your job as a somm, hey?'

Lena rolls her eyes.

I pick up my stem and wave it under my nose. I detect citrus oil, beeswax, pears and smoke. I press the glass against my lips and tilt $10 into my mouth. I let the effervescent mousse coat my tongue and dance against the roof of my palate. I swish the chalky, concentrated wine behind my teeth, even though my dentist has warned me I'm wearing away the enamel behind my incisors, and swallow. There is a confident saline finish. The EFTPOS machine makes its way around to me and I wave my phone over it as I sip another $10.

My wrist vibrates and notifies me I've just spent $58.33.

FUCK. I DID it again.

I run my hands over my body and realise I've fallen asleep in my clothes. It feels like someone has pissed in my mouth, tried to soak up the liquid with a bag of sand, poured salt in my eyes and put my brain through a blender. I reach for a glass of water and notice that I emptied out the contents of my pockets on the nightstand. Phone, wallet, keys, envelope filled with last week's tips.

Shit.

There's $50.20 left in the packet. I've spent $450 in one night, and it was meant to last me the week. I let out a groan and chug the glass of water that's been sitting on the table for the last two days.

I take out my phone and check my camera reel. There's a blurry photo of what appears to be a thumb, and a video of me whining along to Alanis Morissette's 'You Oughta Know' time stamped at 3.42 am. I look elated, sweaty and sloppy. I open my banking app to see that Lena, Joe and Dan each transferred $75 to me at 3 am. I must have paid for the karaoke room in cash.

I get up and go through the pockets of my pants, shirt and bag. I pull out crumpled receipts from the past weeks as well as a fresh one from last night. I paid for everyone's drinks and a round of shots at a cocktail bar before they closed. I must have left a hefty tip. Idiot.

I do it all the time. I want to take care of my friends. I want them to know how much I value them. I get generous. I want to be the big guy. I want to have the upper hand. I overextend myself. I insist. And then I tip. Who the fuck ordered the zombies?

I bring up the calculator app on my phone. The restaurant is closed for the next twenty days. My pay, which will come in two days, is $950 plus change. I'll get another $500 in tips from this week. Hopefully more, because people were in the Christmas spirit – though people are also notoriously stingy during the holidays after spending on presents. That's $1,500 to last me the next twenty days, which is $75 a day. Thank God I've just paid rent.

A notification goes off on my phone. Kathy's hosting orphan's Christmas this year and it starts in an hour. She said not to bring anything, but no one who has ever said that actually means it. What she really means is don't bother if you're going to bring something cheap and cheerful. I walk over to my cellar, which is just cardboard boxes stacked on top of each other in my wardrobe, and start unpacking bottles. This is my secret stash of wine that I've managed to purchase by ingratiating myself with suppliers. The bottles start at a hundred, landed. I don't even want to think about the top end. Every bottle is under allocation and needs to spend years lying down. I could have gone on a fancy holiday with the money I've put into these boxes.

I line up a few options and end up chilling a chardonnay in my freezer while I shower. I have to play it smart with the hospo crowd. I need to impress without being showy. It has to be considered without being pretentious. Distinctive without looking dickish. This is the safest bet.

I put on a vintage Ann Demeulemeester dress that I'm still paying off from The RealReal and the new Rick Owens x Converse shoes I was lucky enough to be gifted by a regular. She was sent the wrong size and didn't want to pay the postage to send them back to the PR agency, so gave them to me in lieu of a tip. They're not my size either, but that's what an inner sole is for. She told me they're not going on the market until February, and every time I've worn them I've felt invincible. Unlike cash tips, I don't have to split shoes with the rest of the crew. I shove my headphones, wallet, keys and the bottle of wine in my bag and realise the only thing that I'm not still paying off is the wine and my keys. Even my bag isn't my bag. Not fully; not yet, anyways.

WHEN I GET to Kathy's, the gate to her Victorian terrace and her front door are wide open and everyone's either hiding under the air conditioner inside or trying to assert their dominance over the hibachi outside with cardboard ripped from old boxes used to fan the coals. Thankfully, the grill is just heating up. Everyone knows you should never let a sommelier cook, a chef make cocktails or a bartender choose wine.

'Hey, I didn't expect you here on time. Thanks for bankrolling me last night, moneybags. If you weren't so insistent on having my company, I would have felt bad.' Kathy was the one who ordered the zombies: I'm hit with a flashback to her yelling, 'Go hard, go early,' as she jumped into her Uber.

'No worries. Where should I put this bottle?' I say, gesturing to my bag.

'I told you not to bring anything. But the drinks fridge is over there.' She motions towards the shed next to the hibachi. 'You can measure dicks with the wine wankers from other restaurants outside.'

Bring it. I open the sliding door and step into the heat.

'What, a Friday night off where you work? How'd you swing that?' The more you can get away with, the higher up the ladder you are.

'He's lying,' Chris whispers to me. He is Ross' manager and oversees the wine team's rosters.

'Excuse me,' I say, weaving past the boys with my bag resting on my front.

'What do you have there?' asks Pete.

I dip my arm into the leather and pull out the bottle that has buried itself under all the pens, bottle caps, foils and corks that have collected since the last time I emptied it. 'What do you think?'

Pete takes the bottle from my hand and examines it carefully, angling it away from the glare of the midday sun. 'Whoa, nice. Take a look.' He hands it to Ross.

'I just grabbed it from my cellar,' I say, trying to sound nonchalant.

'Great producer,' says Ross.

'Only 720 bottles produced. New French oak. Cool climate, single vineyard origin. Whole bunch pressed. Wild ferment in new demi-muid. Twelve months on lees. Unfined. Unfiltered,' I qualify.

'Very cool,' says Chris, 'but that's nothing.' He motions for me to get out of the way and opens the fridge. He takes out a bottle and stands it on the table next to the hibachi, and it's so hot I can already see the glass bursting with condensation. 'Look at this.'

We all lean forward to inspect it.

'That's really nice,' says Pete. I clench my fists and my jaw simultaneously to control my anxiety.

'Giaconda Estate chardonnay,' Chris says, to make sure we all know what we're looking at. 'What do you think?' he directs to me.

I am barely able to contain my envy; I've been holding my breath the entire time. I manage to let out a whisper: 'Nice.'

Ross takes the bottle off the table, bringing it closer to his line of sight so it catches the light in a way that he can read the label. 'Jesus, this is super. The '98, too. How did a nitwit like you get so tasteful?'

He sets the bottle down next to mine and my retinas sear the image into my brain. I find myself comparing their merits and rarity. Sure, it's a great wine, but it's so obvious. It's so lazy. I can't believe Ross prefers Chris' bottle to mine.

'But wait,' says Ross, 'You ain't seen nothing yet.' He walks over to the fridge and takes out his wine: a Cullen Kevin John chardonnay. 'Didn't know what was on the menu, but this can go with anything from shellfish to chicken. Typical Christmas stuff.'

His wine is an exceptional choice. 'Impressive,' I manage to choke out. 'Let's see what else is in there.'

Chris crouches in front of the open fridge and pulls out an unmistakable bottle. Yellow wax. Eggshell label. Even with the sun reflecting off it, I can tell that it's Raveneau. My mouth dries up and I struggle to swallow. I can feel my pulse in my fingertips. My God, who could even source a bottle like that this time of year? Who has the money for Raveneau? I feel my hand start to shake.

'Pete, did you bring this?'

Pete nods at Chris with a smirk.

'You're such a baller.'

'I got lucky at a wine auction, so goodbye yearly bonus.' He chuckles.

'Hey, is something wrong?' Ross says to me. 'You're sweating.'

I'M FINALLY BACK at work, which means it is seven days before I get paid. Just in time for rent. I've almost made it. I have just under $100 left to my name. My phone bill will automatically deduct from my account in the next couple of days. In the meantime, I'll have staff meals to get me through the day and knock-offs to finish off the night. I almost miss the not-quite-right flavour of those skanky beers.

'Looking good,' says Kathy. I haven't seen her since Christmas.

'Thanks. It's the minimum-wage poverty diet,' I say, sucking in my cheeks.

'As if. Dan told me about that afternoon of martinis and oysters.'

I wonder which time Kathy is talking about. Every time Dan and I met up 'for a quick one' we ended up drinking several martinis and a bottle of wine, as if our order could differentiate us from all the rich kids who'd decided not to invade Sorrento, Lorne or Rye over the break. It was important that other hospitality workers knew we were also hospitality workers. The problem with that was it meant I had to survive off instant noodles, cans of tuna and water for the next few days.

'Is that new?' Kathy rubs the cloth of my shirt between her fingers. 'It's really nice.'

'Oh this? I bought it ages ago, but I haven't worn it yet,' I lie. It was a drunk, Boxing Day online-sale purchase and another addition to the list of things I'm paying off. It is also non-refundable. Just four fortnightly instalments of $83 until it's mine. It's a bottle of wine a month. I could have one less bottle of wine a month. That's what I told myself at the time, anyway.

'You're so cool,' she teases. 'All the it kids are wearing this label now, but you were an early adopter.'

I unbutton my top and change into my work uniform, leaving the shirt crumpled in the bottom of my locker.

The shift is rough. I placate a table who insist on ordering Pacific oysters even though we don't have any available because they spawn during summer. I reluctantly serve a woman a dense, jammy shiraz from South Australia – which should spend about twenty more years in the bottle – with her kingfish crudo, and she complains to my manager that the wine smothered the fish. A man whinges that his 350-gram steak is taking too long even though he wants it well done. A couple on a date swear that their manhattans have too much alcohol in them, and a man on the keto diet tries to finish his meal with an old fashioned without sugar. Each table thanks us profusely for our service, which always equates to a horrible tip.

'This is worse than I remember,' I say after pack-down as I guzzle a beer.

'The job or the beer?' asks Kathy, ''Cos that shift was painful.'

'Both.' I'd quit if I didn't need the money so badly.

'The job's not that bad. I've had much worse,' says Graham. 'But this,' he holds up his half-empty bottle, 'this is truly toilet water.' He smacks his tongue around his mouth in disgust. 'This won't do. Wanna get a real drink?'

'Not me,' says Kathy. 'I'm saving–'

Graham waves his hand in the air to stop her from finishing the sentence.

I take a deep breath and think about the $92 I've got left. There's my impending phone bill. There's also my shirt, the Ann Demeulemeester dress, my headphones, my bag, my rent, the internet, the electricity, the water.

Graham senses my hesitation and says, 'A quick one. I'm buying.' He doesn't give me time to respond, but instead takes my beer with one hand, tosses it into the empty bottle bin and links his other arm with mine, guiding me into the sleepless expanse of the city.

Jess Ho is a freelance writer, journalist and critic. They were previously the food and drink editor of *Time Out Melbourne*. They have also been published in *Gourmet Traveller, Eater, The Guardian, The Age Spectrum*, the *Financial Review, Good Weekend, frankie* and *The Big Issue*, among many others, as well as a number of cookbooks and guides on Melbourne. They are the host and producer of the SBS podcast *Bad Taste*. Their first book, *Raised by Wolves*, was published in 2022.

IN CONVERSATION

Put your house in order

Possession, assembly and the art of collage

Pascalle Burton and Carody Culver

Poet, performer and musician Pascalle Burton has always been compelled by the visual possibilities of language and the imaginative dynamism of collage. Her multimodal work, which often draws on conceptual art and cultural theory, evokes a playful intelligence and a thrilling plurality of perspectives and ideas. Her recent project, What has been said by many and has often been said (after Cicero's first and second speeches on the Agrarian Law)*, is no exception: it combines and rearranges text by Cicero and images of 1970s modernist Australian homes to explore notions of possession, power and profit. Burton talked to* Griffith Review *Editor Carody Culver about the collaboration that shaped the work and the process of creating something new from something extant.*

CARODY CULVER: The images in this beautiful piece are taken from the book *Australian Housing in the Seventies* by Howard Tanner – and oh my, what houses they are! How did you come across this book, and what was it about the images that resonated with you?

PASCALLE BURTON: Those houses are just gorgeous, aren't they? The architecture is stunning aesthetically, but I also love that the photographs have such a direct purpose – their job is to showcase residential architecture.

I collect second-hand books for their potential to turn into something down the track. It's rare I find material and know how to use it immediately. And I can't always recall where I encounter them but I do know where I found *Australian Housing in the Seventies*. I was teaching at a high school years ago and the library was culling old books, so this one ended up coming home with me. If I look at the library slip at the back, it was last borrowed in October 1981 – it's been patiently living on the shelves for a long time!

CC: The poem accompanying the images uses text from Cicero's first speech to the Roman Senate on the Agrarian Law. He opposed the law, which, as I understand it, proposed to redistribute agricultural land. Centuries later, we're still talking about land – our purported right to it, our desire for it, and the economic and ideological status with which we invest it. Why did Cicero's words resonate with you?

PB: Yes, the poem is an erasure of Cicero's first speech and the collages incorporate the second speech. The truth is, I wasn't drawn to this text through my own efforts. It was sent to me by an excellent poet and friend, Andrew Galan, for a project we were doing called *Author Unknown*.

Over the past few years, David Stavanger (another wonderful poet and dear friend) and I have been collaborating with around fifty artists to co-create works using a selection of poetic constraints. It was born out of a need for community following the outbreak of the pandemic. Some of the results are straight-up poems and others incorporate visual poetry. Red Room Poetry has been publishing the work online and I'd definitely encourage your readers to explore them.

I feel ridiculously fortunate to have been involved in the project. I love collaboration. You end up with something you never would have created by yourself; I mean, it's you but it's more than you. And I really have Andrew to thank for spurring on this particular work.

He posted me this beautiful old book of Cicero's orations with a note inside:

> Interpreting Cicero's speeches were some of my earliest efforts at applying theory and ideology to text. I like to take different theories and use them in pieces on ideas or concepts. Doing this with overtly political writing, such as Cicero, was for me a useful starting point, and I find it still has application today; although it does slow me down, as my life can feel like it is question marks. I know we have discussed my frustration over the use of the term 'apolitical' without full and exhaustive exploration of the word, and how and why it has been chosen to apply to public servants. That I enjoy applying

> theories to text that is attempting to hide or misdirect on its politics, or doesn't acknowledge its politics [...] for me, started with reading classical literature.

So Andrew had the connection to Cicero's speeches and it was my task to respond to it in some way.

CC: What made you connect Cicero's text with the images in *Australian Housing in the Seventies*?

PB: For me, collage is about relationships. I'd written the poem using Cicero's first speech but sensed there should be something more. And I was just so in love with the Latin text on the left-hand side of the book that I wanted to do something with that. I spent some time going through my book collection, stumbled upon *Australian Housing in the Seventies* and made the connection.

Making collages and treating found texts is another form of possession, where I'm using something for my own purposes. I take the process seriously, both in erasing or extracting from texts and in occupying the collage space. I pay attention to what the texts are saying. That means not only when they were written, but what are they saying today? How do they echo back to the world? How should I represent them?

CC: How do Cicero's speeches contribute to the predicament we find ourselves in today? How do these gorgeous houses from the '70s interact with the current housing crisis?

PB: Capitalism has dragged housing on a trajectory where 'winners' are those who exploit as many people as possible to maximise their returns. How did owning a home become about owning investment properties? Well, the Howard government, for starters. There's a chasm between property developers and speculators – who seem to drive policy – and those who are priced out of entering the housing market or are facing rental stress; between people whose concerns are renovating their house or building investment portfolios, and people with the basic need to keep a roof over their head. It perpetuates poverty and inequality because the exchange of money flows one way, from renters to landlords.

In the introduction for *Australian Housing in the Seventies*, architect Philip Cox seems somewhat critical of Australia's response to meeting the needs and realising the potential of housing in 1976. This was published in a time when the Australian government was more invested in social housing; when wages and house prices were on relative speaking terms, compared to today. The houses in the book are clearly status symbols, and Cox acknowledges they are affordable 'for middle to high income groups and not within the purse of Joe Citizen on a low income'. So the divide in 1976 is already apparent and primed to loom larger.

Having said all that, I still like to keep my art open to interpretation and I generally prefer readers to come to their own conclusions about what it could be about.

CC: I love what you've done with the images – the collage work is subtle but striking. Rather than cutting up the houses and changing the way they appear to exist in space, you've found existing areas in the photographs – roofs, a pool, sections of garden patio – to fill with fragments of Cicero's text in Latin. I'm interested in the preservation on both sides here – preserving the original Latin in the textual fragments and preserving the structural integrity (for want of a better phrase!) of the houses. What guided these choices?

PB: Thank you! 'Structural integrity' is hilarious. Incorporating text in collage is something I have done before. It can reframe how we consume language and images. I describe myself as a poet but my work is often multi-modal. Maybe my approach is a collage of artforms, layering poetry with sound, art or film to disrupt what people think poetry should be. Either way, I usually take a minimalist approach.

The visual aspect of language is so compelling. I love artists and poets who use language assemblage in their work, like Natalie Harkin, Sandra Selig, Erica Baum, Madonna Staunton, Liliane Lijn, Rosalie Gascoigne, Vernon Ah Kee and Robert MacPherson. Their visual language might be sculptural, two-dimensional or incorporated into collage.

And collage is such an evocative medium on both visual and brain levels. Some of my favourite collage artists are Jhonny Russell, Bella Li, Mickalene Thomas, Robert Pollard, Helen Adams, Frida Orupabo, Hannah Höch and John Baldessari. I particularly love what minimal collage can do. I'm a huge fan of John Stezaker, whose expert yet seemingly effortless placement of images is sublime.

CC: The names of places and people are deliberately left blank in your text, which for me gives it a stronger sense of universality – these themes of possession, greed and abuse of power can be applied to so many different situations involving land and houses and ownership. Were you deliberately seeking to evoke a universality here, or were there other motivations and ideas at play?

PB: Thanks for picking up on that, Carody! You're right, they're intentionally redacted to imply that this act of possession occurs in different ways and contexts. It resonates in the multilayered and ongoing consequences of empire, expansion of land by conquest, the establishment of colonies, occupation, money, power and the world's hunger for *more*.

These concepts are at play in Australia's need for social and affordable housing. They're at play in the ongoing colonial land-grab of Australia, through the dispossession and over-incarceration of First Nations people, and they're at play in the military occupation and genocide of Palestinians.

It feels so discordant that our world simultaneously exists with a brutal genocide in Gaza, ever-increasing worldwide housing insecurity and, at the same time, TV shows about home-flipping for profit or *Grand Designs*. It's wild.

Pascalle Burton is a Meanjin-based experimental poet and performer with an interest in conceptual art and cultural theory. Her collection *About the Author Is Dead* is available through Cordite Books. She also plays in the band The Stress of Leisure.

What has been said by many and has often been said

PASCALLE BURTON

I
stirring up trouble
putting up a notice of the sale
this forest in the list of neglected possessions
it is unfair

II

HE does not let a single item pass
the sale of what belongs to the ______
THEY order the lands of the ______ and ______ to be sold
the territories in ______ acquired by the ______
that most excellent and fruitful land of ______ added to the revenues of ______
and afterwards the lands in ______, which become ______'s possessions
then THEY sell the ______ itself

A view from across the street.

III
to sell wherever
to sell piece-meal
to sell *them*
to take money for not selling

THEY left the city as private individuals
on private business
excessively avaricious
unrestricted and unlimited

IV
listen, listen
they hope much so that *they* may be free
but the law attacks

so carefully hidden, THEY are draining
THEY are laying violent hands upon
let loose on the world with great power
(as if *we* do not understand)

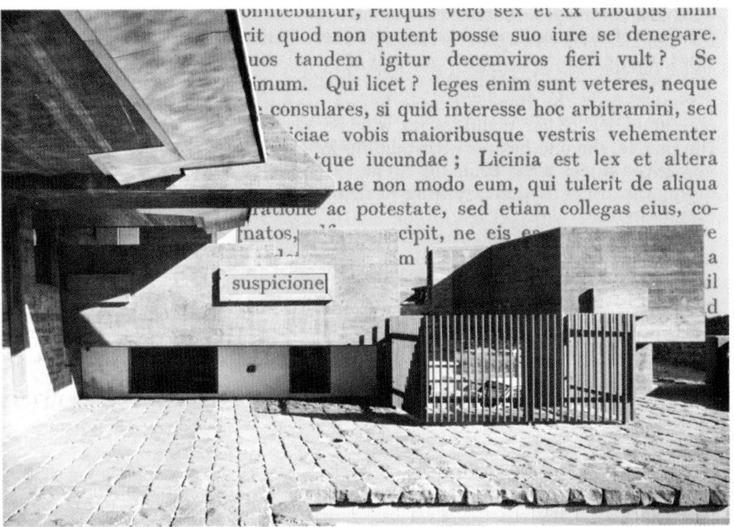

V
first, who can fail to see?
secondly, *I* am afraid.

VI
a place which is said to have given birth to
pride and cruelty
to rank and fortune
henchmen and insolence
walls and tyranny
wholly disastrous

VII
how is it armed?
the law itself allows ______ to conduct as THEY wish
in any towns THEY please

it does not lose its value in time of war

VIII
such things as these
THEY have given hope to the wicked

in the midst of this confusion
we shall find nothing
but the cunning fraud of the law

IX
be prudent in the midst of danger
the danger of the internal and domestic
hidden wounds are formed
what power is
to be restored

NOTES

The full title of this piece is *What has been said by many and has often been said (after Cicero's first and second speeches on the Agrarian Law)*. Collages and poems are composed of text from the Loeb Classical Library edition of *Cicero Orations* (first published in 1930 with an English translation by John Henry Reese), and images from Howard Tanner's *Australian Housing in the Seventies* (Ure Smith, Sydney, 1976) with photographs commissioned by Bruce Rickard and Associates (page 58), Philip and Louise Cox (page 83), Vivian Fraser of Ancher Mortlock Murray and Woolley (page 102), Guilford Bell (page 26), Enrico Taglietti (page 42), Terry Dorrough and Heather Dorrough (page 65), Edgard Pirrotta of Morris and Pirrotta (page 46), Ancher Mortlock Murray and Woolley (page 96) and Allen, Jack and Cottier (page 38). Attempts have been made to locate, seek permission from and acknowledge all copyright owners of the images incorporated into this work. If any omissions have occurred, rights-holders not credited are invited to get in contact with the artist. This piece was created as part of *Author unknown*, a collaborative writing project co-edited with David Stavanger, supported by Australia Council of the Arts and Red Room Poetry. Thanks to Andrew Galan for offering Cicero as a stimulus. Many thanks to the architects and their family members who generously shed light on the houses.

NON-FICTION

Birthmarks

Deliberate intentions in mending and heritage

Bebe Oliver

THERE'S A STORY my mum would always tell. In the days after I was born, as I was making my innocent acquaintance with the world in the old Kununurra hospital, two old Aboriginal ladies walked through the maternity ward.

'Ayyyy, who blungem baby dis one yow?' one of them asked to the room of new and familiar mothers.

'That's my baby,' responded mine.

Pointing to my birthmark, the small patch of blonde hair that sat among the dark brown nest on my head, the old Aunty said, 'He gunna be proper wise boy, dis one.'

I never forgot that story – and not just because it was told at every opportunity for the first twelve years of my life. It was the first of my scriptures, dictating what my future could – should – look like. So it shall be written, so it shall be done.

MY EXPERIENCE AS an Aboriginal boy growing up was equal parts honourable and confusing, exciting and terrifying. A downside to having an Aboriginal mum and a white dad is that a high level of melanin isn't guaranteed, so unlike my two eldest siblings, my sister and I were born white. It was this that made me eager to be different: more like someone else, and less like me. That small boy, although *Blak*, wanted to be Black.

Indigenous people are built differently. Our ways of thinking, our viewpoints, the relationships we form and how we maintain them, our communication, even the way we breathe, are different to white folk. It's something I celebrate, knowing there's an ancient bloodline running through me, connected without fracture to the ground I stand on, the sky I live beneath and the water I swim in.

There was, however, a sense of displacement that didn't present itself until I was older. My heritage belongs to the Bardi Jawi people of the niimidiman (inland Country) and jardagarr (coastal Country) near Ardyaloon, but I was born on Miriwoong Gajerrong land and raised in the wild of the Nyikina. I grew up speaking the wrong language. My mouth wasn't meant for the weight of English words; my tongue needed to know the soft teeth touching of Bardi. Even now, as I approach my mid-thirties, I'm unable to speak fluently in my native voice and instead interweave a collection of cross-tribal words and phrases I've harvested over my life. When people get to know me, they ask, 'Can you speak your language?' It hurts and shames me to respond, 'Not entirely.'

There's no denying the pride and glory that comes with being born Aboriginal and knowing it, along with knowing the history of my culture. Yet with this comes a weight, attached by invisible rope tied by the hands of colonial settlers. Aboriginal people live with the death and damage our ancestors have experienced since 1788, while trying to outweigh it with the strength we inherit from the 2,000 generations that came before us.

A sadness exists deep within Aboriginal communities, where the impacts of death and loss are never forgotten. They manifest as omnipotent behaviours and habits that can be observed intergenerationally. An appalling ordeal in the childhood of someone's great-great-grandparent can create a devastating environment for them today, where actions and habits can no longer be claimed as personal choice but forced legacy.

My primary school was scattered with other Aboriginal children. Trevor, one year older than me, left a memory I'll never forget. He burnt with energy, had a smile full of glowing white teeth, and his long legs always made sure he conquered athletics events. For a kid who never missed a day of school, his absence was obvious one morning when my teacher told me and my peers that Trevor was dead. I came to learn he suicided, undeservedly helpless and unfairly swayed by domestic violence. Trevor was nine years old.

The consequences of white invasion are still fresh. Aboriginal children continue to be taken from their families and placed into unsafe, white systems. Our people, regardless of age, are being thrown into prison cells for the pettiest of reasons. We're dying younger because of untreated illness, poverty, murder and suicide. Aboriginal communities are still denied meaningful opportunities to access equal land, health, education, employment and housing rights. This is the reality that decided my career path and the channels of my work, passion and voice.

Following in the much deeper footsteps of my grandmother, I've chosen the important – albeit perilous – task of intruding on organisational structures and redesigning them to validate the experiences of Aboriginal people and place them on the frontline of advancement. From national health services and hospitals to local and state government bodies, from arts festivals, civic and cultural centres to literary organisations, it's my duty to clinically assess symptoms in society and business and diagnose a cause for treatment. I refuse the myth that the impacts of colonisation, invasion, dispossession and massacre are too deeply ingrained in the blood of Aboriginal people to ever be eradicated.

Looking back on what set me on this path, there are many things I can identify as catalysts for my own anxieties and the pressure to be 'something' or 'someone'. Even then, what takes a person from existing to being a 'someone', and what makes someone a 'something'? I've spent years interrogating the child inside me – seeking momentary triggers, evaluating my life's relationships, reliving millions of meaningless moments that meant the most to my being – to find my true, simple identity.

I WAS ALWAYS a skinny kid: tall, lanky and athletic (despite my chubby cheeks). But by the time I was sixteen and ate as much as I smoked, drank and partied, that frame of mine was only a memory, immortalised in photos.

As a teenager, I worked with my dad during the school holidays. While he drove us to get a coffee one day, without breaking his sight of the road ahead, he asked me, 'When are you going to lose some weight?'

I'd been punched so hard in the chest my heart broke. Instantly, I was imperfect and in need of change to be accepted, and as much as I didn't want to care, I did.

My father was (is) a damaged man who inherited grief and destruction from his 'dysfunctional' white upbringing. He furiously beat me several nights a week for years on end, and almost never showed me love and affection. I was afraid of him, and I hated him, but I wanted him to adore, respect and care for me too. Instead, he dragged me by my wrist into the backyard and whipped me eight times with his leather belt and its giant brass buckle for drinking his orange juice. He ran over my brand-new bike to teach me a lesson for leaving it in the driveway. He threw me into my bedroom without dinner and forbade me to come out until the morning, while the rest of my family sat to eat at the dining-room table.

When he questioned my weight, all I managed to say was, 'I don't know.' When we got to the café, he walked towards the entrance and I headed for the marsh surrounding the town. I don't recall how long I walked for, but I remember the horizon being mostly trees, speckled with white and cream from the roofs of the buildings. I stopped, lay down with my back to the burning cracks of salted mud and cried. I wanted to die.

This was the fabric my childhood was woven from. A desire for acceptance tied to a longing to be 'more Aboriginal' and fuelled by pressure to personify a preconceived idea of success. This, in turn, led me to self-harm and destruction, sadness, anger and denial.

I came out at as gay when I was eighteen, after falling in love with a man for the first time. Experience had taught me that the most dangerous person was my father, so I decided he was the first person I would have the conversation with. Sitting in my parents' living room, I confessed to him my identity.

'Dad, I'm in a relationship with Suri.'

'Oh yeah, who's she?'

'*He* is the guy I've been spending all my time with lately.'

'Oh.' He paused. '*Ohh*. Well, I'm happy for you.'

I had thought wrong. In later conversations between us where we both laid bare our feelings and histories, he said he always accepted me and loved me; he only went about being a dad 'the wrong way'. For the next fifteen years, I'd continue mending my relationship with him, resolving my hurt and forgiving his abuse to forgive him. However, time played its part in the healing of my child's heart, and I realised forgiveness didn't promise freedom, so I severed our ties and freed myself of the weight his presence added to my shoulders.

This is only one emotional emancipation I can claim. There have been other, more important (and heavier) encumbrances I've had to work through to declare a clearer sense of self and belonging.

MY GRANDMOTHER, WHO was a pioneer for Aboriginal health services, once told me, 'You might have inherited your ancestors' trauma, but you inherited their strength, too.' The recognition and subsequent channelling of this power is missing from the lives of countless Aboriginal people. So many of us have been conditioned to believe we're lesser than our non-Indigenous peers, perpetuating assimilation, a contemporary form of the White Australia policy.

When you grow up surrounded by grief, violence, abuse, addiction, poverty or other symptoms of a discriminatory society, it's easy to become vulnerable to this seeming fate. My childhood, paired with my Aboriginal trauma inheritance, meant that at twenty-two I was a drug addict who had attempted suicide multiple times. Behind me was a trail of positive, life-changing milestones, proud moments and gratitude, but any hiccups can have immense weight when you make the expectations of others your own, and this was central to my destructive slide.

Driving home from a voluntary intervention, somehow, for a moment, I was able to observe my past, present and future with clarity. I said to myself, 'If you really want to continue living, you have to leave this town.' This was the stimulus that steered me into the clear. One month later I was standing in the graffiti-laden streets of Naarm (Melbourne), 5,000 km away from my family, without possessions but filled with hope, rebuilding from the ground up. I wanted to take control of my fate. Each new morning I woke up on Wurundjeri Woi-wurrung Country, I could feel the hands of my Blak grandmother and all our descendants holding me upright. The knowledge of my ancestry was a lifeline, and integral to my survival – an ever-present, unseen safety in my heritage. Whenever I needed it, my people could save me. All it required was the simple act of remembering my descendance. It was ironic that my origins were leading me to freedom.

Cultural integrity is one of many facets of Aboriginal identity, and a testament to our reclamation of social governance led by our own communities. Aboriginal people recognise the power and impact lore and values have on the body and mind, and the life elements between, and this fuels our fire to design structures that allow our knowledge and history to be at the forefront of the services our people receive. Certainly, this powered my need to be working within the community, to acknowledge and understand the strength we find in the face of difficulty and push it into the valleys of my physical form as an Aboriginal creative.

Still, there are challenges to implementing and maintaining processes whereby Aboriginal and Torres Strait Islander people can make decisions on their own behalf, exercising choice, participation and control. 'Nothing about us without us' hasn't been accepted by all levels of government and society. Programs and initiatives for Aboriginal people are being designed by non-Indigenous thinkers, and senior positions to govern these enterprises aren't being given to Blak leaders.

When I decided to play a small part in ensuring Aboriginal people can freely determine our political, economic, social and cultural development, I didn't foresee some community members referring to me as a 'coconut' and 'traitor'. A natural (and reasonably understandable) stance from some Aboriginal people is to distance themselves from the government and its representative forms. To some, I'd sold my soul to the enemy and was perpetuating the silencing of Blak voices. However, the philosophy of a minority needing to work within the system that oppresses it to change that system applies. While I was led by this idea at the genesis of my work, I realised I've never functioned within a governmental, white organisation to fight it, but instead to discourage colonial, patriarchal aims. This is important work, vital to my own purpose, and I needed to reframe my thinking.

Many see Aboriginal people as an angry, Black community. Yes, we are both of those things (we deserve to be angry) and we're not afraid to exhibit them, but we're also much more. Personally, the more I was able to shed and abandon then discover and claim for myself, the stronger my self-certainty became. No one has permission to write my story for me, and it's this view I want to share with my community. When I rejected Aboriginal stereotypes, I saw the distinction between the world I was born into and the one I wanted to live in. *I'm not who they told me I am, but the truth I embody.* When I'm putting thought into a strategy, policy or initiative framework, I'm armed with this knowledge, so the only voice I channel is the call of genuine needs for Aboriginal people. I don't drive in opposition, but from a steadfast place of fighting for what's best, what needs to be done and who needs to be at a table. I refuse to do otherwise.

THERE IS A territorialism within the Aboriginal community, institutionalised, I feel, by the very thing that bonds us: trauma. The effects of historical and intergenerational suffering lessen the capacity of Aboriginal people to fully participate in our lives and communities in a positive way. For some, this becomes apparent in symptoms such as attachment difficulty, disconnection from family and culture, and social distress. For me, it resulted in a lack of identity and belonging, creating health and social issues; as damaging as this was, there was an even stronger desire to release myself from this trauma, which was no less harmful.

It was through my writing – the repetitive sharing and exposure to encouragement – that I was able to navigate the complex web of doubt, fear, apprehension and cynicism at the centre of my work and sense of identity.

I began writing when I was small as another way to express myself. I was a dedicated pianist, addicted to art and creativity, and I remember understanding the power of words to make the invisible visible at the instigation of imagination. At times my inventiveness blurred the lines of vision and reality, and I positioned myself in an intersectional world between my own familiarities and what I wanted for my life. Not knowing a family dynamic beyond one led by a violent and abusive dad and a passive and fragile mum, I was intrigued by the notions of peace and stillness. They were foreign concepts to me, but interesting and tempting, and formed the basis of my creative flair.

Aboriginal life is a kaleidoscope of emotions and psychological states. I struggle to write about anything beyond what I know, being so heavily influenced by what's shaped my life and view. This, ultimately, is my truth.

I was first published in 2018, at the insistent persuasion of my friend, mentor and 'Melbourne mum', Jennifer. My essay in *Growing Up Aboriginal in Australia* was my first foray into sharing my story with anyone other than my friends around a table or fire. I left my submission until the very last minute – clicking 'Submit' three minutes before the cut-off – because I was riddled with doubt whether my story was good enough for someone else to read, connect with, absorb, learn from, enjoy or even care about. This impostor syndrome has followed me ever since, sometimes silenced by my own inner voice, sometimes amplified.

In 2023, after a couple of years of back-and-forth editing (and indecisiveness about whether I was doing the right thing), I published my first book of poetry.

During a conversation with my publisher, the exceptional and nonpareil Rachel Bin Salleh, I confessed, 'I fear that people aren't going to respond to what I've written, and what this will mean for my creativity and my voice.'

'Bebe,' she answered, 'the greatest thing about being a writer is understanding that your words will touch the lives of people you'll never meet.'

In this moment, my own self-belief was changed, and I knew I had to write. A stark reminder of my identity and my purpose, it was before me in plain sight: I am Aboriginal, I am gay, I am human, and I have a truth to tell, which comes in the form of the words I write.

Yet, as time went on and I met other Blak writers within the industry, I realised that there were certain topics and themes that were always being written about. Resistance, colonisation, the patriarchy, land back: all vitally in need of voice and platform, yet things I didn't find myself keen to write about to the same degree. Despite the healing I'd been able to achieve throughout my life, my insecurity, born from others' expectation, had presented itself again. To me, it's reminiscent of the myth that Aboriginal people have a certain trademark appearance. Still, I'd question myself:

What makes an Aboriginal writer?

Who decides what topics a credible Aboriginal writer should address?

Why do I feel the need to write about the same things as others?

If I don't write about these things, what will they think of me? Will it make me less of an Aboriginal person with a voice?

My symptoms of impostor syndrome can only be treated through reminding myself of my own identity, and knowing that through my words comes truth, and the solid and eternal drippings of my ancient culture. This undoubtedly makes me an Aboriginal writer, and a powerful one at that.

ON THURSDAY 12 April 1990 at approximately 2.40 am, around ten minutes after I entered the world, I was naked, lying on my mother's chest, nested on her white dress. I was comfortable on her, silently trying to adjust my eyes to the bright light in the room. My mother was half asleep, drifting in and out of exhaustion. I took a deep breath, then released my bowels on her and began to slide off towards the floor.

Naturally, I have no recollection of my birth, or even the first few years of my life; this memory only lives in me because I received it from my mum. It's engraved in my mind after countless dinners, barbecues and birthday parties in which family and friends gathered under the passionfruit-vine pergola of my childhood home and, with full bellies, took turns sharing their stories.

My dad held the role of central narrator at our family events. An actor and pretender, he had a certain animation about him, always pulling funny faces and impersonating different people. I put my penchant for storytelling and entertaining down to an inheritance of those particular colours within his personality. It seemed most stories were about me, maybe because I was the most adventurous: always outside, using my innocent imagination to turn flowers and twigs into little figurines in the garden, unstoppable in exploring the vastness of the bush.

My memories are speckled over decaying slivers of time. Morning walks, drenched in sunrise. Searing afternoons under a giant mahogany tree, poking sticks into my Uncle Bob's goldfish pond. Sunsets and evenings over an ebony-and-ivory chess set, incorrectly laying the pieces out and moving them in the wrong directions to race down the board, always making sure my queen won.

I've existed in this world as a gay Aboriginal man for thirty-four years. I've lived and died and been reborn. I've successfully fought for Australia's Indigenous flags to be permanently flown at famous landmarks; led the establishment of agreements between Traditional Owners and government; founded dedicated, annual, Aboriginal cultural programs across capital cities; secured permanent investment for Aboriginal art within world-leading hospitals; and overseen the integration of Aboriginal paediatric clinical research programs in those same hospitals. My work has been underpinned by a goal to build strong relationships and partnerships between organisations and communities, and to collectively chart paths for positive and effective change. I don't recognise boundaries in my connections and have built a strong network of trusted friends and colleagues across Australia, with the hope to create a world of calm from the chaos we've found ourselves in since colonisation.

I've spent my life hacking away at a pearl shell that, at times, seems as though it'll never open. Still, through the burden and blessing of a boldness I inherited from both my parents, I continue to score the shell with my stone. When it finally opens, it might make it all worthwhile: the trauma, the love and its gift of heartache, the internal dissection to find the pieces of me I love and let go of those I can live without. I hope I'll be able to acknowledge what I've invested, to give my community a legacy they'll be proud of and thankful for. Who knows? But when the pearl shell opens, I'll know its release didn't come from the final incision, but from every effort I made before.

The aunties in the old Kununurra hospital meant what they said, and they spoke it with hope, determination and certainty: that from my mother's womb, a baby was born who would lead with authenticity and without fear. Perhaps I've accidentally become the role model Aboriginal people need – the one I searched for as a young person, the one my grandmother tried to be, the one my father couldn't recognise. Or perhaps I'm only someone who has embodied the strength of his culture, using the voices of his community as the energy for his actions. Regardless, this is the path I walk, and although it can sometimes be dark, I wouldn't have it any other way.

Bebe Oliver is a descendant of the Bardi Jawi people of the Kimberley region of Western Australia and an award-winning writer, poet, illustrator, speaker and facilitator based in Naarm (Melbourne). A leader in Aboriginal advancement, he is chairperson of Blak & Bright First Nations Literary Festival and a board director of Magabala Books, Australia's leading Indigenous publishing house.

FICTION

Animal control

Miriam Sved

HER BROTHER WOULD never have got her involved if not for the dog. Stuart, she knew, thought she had a way with the dog. This might have been only because she and the dog occupied similar situational status in the family. Semi-domesticated, prone to impulsive decisions and unseemly hungers. Objects of occasional indulgence but mostly embarrassment.

Stuart said nothing on the phone about the cops. He said very little about anything and didn't even mention their mother. All he did was drop the name of their childhood street from a certain height.

'I'm at Albert Street. Could you maybe…'

It was typical that he didn't round out the sentence, which would have made it an actual request and put him at a disadvantage.

She'd been busy painting the new apartment with Anna, and had just reached that point of the ceiling where the novelty of it all – of prettying up their home together, of wearing the same chesty Bonds she always wore but with legit purpose, and feeling the flex of her shoulder muscles with the simultaneous awareness of Anna's eyes on them – was starting to give way to a persistent and unsexy ache in her neck, her arms threatening to betray her with trembling.

She was, actually, shitting herself a little bit about the whole thing, the whole Anna situation that felt like a not completely deliberate flow-on from the whole lockdown situation. The lockdown situation had broken the bonds of reality and selfhood. Immediately post-lockdown, SJ had felt capable of embodying the optimistic plans Anna had for her, for both of them, but now the betrayal of her shoulder muscles seemed like a foreshadowing of broader collapse. She wasn't completely sorry to see Stuart's name come up on her phone, knowing that it would be something requiring purposeful movement away from the little flat and her girlfriend's watchful dark eyes.

'Go, go,' Anna said, kissing her sweaty cheek. There would probably have been time to shower or at least change out of the paint-spattered Bonds – Stuart hadn't expressed any urgency, although it was hard to know whether that meant anything beyond his refusal to concede to powerlessness or fear. On the day their father died, eight years earlier, it had been the same, his name on her phone, voice deliberately casual: 'Got the call from the hospice…'

TRAFFIC ON THE way to Albert Street was heavy, although she noticed the footpaths were clear, people siloed in their cars to avoid all those bodily permeations. She got stuck behind a tram, which she could see through the back window was almost empty. In the old world it would have added to the aggravation of inching along behind the thing, but she tried to exist gratefully now. She switched on the radio and scanned for a station not talking about the virus. She had an idea that she might become someone who listened to gardening shows. There was a little balcony off the living room of the apartment; she wanted to find out what might thrive there.

Once she got to her mother's neighbourhood the streets were deserted, as if this suburb had decided not to come out of lockdown after all. The houses looked unflappable, unconcerned behind high hedges. A pandemic might go on elsewhere; here we are having a quiet lie-down.

Even though she knew that was unfair. Lots of old folks around here, lots of isolation and probably quiet desperation. Margaret, her mother. Impossible to think of her that way: as one of the frail, the isolated or quietly desperate.

Anna, who was the only person she'd spent time with throughout those months, had been really upset and worried about not seeing her parents. They lived in a country town north of the city; they were relatively healthy but her mother had blood-sugar issues. There'd been long video chats between Anna and her two sisters to discuss the parents and co-ordinate a schedule of phone check-ins. They all seemed to have a rolling knowledge of their mother's blood sugar and any other bodily problems the parents were having – colds and sore backs and new medications.

Margaret's problems had started before the lockdown – but how long before, how bad were they, what was the prognosis? Anna had asked her these questions with complete assurance that SJ would know the answers, which was both touching and unwelcome. She wished she could offer answers with as much certainty as the daily blood-sugar count. The horror was that Anna might come to understand the texture of echoey silence and polite dissimulation – worse, that Anna might catch these things from her, like a virus of the inner life. She evaded the questions about Margaret.

Turning into Albert Street, she didn't see the police car at first because she was distracted by the irritant of Stuart's beemer parked across the driveway, blocking her access. Stuart, she was sure, did that sort of thing not out of simple thoughtlessness but because he would take any opportunity to draw attention to the beemer.

She noticed the cop car when she was pulling in across the street. It was parked in front of the neighbours' house – Mr and Mrs Aldrich's – but she felt with certainty that it was connected to Stuart's forced casual voice on the phone.

Stuart answered the door. He looked older than the last time she'd seen him, back in March. He took her in, probably thinking the same thing, and thinking something about the paint-spattered clothes. As they assessed each other there was some possibility they might hug, but then he said 'Sara-Jane', and she heard the first whinings of the dog, and the possibility passed.

'You'd better come in.' He turned and walked into the house.

'How are you, Stuart?'

'Oh, you know.' Half turning. 'Everything's been hit hard but my area was insulated. Mostly long-termers so clients couldn't pull out at the first sign of a shitshow.'

She'd forgotten, in the long months, his ability to relate every part of life back to his job at the bank. She thought of forcing him into explicitly human territory by asking about Julia and the kids, but there was a slight prickle of guilt about the two girls – no idea how old they might be now. Stuart opened the door into what Margaret called the living zones – lounge room on the right, then the dining room, kitchen and family room.

'Bit of a fracas,' he said over his shoulder. 'But I'm dealing with it. Just have to make these people understand the situation.'

As though to punctuate this cryptic summary there was a volley of high barks subsiding into a whimper. It came from the back of the house.

'If you could just calm that bloody animal down,' Stuart said. 'He's hiding in the pantry. I think he might have shat in there.'

She could hear murmured voices now, in the lounge room. Stuart stopped in the doorway as though he might block her entry, but she stepped around him.

She saw Margaret first, in her reading chair. Then the two cops who were standing in separate corners of the room. It was like a tableau; she had a strong feeling they'd all been waiting for her entrance to continue with some theatrical scene.

She'd seen her mother a couple of times since the lockdown ended, but it was still a shock. Margaret had lost some vital density that seemed ethereal, although it was obviously about her body – the protruding cheekbones, eyes sunk too deep in her head and hair a wispy cap across her scalp. Only her hands looked the same – her piano-playing hands resting neatly in her lap, long-fingered and surprisingly preserved. The rest of her was ghostly, and there was a blink when she looked at her daughter and the lights didn't go on. SJ felt a momentary sinkhole: not that, not yet.

But then Margaret lifted her chin and seemed to draw herself together from some central projection zone, and her voice came out with the quasi-regal quality that used to be impressive or intimidating, or at least convincing, when it fit with her body.

'Hello, Sara-Jane,' she said.

Irritation rushed back in to crowd out the fear.

'SJ,' she corrected, raising a hand in greeting to the two cops, trying to be surreptitious as she clocked and assessed the one with short hair and a large silver fish twisting around one of her ropey forearms. The assessment was going both ways; she could feel it, the cop's blue eyes taking her in. Although she couldn't be sure whether it was purely procedural.

'Constable Wodak,' the dykey one said. 'And this is Constable McGregor,' nodding to the boy cop, who looked about twelve, with wide vulnerable lips and sprigs of acne across his cheeks. It was insane that anyone would let him carry a gun.

A couple of seconds of silence followed, and into it the dog, from beyond the room, let loose an eerily human moan ending in a yip.

Stuart raised his eyebrows at her. 'Could you, perhaps…?'

Her job. But now that she was here, dropped into this room's strange currents that were subtly roiled by the presence of Constable Wodak – who looked at her, she was sure now, with an extra level of interest that might be competitive or acquisitive or both – SJ didn't want to be banished to animal control.

'So,' she said, pretending her brother hadn't spoken, 'how are you feeling, Mum?'

What had happened, she assumed, was that her mother had wandered off and had to be retrieved by the cops. It had happened a couple of times during the lockdown, once in her nighty.

'She's fine,' Stuart said. 'We shouldn't have bothered you.' Nodding towards Constables Wodak and McGregor.

'You didn't bother us, sir,' Wodak said. 'You didn't call us.'

'He didn't call you?'

She turned to SJ. 'No. The neighbours…'

'Ah.' Mr and Mrs Aldrich. 'The neighbours called you?'

'Yes. We escorted your mother home from their house. She was a bit upset.'

The dog, in his background chorus role, gave a sharp series of barks.

'Yes, but she's fine now,' Stuart said, exhibiting Margaret with a flourish. 'This is overkill.'

'Well, yes, sir,' Wodak said. 'But we're obliged to follow up certain types of reports. As I've explained.'

Stuart blew into his closed mouth, filling it with all the things he wouldn't say to the officers, and Margaret, still sitting with her hands folded, let out a hiss of breath.

So Margaret had crossed over into some new realm of the reportable. Weirdness that couldn't be domestically contained. Publicly dysfunctional.

It was horrible, the whole thing was horrible, of course. But SJ was aware of a little flicker burning low inside her. She'd been aware of it at points over the last year as the edifice of Margaret started to crumble. She hadn't examined the flicker too closely but its existence didn't particularly trouble her, it didn't keep her up at night the way worry over Anna and the damage she could inflict there did, sometimes. Why should it? The edifice of Margaret had never been particularly protective of SJ.

She smiled sympathetically at the cops and tried to convey her allegiance – that she would not stand with whatever her brother and mother were trying to do here to obstruct the processes of cute Constable Wodak.

'So the neighbours, this is Mr and Mrs Aldrich?' A little nod from Constable Wodak. 'They called you. Because my mother was…'

'She was apparently a bit disoriented.'

SJ nodded, encouraging.

Stuart said, 'As I've explained, she forgot to take her medication this morning. A simple mistake.'

Wodak's mouth twitched, a little tell of annoyance. SJ raised her eyebrows and grimaced apologetically, face turned from her brother.

'That's a matter for your mother's doctor, sir,' Wodak said. 'As I've said, I'm obliged to follow up on the matter that your mother, that Margaret, discussed with your neighbours.'

Oh.

A matter of discussion.

SJ looked from Wodak to Stuart to her mother. When none of them offered more, she turned back to Wodak. 'What was the…matter?'

'Ridiculous,' Stuart said. 'A waste of everybody's time.'

Constable Wodak looked at her and, in a neutral voice as though reading from a prepared statement, said: 'Margaret indicated to the neighbours that a child had entered her property unaccompanied, and had been with her for a portion of the day.'

'A *child*?'

'A pre-adolescent female child. Isn't that what you indicated, Margaret?'

SJ turned towards her mother, who at the moment didn't look at all like a dementia patient. She looked exasperated, her back ramrod straight, eyebrows slightly raised and eyes averted from Wodak, from all of them, as though the whole scene was too distasteful to bear.

'Ridiculous,' Stuart said again. 'Don't you have anything better to do with your tax-payer salaries?'

SJ looked at the ceiling and exhaled a long, loud breath, pantomiming the frustration that Constable Wodak was too professional to show.

The other one, the boy cop, had shuffled backwards until he'd cornered himself between the fireplace and the bookshelves, his acne flaring pink. SJ wondered if this was his first day.

She spoke directly to Wodak. 'I completely understand. It's great that you'd follow up something like this so conscientiously. But Margaret, our mother, does get a bit *confused*.' Giving an exaggerated grimace, aware of Margaret's eyes on her, of Margaret watching the display of apologetic adulthood. The feeling was submerged, not rising all the way to the surface as a thought: let her feel what it's like to be apologised for. To be the family shame.

What *was* there, all over the surface, was her allegiance with Constable Wodak. SJ, on the side of law and order. Against *Stuart and her mother.* She couldn't wait to tell someone about this – although whom, exactly, she wasn't sure; it couldn't be Anna, obviously, what with the cool blue of Constable Wodak's eyes and the fish-twined tawniness of her forearms. Maybe Constable Wodak herself was the person she would recount it to, at some later date.

The dog, she noticed, had given up his chorus. Perhaps he'd fallen asleep.

Wodak said, 'We don't want to cause any distress. But we need to be sure that your mother hasn't – that it isn't just the problem of a bit of confusion, that she hasn't…that there wasn't a child.'

This was both more and less clarity than Constable Wodak had offered until now, and she looked from SJ to Stuart and back again with a hopeful little smile.

Something fell into place.

'The child,' SJ said. 'The one my mother said she… Is there an actual missing child that fits the description?'

Wodak inclined her head. 'Not the specific description. We haven't been able to establish that. But there is a missing minor. A possible missing minor. An initial investigation into a possible missing minor.'

'Fuck,' Stuart said.

'I'm so sorry,' SJ said, and then immediately felt stupid, as though she'd thought the missing child belonged to Constable Wodak.

'We just need a description from your mother,' Wodak said. 'It's unlikely but we need to rule out the possibility.'

'Of course, of course,' SJ said.

'But Margaret seems quite unsure about the details, so we haven't been able to establish that yet.'

'That's because there wasn't…' Stuart said. 'There's no physical description because there was no child. This is all a horrible coincidence.'

'But they have to *check*.' SJ waved towards the officers. 'They have to be sure.'

Wodak turned to Constable McGregor. 'The iPad, in the car.'

The boy cop nodded, and SJ nodded; yes, yes, they should get the iPad.

He left the room – moving stiffly with all their eyes on him – and the rest of them stayed. The dog started up with the yipping again, which at least provided some cover for the silence in the room, for the awkwardness of Stuart glaring with open hostility at everyone, and Margaret looking into the middle distance with lofty, sneering dignity. (Was she still in there? SJ couldn't see any lack of awareness in her face, but she had a feeling that lofty, sneering dignity would be the very last part of Margaret to leave.)

SJ smiled sympathetically at Constable Wodak and wondered if she had ever used the gun. The idea was a bit hot – although of course she would never have thought that about any other cop, all of whom were in a different category to Constable Wodak. Poor Constable McGregor could get a pass as well.

She heard him outside the door now – he'd come back into the house but not the room; he seemed to be shuffling around in the hallway.

Wodak said, 'I'll just go and…' she flicked her eyes to the door.

'Yes, sure,' SJ said.

To the others – Stuart and Margaret – Wodak raised her voice slightly and said, 'Excuse me, I'll be back in a moment.'

SJ FOLLOWED. SHE could feel Stuart's eyes on her and knew he wanted her to stay so he could bail her up outside the cops' hearing, berate her about the right way to handle things. The deliberate casualness with which she didn't let him catch her eye was a small, pleasant revenge. For not telling her what was going on before she got here, trying instead to handle the situation with his usual controlling smugness. For being so obnoxious to nice Constables Wodak and McGregor. For the bulk of his beemer parked across the driveway and his allegiance to Margaret's code; his wife and kids and job at the bank that their mother never minded telling people about.

SJ followed Constable Wodak out to the hallway where Constable McGregor was standing with the iPad, cradling it in the crook of his arm and prodding it tentatively. He said, 'I can't find the…'

The two cops huddled over the thing for a minute, pressing and flicking at the screen, which SJ couldn't see. She edged closer, feeling that her adherence to them granted her access. It seemed like some game or elaborate puzzle.

They were looking through photos on the screen, moving between albums. 'This one?' SJ could only make out shapes and colours. 'No, this one.'

At last they opened an image that both seemed happy with. Wodak had the iPad now, holding it against her forearm. SJ looked at the screen and Wodak moved a step closer and angled it so SJ could see the picture, the photo of the girl. The whole thing stopped seeming like a game.

'She has Down syndrome,' Constable Wodak said. 'Went missing from school. She'd been at home for so long during the lockdown, just her and her mother. The mother thinks she might have been overwhelmed at school, or confused. Wandered off.'

She made a grimace at SJ, who was trying to settle her thoughts. As soon as the photo of the girl was there – smiling broadly, eyes set back and spaced wide – she'd felt a kind of horror come over her. At this real, specific girl Margaret's delusions had accidentally intersected with.

'That's not the child,' she said to Constables Wodak and McGregor. 'I mean, there wasn't a child, clearly there wasn't. My mother just imagined it. She's got some mental problems, some…'

She waved towards her own head as her adult mind caught up with something, a foothold in the generalised horror. How might Margaret react to the photo? People with dementia became disinhibited, didn't they? A ghost memory flickered in and out of consciousness: walking somewhere with her mother, Margaret's face seen from below, a child's perspective. Her mother's nostrils flaring with something like disgust when they passed a group of children being led, some walking on their own, others in wheelchairs. Margaret's hissed voice, 'Don't look at them.' It had made SJ feel shame – for herself or for the children, she wasn't sure.

How might the warp of Margaret's ideas manifest if she was shown the image of the smiling girl on the officers' iPad?

'I think the lockdown made it worse, made her worse. Her problems.' Appealing directly to Constable Wodak, trying for a moment to evoke their connection, their shared understanding, but it was gone and might never have been there. This was just a strange cop in her mother's house, her own childhood house, and she wanted suddenly, badly, for both of them to take their iPad and leave.

But Constable Wodak stepped around her and took the iPad into the lounge room. All SJ could do was stand in the doorway and watch.

Stuart was near the fireplace. He stepped forward and looked towards the iPad and the cop held it out to show him the photo. SJ focused on his face. She thought she could see a slight twitch of his mouth, and then he looked up and looked towards her. The two of them locked eyes, a momentary understanding.

Stuart turned to Margaret, and his voice came out surprisingly soft. 'Didn't you say that the little girl had blonde hair? A very young girl with light blonde hair.'

Margaret, who had been looking from Stuart to Constable Wodak with her face closed and back straight, seemed to wilt. Everything about her was suddenly, bizarrely soft focus: her eyes watery, mouth a trembly smile and body slumped forward in a way SJ had never seen her sit. She was a different Margaret, and she said, 'Oh, yes. Such fine hair and such a pale blonde. You must brush it one hundred times a day, I said to her, but she was too little to do it herself so I did it for her, you know. We went together to find the hairbrush and I brushed her hair a hundred times, until it was soft and shiny as silk.'

Margaret was not looking at anything in the real world of the room with her soft-focus eyes, definitely not looking at SJ – whose hair had darkened over the years and was now a plain mousey brown – but for one slippery moment SJ felt the gentle swish of the bristles. She thought she might cry.

Instead she looked at Stuart, who looked at the cop and flashed his eyes down to the iPad, to the girl there who had straight brown hair and looked nearly adolescent. He raised his eyebrows to say, *You see.*

The cop, Constable Wodak, seemed to accept it; she closed the cover on the iPad and lowered it to her side.

Straight away SJ wanted to see it again, to see the girl. Grief gathered in her chest. What had happened to her? Someone's child, lost. *Oh, I'm sorry.* But it was too late. Her first response would always be there, horror. She would always be Margaret's daughter.

Poor Anna, she thought, painting the little room at the back of the apartment in hopeful pastel.

More than anything she wanted the cops to leave so she could be alone, here at home with her brother and mother.

There was a creaking of floorboards and all of them turned to see Constable McGregor standing in the doorway of the room. He must have gone out without anyone noticing, and now he stood there looking lovingly down at his arms, where the sleeping dog was cradled.

Miriam Sved is the author of two novels: *A Universe of Sufficient Size*, which was shortlisted for the 2020 Colin Roderick Award, and *Game Day*. Her short fiction has been published widely. She is a co-editor of three feminist anthologies, including *#MeToo: Stories from the Australian Movement*. She lives in Melbourne on Wurundjeri country.

NON-FICTION

Healthcare is other people

Understanding medicine's specialisation problem

Jerath Head

IN 1977 A gastroenterologist named Franz Ingelfinger had cancer, a cancer that originated in his gastroenteric tract. He was perhaps the most informed patient imaginable, but that year he presented a lecture at the Harvard Medical School in which he reflected on how difficult it had been to find someone who would take charge of his care when deciding what treatment course to pursue.

Ingelfinger had already had surgery to remove a tumour but could not reach a decision regarding various possible chemotherapy regimens and the question of whether radiotherapy would be useful in treating potential metastases. As former president of the American Gastroenterological Association and editor of the highly regarded *New England Journal of Medicine*, he had the finest minds in his profession at his disposal and fielded opinions from many learned colleagues regarding his best course of action. These opinions became so numerous and contradictory that he grew 'increasingly confused and emotionally distraught', as he put it. A friend who was also a physician suggested that what Ingelfinger needed was to find a doctor who would 'in a paternalistic manner assume responsibility for [his] care'. Only when Ingelfinger followed this advice was his distress alleviated.

This anecdote serves to elucidate one of the key ideas Ingelfinger put to his audience: 'If you agree that the physician's primary function is to make the patient feel better, a certain amount of authoritarianism, paternalism and domination are the essence of the physician's effectiveness.' While this language might suggest otherwise, he insisted that such an 'arrogant' approach must stem from a place of empathy, from an acute sensitivity to the patient's emotional state, and must be communicated in a way that aligns with this state and the patient's own health literacy. He also identified that, in a profession rife with 'non-empathetic arrogance' and suffering from the practical effects of specialisation, such an approach 'may be as difficult as containing medical costs'.

The issue of too many learned professionals and not enough empathy is, it seems, a perennial one. I read Ingelfinger's story for the first time in a 2012 book by Ranjana Srivastava called *Dying for a Chat: The Communication Breakdown Between Doctors and Patients*. It considers the manifestations of this issue in the twenty-first century through the sombre example of a ninety-year-old patient named Mabel Johnson. Admitted to hospital to monitor a mild chest infection for pneumonia, Johnson developed a new infection, and the subsequent combination of medication she received affected her kidney function. The attempt to improve her kidney function precipitated heart failure, for which she was admitted to the ICU, where ten days later her care was withdrawn and she died. Throughout her account Srivastava draws attention to the ways in which the health system, including herself, failed Johnson. An inadequately staffed nursing home lacking the capacity and confidence to care for this patient and thus potentially avoid a hospital admission. Specialists alternating past her bedside, meddling with her medical chart and not talking to each other. The lack of a general physician, or someone thinking holistically about Johnson's health, to monitor the mounting medications and adjust treatment based on a thorough understanding of her condition. Doctors not making time to discuss in clear terms with Johnson and her family what they would want if she took a life-threatening turn. Doctors failing to communicate the almost certain outcome of Johnson being transferred to ICU in a way her grief-stricken family could understand.

Inadequate staffing and heavy workloads were doubtless contributing factors. But Srivastava wants to hold the medical profession to account for its more active failures, wants to draw attention to a fragmented system that is stunted in its ability to communicate. The siloing effect of specialisation breaks continuity of care. Physicians from different disciplines devalue each other. The system races ahead of the problem.

This assessment sits heavy with me, as a medical student and future physician. I organise to speak with Srivastava and ask what she thinks about *Dying for a Chat* now, more than ten years after it was published – whether anything has changed or improved. 'I think the book is as relevant, potentially more relevant, now than it was when it came out,' she says. 'It feels to me as though the fragmentation of the medical profession has continued unabated.' She admits that there appears to be more recognition of the importance of good communication. But beneath this is an acknowledgement that change beyond mere recognition is difficult and slow in such an immense and complex system, especially one that suffers from a persistent presence of, for lack of a pithier term, non-empathetic arrogance.

SPECIALISATION IN MEDICAL care, as in labour more generally, is an inevitable outcome of growing populations and therefore demand. In a 2012 article that asks how much specialisation is appropriate in medicine, Allan Detsky and his fellow authors claim specialisation is the result of three principal influences: 'advances in medical science and technology, professional preferences, and economic considerations.'

By 'economic considerations' they mean the issue of demand driving supply, though they also acknowledge the more personal economic considerations of payment differentials for specialists. In Australia, as in the US, specialists can earn much more than their generalist counterparts, both in the hospital system and in community general practice. This fact features heavily in career considerations for medical students and junior doctors.

A constant refrain I have heard as a medical student is that being a general practitioner just doesn't earn enough money. General practice salaries can vary widely, though recent figures suggest that the median pay for GPs nationally in 2018 was about $190,000, or among the top 5 per cent of earners in the country. But when the two highest individual salaries reported by the Australian Taxation Office are for surgeons ($457,281) and anaesthetists ($426,894), student perspective is often lacking.

By 'professional preferences', Detsky highlights an obvious fact: not all doctors want or should be generalists. Different interests and skills will be suited to a certain speciality, and to a degree this is undoubtedly good for medicine. If I found myself needing an aortic valve replacement and was given a choice, I would of course opt for the surgeon most specialised and experienced in this complicated procedure. This should not preclude the aortic valve specialist from taking account of my whole person and the many systems and associated factors that could be influencing my health and its care. Nor should any scope of practice unduly inflate a specialist's sense of their own importance in the medical field – and yet, it so often does. In the process, 'invaluable technical crafts such as repairing a fracture or inserting a stent have become conflated with the greater mission of medicine, which is to serve the whole patient', Srivastava writes in her *Guardian* column. 'But in relegating ourselves to the role of technicians in service of an organ, we diminish the capacity of intelligent and well-educated doctors to hold more than one view, be interested in more than one aspect of the body and contemplate the welfare of all of society which includes the patients we will never see.'

Detsky's third principal influence, advances in technology, may also seem obvious: if better technology is available then we should use it. But this ought to depend on whether the advances are required for better care. In the US, Detsky notes that the medical system 'has developed more specialization and higher costs without offsetting gains in health outcomes. The criteria for certifying a new subspecialty appear to have been largely technology driven. There has been no requirement for empirical evidence that creating a specialty will do more good than harm.'

Medicine is, at its core, a utilitarian pursuit and this often leads people to assume that activities undertaken in its name must be working towards individual and therefore societal good. But this notion does not always bear out in practice. While physicians may generally be well intended, they nevertheless provide treatments lacking in good evidence or that research has shown have no benefit. 'I routinely see cancer patients in their eighties and nineties who have recently had surgery,' Srivastava tells me, 'and it's not that they should not have received surgery at all, but too often I hear that the conversation about whether it was necessary was never had.' This problem was put in sobering terms in a 2020 article titled 'The three numbers you need to know about healthcare'. Despite 'change [being] everywhere, performance has flatlined: 60 per cent of care on average is in line with evidence- or consensus-based guidelines, 30 per cent is some form of waste or of low value, and 10 per cent is harm.' And this has persisted, the authors suggest, for decades. Advances in technology, then, despite doing wonders for the treatment of some conditions, are contributing to a treat-for-treatment's sake approach.

Such is the reality of our technological society, to borrow from French sociologist and theologian Jacques Ellul. Technology for its own sake is what Ellul captured in his definition of *technique*: 'the totality of methods arrived at and having absolute efficiency (for a given stage of development) in every field of human activity'. Absolute efficiency in this sense is not assessed in qualitative or moral terms, by the good or bad that may result for individuals and groups in society. It is instead a cold logic: practice *y* is newer and more efficient than practice *x*, therefore if *y* was done instead of *x* the world would be a better place.

A MEDICAL STUDENT on rotation in surgery was watching a knee arthroplasty, otherwise known as a knee replacement. When the procedure was nearing its conclusion the consultant surgeon, the most senior of the doctors in the room and the one whom the unconscious patient would likely have considered *their* doctor, announced they were leaving. They had another surgery list soon to begin at a different hospital. The registrar, a doctor who hadn't yet completed the surgery training program, could close the patient's knee and fill out the remaining paperwork. While by no means standard, a consultant ducking out of surgery early is fairly common practice – with the understanding that it is 'a bit naughty', as one of the other doctors present put it. As the person with final say, the consultant ought to remain until the patient has been transferred to recovery in the event of any last-minute issues or complications.

After the consultant had left, the registrar noticed a fracture in the patient's tibia, which had been caused by the surgery – a known possible complication of the procedure. However, no one had the confidence or authority to act on the consultant's behalf. The attending anaesthetist was forced to maintain the patient under anaesthetic for another twenty minutes, waiting until someone was finally able to reach the absent surgeon.

Beyond the additional time spent under anaesthesia, which has its own risks, there were no other adverse effects from this situation. The assessment and treatment the patient received for the fracture were the same as they would have been had the consultant been present. As a result, the consultant was not held to account. And why should they be, some might ask? Everything was fine in the end.

I would instead ask: what is it that makes a doctor think this kind of practice is okay given their responsibility to the patient in front of them?

Efficiency, for one thing. Many people are waiting for surgery and there is money to be made. Assuming a competent registrar is on hand, leaving early is the most efficient use of time. Such expediency is often associated with surgeons, clichéd for being money-oriented and more than a little chauvinistic. A dehumanising element is also inherent in surgery, resulting in part from efficiency processes. The patient on the operating table for a knee arthroplasty is reduced to a knee joint. Layers of sterile surgical drapes cover their entire body minus the extent of antiseptic-discoloured flesh to which the surgeon's tools require access.

The impetus for and effects of such expediency are not limited to surgery. General practice, subject in recent decades to both corporatisation and government funding neglect, is another prime example. Standard consults are fifteen minutes, yet one GP tells me patients often present with chronic or multiple issues, or issues that they only reveal after a thorough discussion, which could benefit from a half-hour assessment. Instead, many doctors and practices try to shave minutes off the standard to fit more patients into an hour and thus maximise the return on their time.

Similar concerns are also visible on hospital wards – namely, public hospital wards. A never-ending stream of patients and staff who don't have enough time to see them all creates a sense of perpetual rush. Doctors rove in packs between bedsides, often surprising the people in the beds and leaving them with little time to think about what to ask or how to ask it. Hospital managers see those people as beds that require emptying, efficiency problems that require solving.

Ben Bravery describes his experience of these two issues – as both patient and physician – in *The Patient Doctor*, a memoir of surviving colorectal cancer and subsequently pursuing a career in medicine. In one section, Bravery recounts an interaction he had with a group of doctors led by a hospital manager. He had been struggling to take in any food on account of debilitating nausea resulting from a post-surgery infection. At one point in their interaction, one of the group 'lowered her notepad and with a tone reflecting her status at the front of the pack said, "You need to start eating or we are putting a nasogastric [feeding] tube in."' The implication that he 'was choosing not to eat seemed grossly unfair. To feel ignored while suffering is one thing, to feel blamed for that suffering is another.'

Bravery also recounts instances of being a passive part of such a group as a medical student on ward rounds. 'I remembered how rushed and awkward these were when I was a patient, and had hoped that crossing from patient to doctor would help me understand why. But I soon discovered that as a medical student I felt just as impotent during ward rounds as I had as a patient… I had to choose between staying back and connecting with the patient or racing on to keep up with the team.' As a student doctor, staying back often meant asking small questions about how the person was feeling, how they slept, were they comfortable. The kinds of questions that would have made a difference to him as a patient. 'Sometimes patients asked me who the person was who had just been talking to them, not because they were delirious, but because the doctor hadn't introduced themselves... Once I even had a patient ask which specialty we were from. How often do patients have no idea who they're talking to or why?'

Increasing specialisation and the insistent push of *technique* and expediency have produced a healthcare system that is high quantity but often falls short on basic measures of quality. Patients' confidence in the healthcare system and therefore their longer term health outcomes decline as a result, and doctors' curiosity for the world beyond their immediate concerns is quashed, their empathy restricted.

'I SEE A lot of junior doctors suspend what I think of as their natural self during training,' Bravery tells me – the self that is patient-centred and came to the profession because they wanted to help people. 'They think that once they get far enough along the training pathway then their natural self will just come rushing back. But often it doesn't.' With this observation, Bravery identifies what is known in the broader education context as the 'hidden curriculum', the unwritten and untaught – and generally negative – behaviours that we see in those around us and learn to emulate to assimilate and excel. In the medical context this usually means a retreat from patient-centredness, a harried and sometimes imperious air, and a concern for money and distinction.

Medical students are told about patient-centred care ad infinitum. We labour over weekly theoretical case studies during our pre-clinical (that is, classroom) years to the constant refrain from tutors to think of the patient's experience and social circumstances. Communication forms part of the marking criteria for our clinical-skills assessments. The intention here is obvious and without fault, but I fear it fades to static for many students through repetition without real-life experience. Moreover, these skills make up a tiny percentage of our overall mark and so warrant little consideration beyond the classroom moment.

Workshops for communication skills also form part of our curriculum, but too few and too varying in quality – and don't contribute to our marks at all. In one such workshop, of only two I participated in that year, the tutor – also a practising physician – talked at us for a while and then asked one of the ten students in the room to take a history from the volunteer patient, a young woman simulating an uncomfortable and reluctant teenager. The student did so, then the tutor asked if someone else wanted to do the exact same thing despite the patient already having told us her story. This not being useful for anyone, we declined and instead discussed bits of information that were missed and different ways of approaching certain topics, all while the patient, a volunteer but nevertheless the alleged centre of this entire workshop, sat looking at her hands, not once asked for her input.

The situation doesn't much improve on the wards, as Bravery's experience can attest. 'Communication is teachable, but it's not rewarded,' he tells me. 'There is no key metric for communication, and so resources aren't really directed to improving it.' This is what led him to pursue training as a psychiatrist. Communication skills are an essential part of psychiatry training – how to sit, how to listen, how to ask questions. 'I wanted something that attempted to elevate that patient, that hadn't forgotten the therapeutic *alliance* between doctor and patient.'

In his lecture to Harvard medical students, Franz Ingelfinger suggested that 'the effects of lectures and conversations are ephemeral and are no substitute for actual experience' when it comes to learning how to skilfully and empathetically engage with 'the perplexity, anxiety, and misapprehension that may affect the patient as [they enter] the medical-care system'. He then made a wry but provocative statement: 'One might suggest, of course, that only those who have been hospitalized during their adolescent or adult years be admitted to medical school. Such a practice would not only increase the number of empathic doctors; it would also permit the whole elaborate system of medical school admissions to be jettisoned.'

I am not familiar with the US medical school admissions process in 1977, but if the Australian experience in 2021 is anything to go by then Ingelfinger is referring to the requirement for exceptionally high marks at multiple stages, often resulting from private education and extracurricular tutoring, and a family or partner who can provide financial support for four years. Either that or the capacity to negotiate work while studying a course so laden with content that a university-issued guide I once read suggested sixty to eighty hours of study per week on top of classes. This skews medical school admissions towards the most advantaged populations.

A study of medical student admissions to the University of Western Australia found that, over a twenty-year period *after* expanding its selection criteria, almost half of all students were from the most advantaged socio-economic decile in Australia, and three quarters were from the three most advantaged deciles. In other words, 75 per cent of medical students at this medical school came from the wealthiest 30 per cent of the country. This may not be surprising, but it is worth considering whether this produces doctors who are best positioned to empathetically engage with the perplexity, anxiety and misapprehension that face the average patient.

HOW MUCH SPECIALISATION in medicine is appropriate? Enough that the general care of patients, and the general capacity of doctors to engage with patients both clinically and empathetically, is not compromised. But how long is a piece of string? A more interesting question, perhaps, is why doctors shy away from the messier pursuits of healthcare – the general, the lacking in clear resolution?

The answer is cultural. In part, this is an effect of *technique*. Generalism is care work and care work has fewer measures that can be subject to efficiency processes, fewer itemised achievements that can be pointed to as measures of success and remittance. It is the sum of all the enterprises we engage in to support health rather than strictly to fix it – and our society fails to incentivise such work in many fields besides medicine. In part, this is also an effect of socio-economic advantage. A training pathway that disproportionately selects students from more advantaged backgrounds will result in a preponderance of graduates who are concerned with their own advantage and less likely to pursue a generalist route. This is not to suggest people from the top deciles of socio-economic advantage do not deserve to be doctors. Many will make brilliant and empathetic physicians. But as Bravery observes in *The Patient Doctor*, 'for others from diverse backgrounds with different health experiences, also brilliant and empathic, structural barriers in our unequal society make medical school a more difficult, improbable prospect'. This has a concentrating effect that isn't necessarily good for patients.

The answer is also structural. Medical training forces junior doctors into centralised teaching hospitals, most of which are in major cities, where their exposure to general medicine and general practice is limited. 'In a hospital system saturated with specialists and subspecialists, it is increasingly difficult to find an old-fashioned general physician,' Srivastava tells me. And 'you can't be what you can't see'. Moreover, medicine fails to incentivise communication and patient-centred care. In most disciplines, doctors are not required to undertake regular training in having difficult conversations, even though such conversations will be a regular feature of at least part of their career. This failure is compounded in public hospitals, where junior doctors do most of their training, by the fatiguing effects of heavy workloads and perpetually inadequate staffing levels.

Many doctors – younger doctors in particular – rail against this, against the indignity of unrelenting demands from institutions that compromise their capacity to provide quality care. They talk of burnout and of leaving the profession early, and many do. In the US, Lisa Rosenbaum has noted a shift in this framing from 'burnout' to 'moral injury', 'the sense of moral transgression clinicians may experience when the system prevents them from meeting patients' needs'. In a January 2024 article in the *New England Journal of Medicine*, Rosenbaum considers the detriment that such framing may pose to doctors as individuals, to the meaning they may ascribe to a profession in which utilitarian meaning is supposed to inhere. While acknowledging that 'meaning is deeply personal' and that it may be difficult to achieve through work for many reasons, she points to 'the strange equation that has evolved in the [wellbeing] discourse where being mentally healthy is equated with feeling good or calm or relaxed' and 'the near religious fervor that the pursuit of wellbeing, narrowly defined, has assumed'. To what extent this applies to junior doctors is an open question, but Rosenbaum's point is that this is not the sort of meaning doctors can or ought to expect from their work, even while they ought to expect more from their institutions. She wonders 'whether the circulating narratives about our terrible work environments dissuade us from seeking out moments of joy'.

Rosenbaum is not oblivious to the affront of pushing responsibility for systemic change onto individuals. Rather than simply chastise junior doctors for being fatalistic she calls on herself, and those like her who are responsible for teaching future physicians, to do better. 'All trainees deserve to be guided by physicians who see in them the possibility of making medicine better. That sense of possibility is critical not just to wellbeing, but to recognizing –and preserving – the joys that remain.' Whatever type of doctor I become, I hope it is one who finds mentors such as these and can do justice to their lessons – lessons about curiosity, about human alliance, about joy.

For references, see griffithreview.com

Jerath Head is an editor, writer, researcher and medical student. His writing has been published in a number of Australian publications, including *Kill Your Darlings*, *Sydney Review of Books* and *New Philosopher*. He was the co-editor of *Griffith Review 56: Millennials Strike Back*.

NON-FICTION

Drowning in a puddle

The anxiety of not being enough

Beau Windon

'I DON'T THINK I can enter that,' mumbles the young woman. She's sitting at a round desk with seven other people and I'm standing at the front of the room, cosplaying as someone who knows what they're doing. I've been invited to facilitate this workshop for young disabled writers – to inspire them and share my experiences as an emerging writer.

'I don't want to take an opportunity away from someone who needs it more,' the woman continues. 'I just wouldn't be seen as disabled enough. Thank you for telling me, though.'

Another writer agrees that she's not disabled enough to submit for an upcoming writing opportunity aimed at disabled writers. Others join in – this seems to be a unanimous line of thinking.

It took me nearly ten hours to plan this one-hour session. All I wanted to do was encourage the attendees to create and share their art. Now I just feel sad. Sad for them. Sad for myself. Sad for the people offering the opportunity for writers exactly like the ones I'm running this workshop for.

I feel the familiar darkness of the hole and begin to spiral down. Maybe I shouldn't have mentioned it at all. Any other instructor wouldn't have let such negativity spread among a group of young hopefuls. The workshop organisers made a mistake asking me to do this. I should've said no. I'm not smart enough. Running writing workshops is for people who have their lives together. My life is anything but. I'm a mess, and I should just admit that to the group right now and walk out of the room.

Self-doubt, self-hatred, self-sabotage. The hole is calling us all. But I force myself to ignore its pull and remember how I got here.

'ARE YOU ALRIGHT? You're bleeding.' My co-worker looks at me with concern – I know this look better than any other human facial expression. It's the one that's most often directed my way. I'm twenty-one and working at a theatre restaurant. When I'm in character, walking among customer tables, I tune out most of the self-destructive noise inside my head. But when I slip behind the scenes, it comes screeching back at three times the volume.

The skin on my hands resembles dry mud – cracked, discoloured – with leaking specks of red. I pretend to inspect them, as if their appearance is new to me and they're not burning because I've just dunked them in boiling hot water.

'Weird,' I respond.

'What happened in the restroom?'

A loss of control? Descent into mania? How do I tell my normie co-worker that I knowingly inflicted this pain on myself? No matter how many times I soaped my hands, no matter how long I held them under the water, no matter how hot the temperature, I couldn't get them clean enough. Even now, cracked and bleeding, they feel off, but I have to get back to work. My obsessive-compulsive disorder and the way it swallows me into irrational rituals presents a unique dilemma: admit what's happening and deal with the relentless questions and enraging looks of concern, or lie to avoid all of it and just be seen as an unreliable employee. I've lost too many jobs because of this predicament.

'I…' – breathe, say it, tell them the truth; actually, don't – '…don't know.'

My colleague's expression grows confused. All I want to do is run away, or push them, or push them *and* run away. My thoughts are so fast and erratic that I can't keep up. I feel gross. I feel ashamed. I feel…

Fuck. I hate myself.

DEAR BEAU-21,

I was thinking about you just now. You've grown a lot since that day at work. Life can be confusing and scary – but you're just like the fictional characters that you turn to for escape. You identified what was hurting you and you put in the work to remedy it. Your greatest enemy may not be some universe-destroying demigod, but it's just as devious – and it lives inside you.

But that doesn't mean that it's a creation of your own design. More than anything, its power comes from the stigma that society has given it to weaponise against you.

When you worked in that restaurant, you were terrified of what everyone thought about you and the odd quirks you couldn't control. So fearful that you'd be branded as *other.* You were other to the neurotypical. You were other to the mentally healthy. You were other to the middle-class white folks you worked with. You were even other to the majority of your lower class peers. There was nothing you could do to change that.

But I suppose you were even more scared of being one of those others. Not because you didn't like them, but because they knew real struggle, and your struggles weren't worthy in comparison. Your struggles were all you knew and you had developed ways to cope. While life was difficult, it wasn't difficult enough for you to stand beside the marginalised others. You felt different: neurodivergent but able to mask it. Mentally ill but able to carry the burden all on your own thanks to what you'd learnt in therapy. Lower class but with an oddly specific interest in fashion and a financially irresponsible attitude that made you blend in with those who weren't struggling. And because you came from a family of Blakfellas, other people just assumed you were bottom of the socio-economic barrel because of their ingrained prejudices.

You didn't belong with the majority, but you weren't enough for the others that you could relate to.

I think about that time a lot.

Your intentions were good but naive. Without realising it, your insistence that you didn't belong was demeaning your community and denying yourself.

One day you'll understand what I mean.

Keep in touch.

Cheers,

Now-Beau

XOXO

THE CHILL OF the wind brushes my hair from my face. The weather is cold but my back is sweaty. I'm twenty-eight, living in Melbourne and sitting on a hill at Flagstaff Gardens that I like to visit so I can sit and think. A bunch of dogs sprint around the grass in front of me.

How long has it been since I last spoke to my father? Probably a year. I stare at my phone and see my reflection staring back. It looks sweaty, shaky and squirrelly. Our relationship is dysfunctional, to say the least. My relationship with my father, that is. But also my relationship with my reflection… and my phone.

A text from my mum pops onto the screen: *Have you told your father yet?*

He never approved of anything I did.

He never approved of anything I wanted.

He never approved of me.

An itch runs up my torso and I do my best to ignore it, but I can't for long. The red splotches appear as panic takes over and I can't help but scratch. An ex-girlfriend once told me that I looked like a druggie in withdrawal when I scratched with such intensity. That's how panic and anxiety manifest in me: an uncontrollable itchiness that no doctor can ever define or treat.

I pull my shirt up, let the wind hit my skin, slow my breathing. My torso twitches as I fight the urge to scratch. I get some disturbed looks from passers-by. I always do. People distrust what they don't know and have a deep-seated fear of erratic people.

Being looked down on feels the same as breathing to me. It's something that happens and I can't change it. But I can do something to control it.

As the itch subsides, I hit CALL on my phone. I need to do this now while the wave of pain is receding. After five or six rings, a grunt blows through my ear.

'Hello?'

'Hey, Dad.'

'Yeah.'

A thick silence permeates the air.

'Are you there?' I ask.

'Yeah. What is it?'

'I just thought I'd call to…chat.'

'Oh.'

I don't know what to say but he speaks first.

'What is it?'

'I just wanted to let you know that I got accepted into university. I'm going to be doing an associate degree of professional writing and editing.'

More silence.

'It's a two-year program at RMIT, which is only a ten- or fifteen-minute walk for me.'

'What did you do that for?'

'It'll help me with the skills I need to be a writer. My support worker helped me with the application and I–'

He grunts and I know what's coming. 'Those things are a lot of money, you know. You'll be in debt your whole life for this when you could just learn it yourself at a library or yarning with others. Isn't that what I always said? These kinds of things aren't for everyone, and they don't like us. It's a stupid idea. How much money have you given them? Even if you drop out you have to pay for it all, ya know? And they convince you that they're helping you when they're turning you into a puppet.'

I knew he would respond like this. He doesn't care for elitist colonial systems.

'I don't pay anything up front,' I tell him. 'And if I don't earn over like $50,000 a year then I won't pay anything back. That could take a decade or more. It's a fresh start.'

'What if you have another breakdown? This isn't a good idea.'

'They have a disability program that'll give me assistance if something happens.'

He laughs. 'Then all your classmates will call you a r3t@rd.'

'I won't let anyone know about my past or any of my head stuff.'

'You can't hide it. You're one of the most annoying people in the world with all your weird shit.' Dad laughs. But I know when he says something mean and then laughs, it's because he worries about me. He sighs. 'Is there something like Kalwun there that you can go to for advice and help?'

'RMIT actually has a First Nations community called Ngarara Willim.'

'You should go see them. They might be able to help you.'

'I'd actually like to keep that to myself so I don't get singled out for it.'

'Nah. Nah. Fuck that. Fuck them. Don't let them make you feel ashamed of yourself. Be proud of that. Find some mob there and they'll have your back.'

I don't feel good. 'I'll think about it. I gotta go. My stomach is hurting.'

'Yeah. Okay. Call more often.'

I hang up. My tummy is grubbling and I worry standing up might make me shit myself, so instead I curl into a ball. People are probably looking at me, but I'm not worried about them approaching because I am very aware that I don't look like an approachable person.

DEAR BEAU-28,

It's not his fault. His distrust of systems that have excluded and alienated him is a fair outcome of being othered by those systems. He shares almost all your diagnoses – minus one, plus two – and grew up in a time when mental differences were less understood. He came into himself when the colonial attitude of white supremacy poisoned his surroundings.

He's harsh on you because others were harsh on him and he doesn't want to see you face that same harshness. He's found purpose in accepting his identity and accepting himself. You will too, with time and reflection. But first, you need to understand why you're unsure. Why you're afraid. Why you're ashamed.

There are core memories that stick to you and are hard to shake. Like in primary school when you told fast Julian that you were Aboriginal and he said 'No, you're not. You have light skin so you're an Australian like me, you idiot.' Or in high school, when you sat in the library reading *Legendary Tales of the Australian Aborigines* by David Unaipon and overheard the year-level bullies, sweaty Ben and big Aaron, harassing another Indigenous kid. You ran and hid in a corner, scared that they might target you next. Even though you were *Australian like them, you idiot*, you were never quite *enough* for either label.

Tell them you're a Koori with pride and they lash out and say you're not dark enough. Tell them that you're *Australian like them, you idiot* and they'll say you're a h@lf-c@$+e little freak. Those who are insecure about their position in society will do everything possible to ensure people they don't understand are isolated and outcast. It's how they convince themselves that they have worth.

But gathering with mob to yarn about your past will expose many similar tales of rejection. When you start to accept yourself, you'll be able to accept that some people just yearn to hate. Is this a devious tactic that's innate to colonial systems? Or is it something the dominant majority witness and replicate for self-preservation? You're not a member of their club, so you'll never find out, but you choose optimism and believe it's the latter.

Your father was right. For all his flaws and his inarticulate conversational choices, he's learnt a lot in his time, and you should remember that.

Where you come from and what was taken from you matters.

Tattoo those symbols of Blak self-love on your body and wear them with pride.

Embrace mob and be there for them like they're there for you.

In a few years, you'll understand that your fear of being part of them and your fear of not being *enough* for them is all lingering trauma from the assault of colonisation.

You got this.

Much love,

Now-Beau

XOXO

[-o-]

I AM TWENTY-SEVEN and alone. Texas convinced me to move to Melbourne from the Gold Coast. A new city for us both – one where no one knew us or our failures at *being*. She made it sound so romantic: take a risk and start over with no jobs lined up and only $2,000 between us for rental bond. I am a creature of habit so I was reluctant for such a huge change, but she convinced me that it would be okay.

'I'll be there for you,' she said with a tone of conviction.

Three months later, she's gone.

Today, as the washing machine speeds up, I find relaxation in the bubbles spreading. It takes an hour and forty minutes to do a regular load. I sit in front of it the entire time, mesmerised.

'I hate it when your autism shows,' Texas said in one of our last conversations. 'If people knew you liked to sit in front of the washing machine and watch it, they'd think you were brain dead and boring.'

'Do you think that?' I asked her.

'I can't say you're boring. But some of these quirks of yours that were cute at first are now…annoying.'

'You're free to do something else.' I never asked her to join me. I knew she didn't understand why I was captivated by something so 'simple'. The swishing, the sound, the repetition, the change of form: it calms me. When I was a kid, we always handwashed until eventually we got a top-loader. Seeing the cleaning in action is exciting.

'I think I need some space,' she'd said and grabbed a half-filled water bottle from the countertop.

'Please don't touch that,' I half whispered, not sure if I should explain that the water bottle was tainted because it had been in the open pocket of the backpack I had taken with me to a café and I didn't want to introduce all the atoms from the café (that had contaminated the bottle) to the environment of our apartment without first putting it through my thorough decontamination ritual.

She tossed the bottle at the wall and screeched like a baby channelling a pterodactyl. 'Fucking hell!'

A week later she flew back to the US. A couple of days after that, she called to tell me that she wasn't coming back to Melbourne. I asked about the twenty-four-month rental contract we'd just signed and she told me I'd find a way.

Without Texas, the rent eats up 110 per cent of my income; it used to be 60 per cent. Moving to a cheaper apartment will cost too much and I can't handle the burden of a housemate in a one-bedroom abode, so I'm trapped. I don't tell many people because it's a shameful thing to be stretched beyond your means, but I find a way to manage. I have to. There's no other option.

The washing machine finishes its cycle and plays a cute little jingle that snaps me back to reality. I move to my computer and open a new Word document.

When your back is against the wall, it shows you how resourceful you can be.

In high school, I competed in wrestling e-feds: online collectives where participants role-play professional wrestlers. Every week we'd have seven days to write our role-play, a promotional scene designed to hype up the match we were scheduled for. The e-fed general manager would then read all the promos and write out the wrestling matches, choosing the winners of each match based on the quality of the role-plays. I became the world champion in a matter of months.

Some might consider the wrestler role-play promos I wrote to be low art. But they showed me that despite consistently failing English, I could string together words in a captivating way. So when Texas moves out, when

I'm desperate for money and working a low-paying, low-hours job, I look to my past for help.

Taking some recurring freelance jobs through Fiverr, I find myself writing erotic short stories for overly wealthy businessmen. All anonymous and organised through a forum: clients explain their fantasy, I quote them, they pay and I deliver a story. The clients assume I'm a woman because I use a gender-neutral profile name with a display picture of a female comic-book character. Most commission requests are accompanied by flirtatious text and financial bragging. I don't know how to tell them that they've misunderstood my identity, so I don't.

Another way I make money is by busking as Captain Jack Sparrow, sharing improvised stories on the streets and hoping for the best. I'm great at talking *at* people – it's when they want to personalise the conversation that I flounder.

I hate both of those gigs. Mostly because of how often my wires get crossed during communication. *I hate it when my autism shows.*

I finish writing today's smut and send it off. It then takes me thirty minutes to go through my ritual to leave the apartment, but I get through it, and it looks like I'll only be five or ten minutes late.

Needing a way to combat my loneliness, I've turned to the app Meetup. So far, I've chickened out of attending a cinema meet-up for fantasy and sci-fi fans and got cold feet the morning of the anime and manga meet-up. But this one…this one seems like it'll be an easier fit. A meet-up support group for people with anxiety and depression.

The walk into Docklands is nice. I could've hopped on a tram and been on time, but I'm so anxious that I fear having a panic attack on public transport.

I make it to the Alice in Wonderland-themed café only five minutes late. I see a large group sitting inside with a flag indicating that they're who I'm looking for and I…lose my breath.

I powerwalk to the park. Pull my shirt off, consciously think about all my therapy and the dozens of breathing exercises I've learnt. Then I break down and cry. The realisation sets in that I'm too nervous to attend a meet-up with people who would actually understand my plight. But would they? I'm suddenly convinced they'll laugh at me. I don't belong with them. I don't belong with anyone, not even Texas, who convinced me to make this big move and then couldn't handle me in the long run.

DEAR BEAU-27,
In hindsight, it's ridiculous that we used to be afraid of what our kindred spirits would think of us. As if they're all worrying about you and what you're doing instead of being inside their own heads wondering what others think of them.

The thought of being accepted is terrifying when you're so used to not being accepted. You expect the worst because the worst is what you've become accustomed to. The people in that meet-up group will become your closest friends for the next year. You'll come to understand that they worry about the same silly little things you do. But those silly little things aren't so silly and they're not so little. We just designate them as such because that's how we've been taught by some of the people around us – who expect us to behave in the exact same way they do. But life just doesn't work like that. Different experiences create different strengths and weaknesses in all of us.

You felt hurt by Texas and hurt by Dad – but Dad was speaking from a place of love and understanding. He wanted to help because he'd been through these things himself. I know you've always wanted to fit in, but you need to remove those rose-tinted, heart-shaped glasses and realise that fitting in isn't about being enough – it's about being present.

You know what *will* make you feel enough? This will sound like a horrific joke, but it's opening yourself up and talking about what makes you feel awkward and shitty. Writing about it. Sharing it. That's how you'll realise that even the people you look up to have moments when they doubt themselves.

Don't let preconceived notions of what you should be drag you down. Accept that you *are*...and that's okay.

You'll get there. Just need a bit more introspection.

Write back – I enjoy these talks.

Hugs and kisses,

Now-Beau

'DON'T TALK LIKE that,' I say to the writing group.

A couple of them look down at the desk, shame written across their faces.

'Sorry, that sounded harsh,' I say. 'I just mean that you shouldn't do that to yourselves. It's hurtful in so many ways that you won't realise without true, deep reflection.'

They look up and I suddenly become aware of their eyes on me. Hopeful, as if they're expecting me to say something that'll change their minds.

Shit. That ain't me. I'm not smart enough or emotionally intelligent enough for–

No, you know what? Maybe I'll just try. Even if I can't articulate it clearly, I can't leave them feeling like this. I need them to understand that they don't need to be so hard on themselves. I need them to understand this because if they don't, how will I ever manage to keep my own inner bully at bay?

'No one has any right to tell you that you're not disabled enough or to minimise your experiences and your struggles. Not even you. I know because I struggle with these thoughts as well. This is just us being victims to a toxic discourse. It's so easy to fall prey to this way of thinking because it is everywhere. We're not *enough*. We need to be *more*. So many people will try to convince you of this. But your feelings matter, your struggles matter, and if you engage with our community – your community – you'll quickly learn that you matter and you'll be welcomed with open arms. You are enough.'

A couple of them smile. The skittish young woman even thanks me.

'No one has ever spoken about it like that.'

It's a difficult thing to speak about. Maybe I should write about it.

Beau Windon is a neurodivergent Wiradjuri writer based in Naarm (Melbourne). He was a recipient of the 2022 Melbourne Lord Mayor's Creative Writing Awards for self-told stories, and in the same year received funding from the City of Melbourne, Creative Victoria and Creative Australia to produce his first memoir. You can follow him on social media @WhoIsBeauWindon or on his website: www.beauwindon.com

Andrew Galan

The National Institute of Standards and Technology

I disappoint myself each day
that I remember my work password
I take it that seriously
that I base my key
on the National Institute of Standards and Technology
system:
- make them long
- make them random
- make them unique
- don't go to Z'ha'dum
- if you go to Z'ha'dum you will die.

then spend a week memorising it
like anyone cares, where's my medal
eventually the system makes me change it
even though the standards say do not,
'individuals who are asked
to change passwords frequently
are much more likely to
reuse, append a number, letter, or special character
and go to Z'ha'dum, where they will die'.

But I do it all again.

Andrew Galan is the author of two collections of poetry, *That Place of Infested Roads* and *For All the Veronicas*, and his work has also been anthologised in the collections *A Line in the Sand*, *Admissions* and *Solid Air.* An inaugural member of the Australian Capital Territory Arts Minister's Creative Council, he won a Canberra Critics Circle Award for his contributions to poetry. His work has appeared widely, including in *Australian Poetry Journal*, *Rabbit* and *Cordite*.

NON-FICTION

Conferral

Down and out in Australian academia

Rebecca Harkins-Cross

I NEVER PLANNED to become an academic. This is what I remind myself in the grim months after my doctorate has been conferred and the automated rejections won't stop coming, first for the lecturing jobs, then for the residency, the scholarly journal, the post-doctorate. In my experience such barrages always arrive when things are desperate, by which I mean I am broke. Each unsuccessful application appears, to my convalescent ego and bank balance, like a snub to my very survival. Each position description includes 'resilience' among the ideal candidate's desirable attributes.

Like many young-ish writers, I conceded to postgraduate study under the misguided apprehension that a PhD was a comparatively dignified method of funding one's first book. And if said book was a bust, well, at least I would surface three to four years later with a useless qualification. It's difficult to pinpoint the precise moment during my seven-year candidature that the Stockholmian instinct kicked in, but apparently I started imagining that academia might also bestow me with a method of living.

Beneath my fantasy of a regular wage is the puerile hunch that if I stay in academia, I can regain some of the nervy possibility I held as an undergraduate student. It was at university that I first met people whose days were preoccupied with thinking, reading and writing, revelatory mostly because they were compensated for these activities with bourgeois trappings and validation. With hindsight, I can recognise that my straining so doggedly to become the kind of person who succeeded according to the university's metrics mainly taught me what bell hooks says is the primary lesson of college – namely, 'obedience to authority'. My early academic achievement made me precociously neurotic and, soon enough, unhappy. Part of me wants to prove to my younger self that, almost two decades later, she might be entitled to a pay-off.

Beneath my world-weary carapace – with which most academics, regardless of their position in the pecking order, steel themselves – lies the soft-bodied truth that I find students' pure, dumb hope charming. Their hope, their righteousness, their posturing, their doubt and anxiety and need and ambition – all of it. The students are a salve to the bureaucracy that permits me their acquaintance.

Eventually I receive a sessional contract to tutor creative writing at my undergraduate alma mater, the University of Melbourne. This homecoming feels regressive. On campus detours over the years I've invariably bumped into former classmates who've never left, presumably trapped in a temporal glitch stymying their entry into the promised land of adulthood. Now I am stuck here with them, and such encounters are overshadowed by the elephant in the cloisters – that, contrary to what the brochures thrust into our smooth hands on Open Day claimed, most of us remain underemployed in casual jobs lasting six months. We completed our terminal degrees only to learn that our 'world-leading' educations have not qualified us for ascension to the next tier of what increasingly resembles a pyramid scheme. Those rare moments of electricity in the classroom, fleeting but compelling, didn't justify our resignation to suspended animation.

Our pact gives shape to cultural theorist Lauren Berlant's 'cruel optimism', their term for attachment to desires that are, in fact, 'an obstacle to your flourishing'. The hope of future security has ensnared us in a decidedly insecure situation.

THIS SEMESTER HAS barely begun when so too do rumblings of another strike. Enterprise Bargaining Agreement (EBA) negotiations have stalled, more than a year after the previous agreement's nominal expiration in late 2021. For sessional staff – who, according to the National Tertiary Education Union, make up 70 per cent of the broader sector's labour force – working conditions are bleak: contracts routinely doled out days before teaching resumes; dangled carrots vanishing when student numbers waver or inter-departmental agendas kick in; untrained tutors tasked with devising 'innovative pedagogy' for units they may never teach again; no leave entitlements, yet none of casual work's avowed flexibility either.

In the preceding term University of Melbourne unionists marched off campus to Trades Hall, rallying with colleagues from four other institutions across the city. Now, the Faculty of Arts is considering ramping up pressure by going out on a week-long picket independently, unable to secure the backing of faculties with lower union density. Comrades stoke revolutionary zeal by proclaiming this will be the longest campus action since the stonemasons who erected Old Arts – the sandstone building plastered across official marketing materials – downed tools to demand an eight-hour workday in 1856. As momentum builds, members from the Victorian College of the Arts, the Melbourne Law School, student services and the library also sign on.

Union membership across the university has been growing exponentially since sessional staff began mobilising the branch. Decasualisation and manageable workloads are now the crux of bargaining, plus gender-affirmation leave, increased Indigenous employment targets and the standard pay rises. This new contingent's campaign over stolen wages, largely linked to impossible time allocations for marking, has resulted in the university shelling out over $45 million in backpay since 2020, setting a benchmark for similar cases across Australia. The university consequently offered several tutors in each department two- or three-year fixed-term contracts, whose provisions made marking hours less quantifiable, but these are also due to expire by year's end. The general mood is that there is nothing left to lose.

I am already buoyed by the prospect of a week off and an excuse to publicly vent my frustration. A persistent ache in my right shoulder has migrated into my neck and become so flagrant that I can now no longer endure sitting in a chair, aka my life's principal pursuit. An MRI scan confirms a bulging disc in C5–C6, the vertebrae bearing my head's weight, which my doctor says could be deterioration from undiagnosed whiplash or from spending seven years hunched over a desk. The dislodged sac is now pressing against my spinal cord, sending waterfalls of pain cascading along my scoliotic curvature at night. She writes me a short script for oxycodone cut with naloxone to circumvent addiction and tells me to rest until my spasming muscles settle.

Tutoring is the only work I can still manage, as I can pontificate standing up. I wake groggy from the opiates that grant me sleep and, on teaching days, counterbalance their haze with a cocktail of black-market study drugs, nicotine chewing gum and prescription anti-inflammatories. When I finally admit this to a colleague, he shakes his head and says, 'That's some Heath Ledger shit.' By this point I am also eager to foist blame on structural precarity, rather than my own poor decision-making.

Also, my mother-in-law is dying. Experimental treatment for the rare cancer her doctors once declared 'an interesting case' has not only failed to keep the mutant cells at bay but also eroded her bowel wall. After they operate to install a stoma bag, her digestion shuts down entirely, and now my husband and his family are sitting vigil in the hospital, waiting. There are babies to distract, meals to prepare, tensions to defuse, stories to remember. My mother-in-law insists that she has no regrets, as her husband of fifty years, three sons and two grandchildren gather around her. Her only advice is to get up and face each day, whatever comes.

So I push on like the cautionary tales I once pitied in newspaper exposés about the Crisis of the Universities. Sessional staff solemnly liken the parlous terms of their labour to that of miners, taking misplaced pride in injuries borne at the coalface: the colleagues who, without leave entitlements, resume work two days after giving birth; who take on eight contracts simultaneously for fear the following semester will be fallow; who go into debt to maintain their careers; who teach in the morning before their parent's funeral and return to campus afterwards to fulfil their evening tutorials. Academics trade war stories as currency, and in this economy my small dramas are cheap.

Often I find myself recalling the opening scene of Christine Smallwood's *The Life of the Mind* (2021), in which the protagonist, Dorothy, an adjunct professor at a private college in New York, is shitting in the wheelchair-accessible bathroom beside the critical-theory reading room. She is still bleeding six days after miscarrying, and adds both the 'dead-end pregnancy' and her body's inability to expel it in a timely fashion to her list of failures. This semester Dorothy is teaching 'Writing Apocalypse' while she is also failing to 'write the sample chapter that would get her the contract that would get her the job that didn't exist': 'She vaguely recalled a time when wanting to do the job she had trained for did not feel like too much to want. Now want itself was a thing of the past. She lived in the epilogue of wants.'

Even in the single-occupancy bathroom, the most private space Dorothy can find between classes to shit and bleed in peace, someone is jiggling the door handle.

AFTER A LONG month my mother-in-law lets go and her funeral coincides with the walkout. The strike fund's conditions, unlike my casual contract's, don't require my weighing up rent money and grieving rites.

'What is happiness, anyway? Does anybody know?' asks a family friend at the pulpit, reciting an essay by Helen Garner that my husband read aloud in the hospital. 'I'm not going to spend what's left of my life hanging round waiting for it. I'm going to settle for small, random stabs of *extreme interestingness* – moments of intense awareness of the things I'm about to lose, and of gladness that they exist.'

Once the instant coffee and freezer-burnt canapés are done, I watch the day's strike processions on Instagram. Smartphone footage pans across an impressive crowd gathered beneath Vice-Chancellor Duncan Maskell's office. A boorish chant to the tune of 'Seven Nation Army' by the White Stripes of 'More Per-ma-nent Jo-obs' confirms a disgruntled workforce who came of age in the same musically circumspect era that I did. I heart photos of my friend Lauren, who holds a placard featuring a game of snakes and ladders, alongside the slogan *10 years teaching @ the University of Melbourne. Same faculty, same school, but not eligible for maternity leave.* She wears a cropped jumper that rides up her protruding bump. Before she fell pregnant she had already decided to retrain from cinema studies to building design, quipping that endless waves of campus redevelopment ensured more jobs in construction than academia.

The next day I attend a union meeting where members are voting on whether the strike will extend beyond the initial week. The room is split largely along terms of employment. Ongoing staff claim to understand the institution's inner workings, repeating phrases such as 'We have already reached peak power' and citing the number of years they were sessional as bona fides. My mind drifts to Frederick Wiseman's documentary *At Berkeley* (2013), remembering scenes of bloated faculty meetings where professors, clearly accustomed to captive audiences, debate how to quell student protests while invoking their own halcyon days in anti-war campus activism. (Earlier this year Berkeley staff went on strike for six weeks, eventually winning a landmark agreement for higher wages to afford San Francisco rents.) The only cogent argument against continuing is that the striking faculties will likely be starved out if they withhold their labour alone, without the collective strength of the whole branch. When the motion to continue striking wins by a single vote the convenor panics and recasts the ballot so the affirmative must now obtain a 60 per cent majority. 'No' wins by default and the room is thick with fury.

We disperse into a grey day and trudge dutifully to watch speeches underway outside the law building. The most rousing contributions come from student services staff, who are reeling from constant restructures, rising workloads and wage stagnation. Students often fail to receive academic adjustment plans or special-consideration outcomes in time to alleviate whatever stressors they're seeking help for. For academics, the rationale goes that precarity is the price of passion, but this flimsy reasoning falls over when applied to administrators working for Australia's richest university. Their average annual full-time wage equates to a fortnight of Vice-Chancellor Maskell's.

A video circulates on social media of members picketing outside a leadership meeting, several of whom catch Maskell sneaking out the back door. The voice behind the camera asks him whether, considering his salary, he's capable of grasping casual workers' needs in a cost-of-living crisis. 'I spent a good fifteen years of my life as a casual worker, but my base salary is a million dollars,' he replies. (He takes home closer to $1.5 million after bonuses and benefits – roughly three times the prime minister's wage – making him Australia's highest paid university executive.)

'This is not just a stage in our lives,' another woman begs him, her voice cracking.

When Maskell tries to flee, someone yells after him that they're forgoing a week's pay because they can't take it any longer. He spins back swiftly, no longer masking his scorn. 'You've gone on strike for a week. That's your prerogative – that's industrial relations. That's *absolutely* your prerogative. By going on strike for a week, you've lost 2 per cent of the 4 per cent pay rise you had last year, but that's okay.'

'We're not doing it for fun,' the voice implores. 'We're doing it because we're crying out.'

I'm shocked to learn later that Maskell hails from the working classes. Raised in North London, his father was a maintenance superintendent and his mother a factory worker. Maskell spent his youth in council housing before a Cambridge education engendered his social mobility. In this fairytale the pauper becomes a prince, his cursed gift a kingdom of subjects now revolting for their share of the riches.

IN THE WEEKS following the strike, I know I am failing my students. How can I be the teacher they deserve without sacrificing my scant resources to an institution who treats us *all* as disposable?

In one class I try to provide a topic that demonstrates the infinite possibilities of creative non-fiction, but in the moment all I can summon is 'back pain'. 'You could write a personal essay about back pain,' I tell them. 'You could write a piece of literary reportage where you visit a back-pain clinic to document a day among its doctors and patients. You could write creative criticism exploring back pain in contemporary literature.' (Now I am among the initiated, I am noticing back pain everywhere.) 'You could write a polemic against the diminishment of women's suffering.' These examples are so deranged that I must also admit that my back pain is occluding any other thoughts.

Lately I can no longer discern whether my malaise stems from my wonky neck, grief, post-PhD doldrums, the long tail of tapering off antidepressants or the fact that each week when I return to class I am faced with the wretched reality of my dwindling prospects. My husband helpfully informs me that I falsely believed this system was a meritocracy when it was working in my favour, and now I am realising it was rigged after all.

I read sociologist Raewyn Connell's *The Good University: What Universities Actually Do and Why It's Time for Radical Change* (2019), which opens on the picket line. Her sweeping study of the global higher-education sector is a continuation of discussions that began during industrial disputes at the University of Sydney. To tackle contemporary crises such as 'outdated pedagogy, exploitation of young staff, distorted and even faked research, outrageous fees, outrageous pay for top managers, corporate rip-offs, corruption, sexism, racism, and mickey-mouse degrees', she says we must study the labour practices required to fulfil the university's functions. Neoliberal business models grate against contemporary ideals that teaching and research serve 'the public good'. 'I have stuck with universities because their capacity for challenge, critique, invention and intellectual growth survived,' says Connell. 'I think it is still alive; but it has to be fought for.'

Connell argues that the Labor government's policies to widen access to tertiary education in the late 1980s, which included reintroducing tuition fees and establishing the loans system known as the Higher Education Contribution Scheme, in fact ushered in the current 'market regime'.

Simultaneously, government funding fell from approximately 90 per cent of university budgets in the 1970s to 42 per cent by 2010. Reframing universities as corporations competing in a market – and students as consumers purchasing a product – makes a university's value proposition 'access to a variety of privileges': to institutional reputations, to prestigious networks, to 'future advantage in the job market'.

While student enrolments have exploded in recent decades and will continue to increase – the government's new Australian Universities Accord recommends that by 2050, 80 per cent of Australia's workforce should have attained a tertiary education – these corporations now displace the risks of market fluctuations onto gig workers at far higher rates than the Australian economy overall. The careers of young academics stall before they've even begun, more likely to burn out before they progress; scholars Megan Kimber and Lisa Ehrich have dubbed this a 'lost generation'. Meanwhile university councils are increasingly stacked with businesspeople, rather than senior academics, and the economic gulf between management and the precarious staff who perform the university's primary activities grows ever wider. Extrapolating a possible future where universities become 'proper firms', Connell imagines 'the most profitable universities [will] have no campuses at all, just brands, managers and online systems'.

But the student-consumers aren't satisfied, either. The University of Melbourne is the highest rated Australian institution on the Academic Ranking of World Universities yet scored lowest of 139 local higher education providers in a 2021 Student Experience Survey, an outcome executives were quick to blame on the pandemic.

Trying to remember what a 'good university' looks like I return to bell hooks, whose theory of critical pedagogy has always been a beacon. hooks' career strived to overturn what her intellectual mentor Paulo Freire called the 'banking' model of education, inspired by her early schooling prior to desegregation in which she learnt that education could enact 'the practice of freedom'. Her radical approach recentres joy and excitement in the classroom, fostered not by the teacher who stands at the lectern but by the community of learners she sits among: 'Making the classroom a democratic setting where everyone feels a responsibility to contribute is a central goal of transformative pedagogy.'

In this spirit I try to speak to my students plainly about how staff working conditions are their learning conditions, as the union's motto goes, but my words come up short. Can they tell that I am incapable of uttering the endearment 'comrade' without the egalitarian moniker catching on my tongue?

Each week they ask eagerly, 'Has the university met your demands?'

THE UNION VOTES in favour of another week-long strike, this time supported by the entire branch, and resentments that are usually subterranean rise to the surface. A deliberately atomised workforce has, for this semester at least, an eye to our collective struggle.

I'm ashamed to realise how much the university's logic of competition lives inside me. How in early meetings I googled my peers, sleuthing to deduce where each of us sat in the queue: where they did their PhDs, who had how many papers and prizes, their track records of teaching and industry experience. I cannot find answers to the more slippery question of who is in which permanent staff's favour. What is now apparent is that the terms of this losing game are impossible to wager. It doesn't seem to matter if you are the department's star student, if you won the prestigious grant, if you have oodles of publications or have received awards for your teaching practices, if you spend each Friday night propping up the bar at the Clyde, if you are a sycophant or a genius or a saint. Everyone is coming up short.

This time around I walk off with my colleagues and the day is bathed in golden light. As the march assembles I spy George, a diehard beat scholar with whom I attended an American literature reading group during honours. I'm overjoyed that George has survived, that they haven't quashed his Haight-Ashbury faith. He holds a sign citing hooks: *The classroom remains the most radical space of possibility in the academy.*

Inside the Faculty of Science, Maskell is giving a public address, soon drowned out by union songs, speeches and boos from the foyer. Members weave through the assembly to take selfies with an effigy of his bulbous head, with piggy-pink cheeks and dollar signs for eyes. A newly activated mathematician takes the microphone, speaking passionately about the divide between peasants and landlords. He glows with arrant pride as we cheer. I tear up seeing my course's co-ordinator in the front row, her fists aloft.

All week I bump into lost acquaintances and we are momentarily liberated from our shame. Soon enough, someone admits culpability for their circumstances: if they hadn't stood up about that injustice, if they weren't so embedded in the union, if they hadn't wasted their adolescence sculling beer from shoes. My own defences default to shaky class credentials, possessed by the teenager who received an Access Scholarship 'offered to undergraduate students who are experiencing disadvantaged circumstances'. The dreams of that girl were small and base. She aspired to be the diner ordering surf 'n' turf, rather than the waitress ferrying the burning plates. When I feel threatened, the teenager returns to play make-believe that anyone who succeeds must be buffered by a safety net, still terrified that one false step will relegate her to scraping leftovers into the trash.

As the semester winds down there is a legislative change to inhibit rolling fixed-term contracts for ongoing positions. On edge, the university's lawyers jump the gun and many tutors in fixed-term teaching specialist roles are granted permanency, before the union announces that this ruling won't yet apply to the tertiary sector. I'm thrilled for my peers and still crushed to see plainly that our fate is random. One colleague has an unceremonious farewell meeting with his manager, before being called back days later and begrudgingly given an ongoing job; he's mostly relieved that he will receive parental leave when his first child arrives in the summer. Another cries when she divulges the fixed-term contract she was informally offered has been rescinded. She was told in assessment week and expresses surprise that it impacted her ability to keep marking. 'Of course it did,' I say weakly. 'You're a human being.'

In the new year, union members vote to endorse the EBA. Negotiators have secured permanent employment pathways, minimum research allocations for new continuing academic positions, workload reviews and substantially increased Indigenous employment targets; other claims such as sick leave for casuals have had to be abandoned. My cynicism melts as the sessional staff who ran the wage-theft case insist that the EBA is only a piece of paper – that having these changes enshrined will provide grounds to champion further campaigns.

I admire their fortitude, their belief that another university is possible, but I'm not sure how much resolve I have left. One more semester, I tell myself, and then I'll reassess.

WHEN I AM drafting this essay a recruiter calls to say I am the chosen candidate for a permanent role at another university. I accept immediately.

I'm under no illusions, however, that my fortune proves the system works after all; my new branch is currently gearing up for a week-long strike of their own.

What scares me most about reaching the other side is whether you can resist the institution's logic once you become its smiling face. Will I tell another generation that this is how academia has always worked, these are the dues you must pay, that your capacity for routine humiliations and broken promises are measures of your commitment?

What I have learnt is that the university's reliance on insecure labour creates a system of patronage particularly vulnerable to exploitation, where allegiances across the ongoing and sessional divide are tainted by power imbalances. Excessive and often ill-remunerated labour is proffered as a gift, adding another line to your CV that might eventually set you apart from your peers. Everyone knows that refusing is to risk falling out of favour, and there is always another warm, more amenable, less broken body ready to take your place. Competition corrupts us all and nobody comes out clean.

I return to hooks again, who writes that when she awaited tenure, she was more frightened of receiving it than of not. Part of her job became reassessing her relationship to power, because denying her possession of it was no longer an option. Those from the working classes, who 'have so often seen those with class power coerce, abuse, and dominate those without', must discover another way of occupying its good graces.

My hand-wringing is futile – and besides, these questions demand actions, not words. I get up each day and swipe my security card, safely assured that the door will open.

Rebecca Harkins-Cross is a lecturer in creative writing at RMIT University. Her essays and cultural criticism have been published widely in journals and periodicals across Australia and the world. Her debut book, *The Headless Woman*, is forthcoming with Fireflies Press.

FICTION

the road of ghosts

Saraid Taylor

I AM ON the haunted road and then I am inside a memory and the memory is of all those cold mornings. In the memory, I am remembering: the gnarled hand flicking forward, baronial, holding mine in front of my face, mimicking the angle of his wrist. The memory inside the memory is distilled to the word *fingertips*. That is all I have to remember, I tell myself as I walk towards the stadium, *fingertips*, *fingertips*, *fingertips*, and a cocked wrist. It is his voice speaking through me. I listen. I am an adult and I harbour the child. She always listened. The stadium is empty except for the cleaner. I wave to him. He unlocks the automatic doors for me with a smile. Out on the court, the leather scales of the basketball are soft. I grip them tautly with the fingers of my right hand. I dip. I flick and snap my wrist. The ball moves: fleeing, falling. It drips like water through the net. I breathe. *Fingertips, fingertips*, the voice whispers. *Finger*, it screams, *tips*. There is still an hour before anyone else from the national league squad arrives for our team training. I walk to the bathroom. I can no longer breathe. I am sobbing, breathless, for no reason. My reflection surveys my wet face in the mirror. I tell her to breathe. She smiles through the tears catching on her eyelashes.

I SLITHER OUT of this memory. I am on the road again. Looking back, I can see all the little shreds of bleeding skin I have left behind. I look at my bruised forearms and the scabs turned scars on my legs. The marks are now tiny memorials to forgotten moments. I glance backwards again. The start of the road leads to him: a man only of my memories, but still I can hear his voice. It is a voice that carries and deepens and booms as it enters me. He is a mentor, the skills specialist, my shaper. He is his own contradiction: calm and briskly furious and gentle and brutal and cold and humorous. If I cast my eyes far enough down the long road, I can see him – Graeme – as I first saw him, but only because he has never changed appearance. The ghost that stands watching on the yellow lane line thirty metres in front of me still looks like him.

I bend to touch the asphalt and let myself drip backwards ten years: I shiver in a foyer after the first tournament game with my new team. Graeme stands in the middle of our huddle. He is stooped over with creaking bones, but he is still huge: broad shoulders, long legs, a deep slow voice. He was an athlete once. Now he is seventy and has coached for decades at international level. He is consistently noble: both a hired coach in the country's professional league and a volunteer at the junior level, co-ordinating his club's under-sixteen girls' program and coaching its first team.

'I put you in this group for a reason,' Graeme booms suddenly at me and I flinch in surprise. 'Because you're good enough to be here.'

I am the youngest of his three bottom-age players. This means I am thirteen. The two next youngest have already turned fourteen, and the other girls are nearly sixteen. I am also ugly. I wear large blue kneepads as a reminder of an injury two years before that fragmented the lower bones in both my knees. I have crooked teeth in thick metal braces. My ponytail is a tangled knot of curls my mother insists I wear high on my head to make me look taller than I am. My shorts are long.

The other girls' shorts are not long because they roll them at the waist. They do not wear kneepads. They wear mascara. Their hair falls, sweeping and smooth, down their backs. The girls talk of boys and dates and favourite positions and are confident enough to shoot three-pointers.

'But, *goddammit*' – Graeme scowls kindly at me and I tremble in my ugly skin; I nod desperately, hoping it will placate him – 'stop looking like an animal caught in headlights. Stop!' His voice gets louder as he waits for me to relax. 'Look at the size of your fucking eyes! Loosen up, would you! You're here for a goddamn reason.'

I am still nodding. 'Thank you,' I manage. 'Thank you.'

I RETURN TO the road but it rushes me into the memory of a month later when I am on the cold court in Graeme's gaping stadium. The basketball is trembling in my hand. I push it away, into a pass, and it is intercepted.

'*Goddammit!*'

I freeze. The team freezes. I swipe small, sweating curls off my forehead. There is silence as Graeme glowers at me. He waits for the rest of the team to stare at me, too.

'Why,' Graeme roars finally, 'did you *do* that?' A white fleck of saliva spits from his lips and hits me on the cheek.

I resist the urge to wipe it away. I clear my throat. 'I'm sorry, I thought–'

'That was a fucking *stupid* decision.' He hunches over me and I wince into myself.

'I–' My heart is violent in my chest. I can feel the damp of the saliva fleck. 'I didn't–'

Graeme softens and shakes his head. He smiles and I breathe again in relief. 'Something tells me you're not the type to be winning any academic awards at school,' he says.

I return his smile instinctively, then my face heats as meaning crawls slowly after his sentence.

'Are you?' Graeme asks. He is waiting for an answer. There is that smile on his face, even as his words stay hard. '*Are* you?'

I eat the tears before they can be seen. 'No,' I think I say.

MY MOTHER IS tied like a corpse to these memories. She is there when Graeme says this. She is there most of the times he screams in my face. Her eyes are distressed as she watches. She is silent. None of the parents ever say anything. None of the other coaches either. The hulking reputation of Graeme is not something that invites critique.

On the haunted road, my mother appears as many beloved ghosts. She played basketball. She has a degree in physical education. She appears somewhere near where the road starts when I am five, as my original coach. She spawns into another self as the under-twelves assistant coach my first representative season, and then another self in under-fourteens. She splits into a new blanched wisp when Graeme asks her to be his under-sixteens assistant coach. Outside basketball, Graeme is a secondary school teacher. He teaches literature. My mother drives us fifty minutes every Wednesday to Graeme's school because he gets access to the basketball courts for free. She listens to him on the phone for hours afterwards. She is both afraid of him and almost friends.

On the road we share together, I can detect the other two bottom-age players from that year trailing me, but their skin is coldly translucent. Jasmine is a player who was heralded as a prodigy when she was ten. She is no longer as tall. Graeme does not like Jasmine. Jasmine is scared of Graeme. Avery is similarly a natural talent, but that talent has evaded the constraints of her height and clutched to her skill. Graeme very much likes Avery. Avery, who is indifferent to basketball, is also indifferent to Graeme.

'You are embarrassing,' Graeme sometimes says to Jasmine, shaking his head. 'You are such an embarrassment. I don't know why I picked you.'

'You are going to play for Australia,' Graeme often says to Avery. 'I have coached a lot of players and I know how to spot talent.'

These two young ghosts are almost transparent because both Jasmine and Avery stopped playing basketball the following season.

FOR GRAEME, I am somewhere in the middle. I am not as irritating as Jasmine, not as gifted as Avery. I ask to do a lot of individual training sessions so he welcomes me into his wrinkled arms. He thinks he knows me, and he is very convincing, so I believe him. 'She needs the criticism,' he tells my mother. 'Some players cannot take it, but that's how she responds.'

Graeme works with me almost every day of each school holidays. He conducts sessions that stretch from an hour into two. He teaches me how to shoot; he splinters my form down into nothing and then restructures it until it is exact. Fingertips: the ball slides through the air into the ring. He shuffles after each rebound, his returning pass precise. Graeme pours himself into me. He is patient. He is generous. He is firm, like a grandfather.

I make thousands of shots with him. 'Her clip is now as consistent as one of my national league players,' Graeme proudly tells my mother. But to me no shot is ever exactly right. 'The ball did not spin backwards fast enough,' Graeme advises even after the ball swishes through the net. 'Now it did,' he says, 'but your elbow stuck out slightly too much to the right. Your guide hand just interfered! And then your fingers were not spread.' He frowns in displeasure and I correct myself, over and over. I remember each instruction. I collect them in my head until it aches. 'That was perfect,' Graeme says finally, 'except the ball touched the edge of the rim. You want it to swish through the net.'

I BECOME A top-age player in Graeme's under-sixteen team the next season, but I still miss every three-pointer I take in a game. My body spasms in shame each time. The ball never even hits the ring. 'Here,' Graeme drawls one Friday night after another win.

I feel fear but I accept the basketball from him as he moves to wait underneath the basket. I step outside the three-point line.

'Don't think,' he says. 'Just shoot it.'

I make myself breathe. The shot moves along the air and falls gently through the net.

He smiles. 'See?'

'But why,' I groan, 'am I completely missing every single game three when I practise them *so much*?'

'You're over-thinking everything,' Graeme says playfully. 'You need to just relax and shoot it.'

'I really am trying,' I say.

He pats me on the back, then I feel him remove his hand to point at where some of my teammates still stand. 'You're a main leader in my group now. Act like it, because the younger players look up to you.'

One of the younger players is Lucia. She was born six months after me but is classified as bottom-age. I never need to retrace my footsteps back along the road to find her. She glides past me every day in various forms. Her first ghost looks like a fragile little girl with blue eyes and shimmering golden hair. I can see her mother, too, imploring Graeme to take it easy on Lucia as she has not been getting enough sleep. But Lucia's mother only says this after the first practice match of the season.

The road deposits me into the memory of that game. 'Don't you goddamn cry!' Graeme is bellowing at this little blonde-haired girl. 'You shouldn't have taken that shot! It was *dumb*.'

I feel my own eyes water as Lucia's face crumples and her shoulders begin to shake. My heart hollers within my ribcage. I want to move to her, but she is Jasmine or me or any of the others and none of us can prevent her doing her time. The team watches in sad silence as she sobs.

Graeme's expression contorts. His voice softens suddenly to gruffness. 'Stop crying,' he tells her. 'You're okay.'

I swallow as he pats her gently on the shoulder. My chest has tightened. I have gravel crawling into my skin. *All those times*, I muse to myself, *I should have cried*.

THERE IS ANOTHER ghost of Lucia who stands on the side of the road. I watch her beckon me towards a different memory. It is of her stalking into the stadium bathroom only two months later. The door hits the wall hard behind her.

'He's fucking ruining my shot,' she mutters as she slaps a hand against the tap at the sink and begins to splash her face.

I stare at her from where I fill my water bottle. 'Who?'

'Graeme.'

'*Graeme?*'

'Yes, Graeme is trying to ruin my fucking shot!' Lucia says. The long blonde strands of her hair flick angrily in her ponytail. 'He keeps forcing me to change it.'

'I – I think he's trying to help?' I try.

Lucia says nothing, only shakes her head again. She whirls out of the bathroom without waiting for me.

That night, after team training and our individual shooting session, Graeme asks for a chat. I am still dripping with sweat as he gestures for me to sit next to him.

'I hear you tried out well yesterday,' he drawls.

He is talking about the first set of try-outs for the state-wide under-sixteen team. From the hundreds of children across all clubs who attend, the selectors choose forty to progress to the next phase. I ask nervously how Graeme heard.

'One of the selectors is a mate,' Graeme says. 'Do you know what number he said you were selected at?' He speaks the sentence like he is singing.

I shake my head.

'Number one. The coaches unanimously had you down as number one. But this is your warning.' Graeme shoos me towards my mother. 'It's not the time to stop working.'

I DO NOT make the final ten for the under-sixteen state team. I am chosen as one of the five emergency players, like Lucia. It is an achievement for her. For me, as a top-age player, it is an unexpected failure. My parents want me to get angry. They want me to cry. Instead, I say I will make the under-eighteen state team as a bottom-age player the next year. Graeme taps me tenderly on the head when he sees me and then orders me to get on the baseline. He counsels me pre-emptively against sulking but later tells my mother I should be the state team's fucking captain.

State trainings are for two hours on both a Saturday and Sunday afternoon, dotted between a Wednesday night club training, a Friday night club game, a Saturday domestic game and the two hours of club training early on Sunday morning. I accept the emergency position and for weeks attend the trainings, but the state coach is apathetic to the combined workload and the sessions are severe: sprinting into drills into further scrimmage. I go to school on Monday morning with each vertebra in my back aching and the tendons in my knees sore.

My father, also once an athlete, is a frequent spectre on my winding road. He carries the phantoms of his dreams and his injuries and offers them all up to me. He advises me on career longevity and my mother urges sensible persistence, then they inform the state program of my withdrawal. Over the campaign, four athletes develop stress fractures. Lucia is taken to the national tournament as one of the substitutes. Graeme tells my mother it will not change her hierarchal position in our club team. She is still the tenth player. She cries too much when she does not get her own way, he says.

I TWITCH OUT of the memory. Samuel stands shimmering under a gum tree in front of me. He is a similar height to Graeme, but wider and younger so less hunched. He is the head coach of the under-eighteen state team. He has the quietest voice. It makes me trust him. Samuel offers me an emergency position in his state team as a bottom-age player. It is not exactly an accomplishment, but it is close.

On the bitumen now, Samuel the apparition is nudging me towards Graeme again. It is my least favourite memory of Graeme and I try to refuse, but Samuel insists.

'Here,' this form of Graeme drawls. He waves a basketball at me and my stomach constricts. It is the last night of our club's under-eighteens trials and my friends are gathering drink bottles and bags. Graeme has run each of the four sessions. After almost a decade coaching the under-sixteen girls, he has decided to move up a year level.

Graeme tosses me the basketball then points outside the three-point line. Even after four years of knowing him, I still find myself grimly scared. 'Shoot it.'

I would like to politely decline but he would never let me, so I take the ball. My hamstrings clench with my stomach as I shoot. Everything is flat. My breath is empty. The ball drops sharply before it clears the ring.

Humiliation and panic roll through my heart as Graeme turns to me. There is that strange smile on his face. 'You've just stopped working hard,' he says. 'Haven't you?'

The blood dances in flames under my cheeks. 'I feel like I still work really–'

Graeme shakes his head, not unkindly. 'You used to work so hard but now you've stopped. You've dropped off and others' – he says the word meaningfully – 'are surpassing you. They might have already surpassed you.'

I stare at him in disbelief. I thank him for the session. Then I pick up my bag with quivering fingers and leave. The night sky retreats as I pull my father's car door closed. I slump backwards in the passenger seat and cradle myself.

'How'd you go?' My father looks over at me. His face changes. 'Are you okay?'

'I need to leave,' I whisper. 'But it is going to break my heart.'

'What happened?'

'I've been at this club since I was seven, and now for my very last junior season I have to leave.'

My father's voice rises. '*Tell* me what happened.'

I stare out the windscreen, struggling not to cry. 'It means I won't win the championship with my friends. And it will hurt him and he will despise me. But there is no choice. He's helped me so much but now he's damaging me and I can't stay and be coached by him.' I look at my father and cough to hide my voice breaking. 'I really don't think I can do it, Dad.'

SAMUEL ALSO COACHES the senior team at a neighbouring club that always loses to my club. I understand the optics of moving to play for the under-eighteen state coach. I suspect I will not be selected in the state team because of them. But it seems the only choice. Samuel feels almost familiar. The volume of his voice is at least gentle. I smother different versions of myself – the ambitious one, the proud one, the loyal one – to attend his club try-outs.

My parents have formed a plan to stop me from severing my basketball career: avoid playing Graeme and my old teammates by skipping my last year of juniors and competing only in the higher age bracket, and from there eventually audition for a professional position in a national league team. But I am tugged out at the end of the session because of the club's policy: young athletes cannot play seniors unless they also participate in the juniors program. I am taken straight over to the club's under-eighteens try-outs. This team is ranked second last. Their coach, a man who smiles with his mouth and eyes, explains to my mother that with me the team could finish top four. My mother tells me this in the car on the way home and I finally cry.

MY FEET ARE bare. They scuff against the unholy road. When I look up again, my floating mother is back. She has extended her arms as if to hold me but maybe she is really holding herself. The road owns me. It owns her too. My mother's remembrances are paved alongside mine. She sees Graeme at a regional stadium a week after we make the decision for me to leave. She is coaching my sister's under-sixteen team. He is coaching his under-eighteens on the court next to them. My mother smiles a polite greeting at him.

Graeme does not smile back as he creaks towards her. 'You have no right to speak to me after what your family has done,' he snarls.

'Graeme–' my mother says.

'You are a fucking disgrace.' His voice is rising until the white spittle flecks at his mouth. 'You *and* your daughter. She will never make it. You should be ashamed of yourself. You are both entitled and pathetic.'

I do not make the under-eighteen state team as a top-age player. I am, again, offered emergency. Graeme tells his team this is embarrassing, as I only moved to Samuel's club to make the state team. Lucia is selected in the ten as a bottom-age player. A friend informs me Lucia thought it was bad I had left. 'She was saying it was just so disrespectful when Graeme did nothing but help you. Like, worked with you so much and did so much for you.' She tells me this and I think of tiny Lucia crying on the court and complaining in the bathroom, and say nothing.

I feel humiliated as I accept the emergency position, but I convince my parents that the extra training is beneficial. 'For your heart?' they want to know. 'For your soul?'

Graeme, who has been appointed as mentor to Samuel during the state-team selection process, appears at trainings sporadically. It is another thing to fill me with dread. He mostly ignores me but, other times, lumbers over as we shoot free-throws and begins to break my shot back into form. Lucia watches with the other girls for a while, then they move and still Graeme holds me: holds me as I hold the ball in my palm. He makes me turn my wrist, position it cocked on my fingers, flick it through hard. His breath is warm down the back of my neck. I am ravaged with guilt and shame and pain. It lurches me back to the road.

Samuel is there again, under a different tree. I sit next to this ghost and then I am sitting at the seniors training where Samuel asks me about Graeme.

I take a big breath. 'I have some bad memories with him,' I confide finally.

Samuel laughs. I watch the anguish in my words flit away from him, unseen. 'Oh, Graeme is tough, that's for sure.'

'Not just tough,' I almost plead. 'I can take tough. He was not always…kind.'

He laughs again and his voice is suddenly a sneer. 'What, did you come here to run away from Graeme?'

I WONDER SOMETIMES whether I should find a non-ghost Graeme to apologise to, or to thank again because maybe I never did enough. There is this little shadow slip under my heart that I carry him in. Each time I walk into any basketball stadium, into any sporting arena, along any length of the aching road, he is the memory I hear. He never touched me with his hand but I feel him still: his words etched deep into my skin that I bear on this broken bitumen that does not seem to be leading anywhere. I walk anyway, alone and visited.

'Not about talent,' my father once said. 'The ones who are successful are often the ones who can hang in there the longest.'

The road is full of ghosts; I am made of them so I am one of them. The road haunts me and I haunt it by clinging to the wisp of myself that is a semblance of movement forward.

Saraid Taylor is a writer and athlete living on Wurundjeri land. Her debut novel, *Flinch*, is forthcoming with UQP and she is signed to the Melbourne Demons in the AFLW. You can find her at: www.saraidtaylor.com.

NON-FICTION

Finding the right phenotype

On (not) being autistic

Sam Elkin

I CAME A little late to neurodiversity. It was a 2021 episode of ABC's *All in the Mind*, which promised to uncover the hidden histories of late-diagnosed autistic adults, that first piqued my interest.

The host described the changing conception of autism in the twenty-first century from a condition that affected a small minority of non-verbal boys to a more kaleidoscopic neurological experience that those raised female tended to be better at masking.

Describing herself as a child, Dani from Melbourne said, 'I was too sensitive, I was too enthusiastic, I was too much… I was a little psychologist from day one because I was constantly watching and trying to figure out what was going on between people.'

A lot of what Dani and the other interviewees described, from sensory overload and chronic anxiety to an aversion to eye contact, sounded achingly familiar to me. In outer-suburban Perth in the early '90s, I'd also grown up feeling like I didn't fit in and I never quite knew why. My classmates and teachers considered me strange. I assumed this was mainly due to my gender. I was certain I was a boy and renamed myself accordingly after the cartoon hero Fireman Sam. Fixated on professional wrestling when most little girls were captivated by Polly Pockets, glitter wands and *The Little Mermaid*, I struggled to accept the sex apartheid of primary school.

But I also had big, difficult emotions that I could hardly explain, as well as pushy, repetitive thoughts. Every time the opening lines from an advertising jingle for the local ice-skating rink came on the car radio, 'Just think ice rink', I'd be overcome by a wave of anxiety. It felt vital that I immediately recall where and when I'd last heard the song. If I couldn't, I'd sob until I was balled up on the back seat like a grey slater. I had few friends and spent much of my time in the backyard playing with snails, poking them until they glistened with sticky, frothy slime.

As I got older, I tried to hide my odd habits and unusual proclivities through mirroring my friends' interests and drinking copious amounts of alcohol. My hair care left a lot to be desired. I was completely fixated on Mulder and Scully from *The X-Files*, creating dozens of scrapbooks filled with every magazine article about them I could find.

As the interviewees described their own similar experiences, I started to wonder if I too might be autistic. But, my mind countered, surely my experiences were not so unique. Wasn't childhood hell for everyone in their own special way? Being drunk, obsessive and eager to fit in were surely typical experiences for an Australian teenager.

It was in this state of mind that I picked up Clem Bastow's 2021 coming-of-age memoir, *Late Bloomer: How an Autism Diagnosis Changed My Life*. A wry, chatty book, *Late Bloomer* tells the tale of Bastow's journey from awkward, anxious outsider to Hollywood entertainment journalist, interviewing the likes of Kristen Stewart. The culmination of her tale is being diagnosed as autistic at age thirty-six, which was a profound experience. As Bastow puts it, 'It's hard to qualify just how life-changing it is to receive an autism diagnosis well into adulthood. Suddenly, it was as though I had a road map, translator and code-breaker all in one.'

I enjoyed *Late Bloomer*, especially Bastow's touching portrait of '80s pre-gentrification Port Melbourne, but it brought up some uncomfortable feelings. As I read about her childhood obsessions ('no five-year-old knows more about dinosaurs than I did'), meltdowns and picky eating, I kept thinking that it was all too normal to be autism. Wasn't Bastow just describing run-of-the-mill, awkward kid behaviour? If this was autism, I felt there was precious little room left for human eccentricity outside the prism of a medical diagnosis.

In the not-so-distant past, sin was the cause of aberrance. Women were burnt at the stake as witches, and to explain why some children were different, myths were told of them being kidnapped by faeries and replaced by evil changelings. Had our twenty-first-century Western explanations of unusual behaviour simply replaced the devil with the doctor?

I decided to put the issue to bed. Bastow may be autistic, comedians Hannah Gadsby and Josh Thomas too. Even Emily Dickinson had just been posthumously diagnosed. But not me. I was just an undistinguished, middling-level weirdo.

Then my mum told me that she'd diagnosed herself as autistic. She'd read Devon Price's *Unmasking Autism: Discovering the New Faces of Neurodiversity* and seen herself in it. I could see there was a case for this. My mum, despite being able-bodied and intelligent, has long struggled to find and keep a job. She's terrified of crowds and social events, hates driving and making phone calls. She never kissed or hugged my brother and I when we were little, and even bluntly told me once that she wished she'd never had children.

Her confession brought up a memory of one of the most painful and confusing moments in my life. At the beginning of the final year of primary school, on Valentine's Day in 1994, I handmade thirty love notes for each of my classmates, stuffing them into the trays of each desk before school in an attempt to play matchmaker. I paired each classmate up and wrote love letters to each other in what I hoped was thirty unique handwriting scripts, using my non-preferred hand to impersonate the messiest boys in my class. I must've been caught, because I was sent to the sick bay for the rest of the day. Due to malice or oversight, I'll never know, I was left there lying on a single bed on my own for the day until the final school bell rang out.

After my day of involuntary detention, I was so distressed that I refused to return to school. My mum, who had always drilled into my brother and me the value of education, let me lie in bed reading young-adult fiction for an entire month before the Department of Education intervened and insisted that I return or be enrolled in another primary school.

I'd never been able to square away what happened in my mind. No doubt, both my behaviour and my mum's had been strange. It was certainly dysfunctional that she'd never sat me down to discuss what had happened. But was any of this evidence of her autism or my autism, or was it just our own interconnected trauma?

I paused to consider the possible benefits of a diagnosis. If I was autistic, my disinclination towards hugging, eye contact and small talk would stop being seen as a sign of my underlying coldness and instead be considered a legitimate accessibility need. I imagined a whole new world where the federal Disability Discrimination Act (1992) would be my shield, protecting me from the scourge of 'camera-on' Teams meetings. Could I insist on my own four-walled office at work, and get out of the cacophony of the modern open-plan office too? Maybe my new condition could even explain away my patchy work record and reluctance to accept underwhelming authority figures.

But I already had a label. One that, like autism, regularly stirred up moral panic around wokeness and social contagion. As a recently diagnosed transgender person, I was already part of a highly online, over-educated and underemployed cohort, routinely blamed for stifling free speech as well as both maintaining the gender binary and destroying it. The alt-right discourse was already aflame, decrying the social scourge of everyone wanting to be seen as a 'special snowflake' and the creeping 'politics of victimhood'. Did I really need to inhabit a second suspect identity? Did I need another personal attribute I felt deeply ambivalent about to become a public part of my persona? It would just be another thing I had to affect a state of pride about.

I found something uncomfortable about the dual advocacy of deficit mentality and pollyanna-esque fulfilment in both the transgender and #ActuallyAutistic scenes. Perhaps we had gone too far and made a virtue out of a failure to fit in.

There were other resonances between the discourses around autism and being transgender. The memoirs (and there were suddenly so many) all told a familiar tale of feeling different as a child, of being a square peg in a round hole at school. Of being told by family and teachers to 'be more normal' and to try harder to be neurotypical or cis. The writers would muddle their way into adulthood, struggling to hide their secret, before finally having a eureka moment, often in the context of an official medical diagnosis. They were free, no longer required to mask or pass, and could connect to community, often online, where they could research their new identity and treatment options to the nth degree.

Being officially transgender had already made me deeply suspicious of the psychiatric system and its ever-changing bible of mental illness, the *Diagnostic and Statistical Manual of Mental Disorders* (DSM). It wasn't until 1973 that homosexuality was removed as a psychiatric condition from the DSM. In 1980's DSM-III, 'transsexualism' popped up as a new diagnosis, which then morphed into 'gender identity disorder', until the condition became known as 'gender dysphoria' in 2013. In 2019, the World Health Organization declassified transgender health issues as a mental or behavioural disorder in their global manual of diagnoses. While optimists saw this as a sign that the medical profession was headed in the right direction, in an era of global backlash against trans rights, by the time the next DSM comes around again it may be that being transgender will be reclassified as a psychiatric condition.

An unexpected benefit of being on testosterone is that now I am read as male, my socially avoidant behaviour seems to be seen as less aberrant. Perhaps my problem had never been autism, but being an introverted, gender-nonconforming woman.

WHEN NEW STATS came out saying that trans and gender-diverse people were up to six times more likely to have autism, I succumbed to the zeitgeist. I booked in the next available fifty-minute autism assessment appointment with the only clinical neuropsychologist in Victoria who explicitly stated that they were interested in working with trans and gender-diverse clients. It would cost $220, and I had to wait six months.

Every time I saw the appointment looming in my calendar, I thought about cancelling. I was sure I wasn't *really* autistic. I'd been working since I was fourteen, was maintaining a fulfilling relationship, had friends and was a full-time carer to my niece. If I received a diagnosis, what would that do for me? It wasn't like I could take medication to cure me of my condition or quit my job and get on a benefit. I'd already spent many thousands of dollars and numerous hours in enforced psychological sessions to medically affirm my gender. It seemed bizarre that I would actively seek out another costly label.

But I didn't cancel. On the big day, I battled a freak torrential downpour to make my allotted time with Peta, a non-binary clinical neuropsychologist. I was late because it had taken me ten minutes to park in the absurdly tight parking spot out the back of the clinic. Peta had a welcoming, heart-shaped face and didn't seem to mind that my jacket was dripping all over their plush, deep-sea-green carpet.

Over the next hour, I tried my best to faithfully answer Peta's questions.

'Have you had any difficulties at work?'

I described my work history, full of stops and starts. In my mid-thirties, I've had three distinct careers and rarely stayed in a job more than two years.

Some of my colleagues have liked me, but some of them most certainly have not. I am sometimes considered blunt to the point of rudeness. I loathe office politics and all forms of hierarchy, and prefer to eat on my own in a park away from the noisy, overwhelming communal kitchens. I hate open-plan offices, and am always being mildly scolded by my managers for being antisocial due to wearing my noise-cancelling headphones at my desk.

'Do you enjoy mixing with people?'

My first impulse was to say yes, because I find many individuals fascinating. But then I thought of how much I struggle through gigs or house parties without guzzling glass after glass of red wine.

'Do you enjoy being hugged?' Peta asked, face perfectly neutral.

I thought of how many times my partner has tried to cajole me to hug and kiss her nonna, who I like very much, and how an old friend had recently described my efforts at embracing her as 'limp'.

I felt certain that Peta and I were sailing towards a foregone conclusion. But then Peta asked me if I had any hobbies.

When I told them I hosted a weekly radio show, I saw a flicker in their expression.

'Can you tell me a bit more about that?' they asked.

I explained that I co-host an hour-long talk show on Triple R where we interview two guests about their lives as LGBTIQA+ creatives. I described the back-and-forth discussions we have as it's broadcast into thousands of car radios and headphones all across Melbourne.

But I had the strong sense that all of this wasn't sounding very autistic.

'And what about your quality of life?' Peta asked.

'I'd say it's pretty good, yeah,' I replied.

Perhaps these were simply the last questions on the test. But it seemed to me that between the radio show and me saying that my life was going well, Peta abruptly reached their conclusion that I am not, in fact, autistic. At best, they thought, I might be a 'BAP'.

Peta explained that BAP stands for *broader autism phenotype*, a descriptor for a range of traits that resemble autism but are considered subclinical, or not enough to qualify for a diagnosis of autism spectrum disorder.

'This is just a provisional diagnosis, of course,' Peta said.

Peta went on to explain that if I wanted to undergo a full assessment it would cost me $2,640, with a $220 rebate claimable under Medicare if I possessed a valid mental healthcare plan. And that was the special discounted rate for the trans community.

AS I WALKED back to my car, I felt slighted. This confused me. I hadn't *wanted* to be autistic, had I? So why was I upset that Peta had (provisionally) confirmed that I wasn't?

I started the engine and began a hundred-point turn to manoeuvre out of the car park. As I jerked the car around, terrified I might hit the adjacent BMW at any moment, I tuned in to the soothing sounds of an afternoon interview with a poet on Triple R. As I listened, I began to wonder if Peta had a fundamental misunderstanding about what it's like making radio. While it's outwardly viewed as a very social activity for extroverts, it's actually got a lot of attributes that make it a highly desirable form of communication for people with autistic traits. It's much more heavily scripted than real life, for a start. Even if you ask all your interview questions off the cuff, you need a solid pre-written intro and outro to describe your guest and whatever they're spruiking. You can research the topic to your heart's content beforehand, and you have the opportunity to seek out people who are similarly excited about your special interests. Conversations with guests are short and sharp, and you don't have to make constant eye contact with them while recording. Radio studios are also a delight: a quiet, low-sensory room where you can actually hear one another, unlike bars and noisy cafés. If your interviewee's a little too loud for your liking, you can turn down their mic without them even knowing. What I love most about hosting a radio show is getting to reach out to interesting people I admire without having to first wade through excruciating chitchat at taxing book launches or art openings.

When I was growing up, my mum almost exclusively listened to Leonard Cohen and similarly dreary male musicians. She was categorically not into commercial radio. But one week, I spotted a full-page advert for a tiny battery-operated FM radio. It was so cute and small, and the thought of being able to listen to whatever I liked in private was immensely appealing. I begged my mum to buy me one for my twelfth birthday.

At night, listening alone in my bedroom, I discovered Dr Feelgood's *Pillowtalk* on my treasured mini radio. Dr Feelgood (aka Dr Sally Cockburn, a Melbourne GP) ran a national radio talkback show in which worried members of the public called in to ask for guidance on their sexual desires and relationship issues. I came for the sex talk but stayed for the conversations about how to discuss difficult topics sensitively, how to be assertive about your needs and how to sit with confusion and uncertainty. It was all perfect intel for me, a 'little psychologist', always seeking new information about how humans behave.

When I got home, I looked up the diagnostic criteria for autism in the DSM-5. To be diagnosed, you needed to be found to be deficient in 'social-emotional reciprocity', non-verbal communication and developing, maintaining and understanding relationships.

On the one hand, it was good to know that I was unlikely to non-consensually talk someone's ear off. On the other hand, without a label, my avoidant and awkward behaviour didn't have a neurological basis. I was just rude, or shy, or socially incompetent. Emotionally, I felt as though I'd been thrust back to all the rejections of childhood. I wasn't going to be admitted to the club.

I DIDN'T COUGH up for the full assessment, deciding that I would prefer not to have medical confirmation that in the binary of mad or bad, I was bad.

Since my non-diagnosis, there's been a plethora of articles decrying both the surge in autism diagnoses and the ever-increasing costs of seeking one. Many commentators have linked the increase to the introduction of the National Disability Insurance Scheme (NDIS), which requires a diagnosis and extensive medical reports about a person's functional deficits to access the scheme. Adults with autism are now one of the fastest growing groups on the NDIS, and 35 per cent of participants in the $42 billion program have autism as their primary diagnosis. As the cost of the scheme has blown out, the federal government has sought to curtail costs via legislative change and by making drastic cuts to hundreds of thousands of people's support plans. In this light, it's perhaps unsurprising that there's money to be made decrying the surge in autism diagnoses.

I am well aware that many people, my mum included, identify as autistic without receiving a formal diagnosis. There are clips on Instagram and TikTok encouraging people to consider diagnosing themselves, and a plethora of internet quizzes that will do it in under thirty minutes. To date, I have not gone down this route. I have not added 'autistic' to my social media profile or #ActuallyAutistic to any of my posts.

I don't attend specific events held for the autistic community, but I appreciate the accessibility measures implemented by many events and venues to cater to this growing subsection of their audience, particularly within the queer and trans community. I am relieved when I read posts providing clear information about when events will start and end, descriptions of entry and exit points and the provision of low-sensory chill-out rooms at parties.

A world full of complimentary fidget spinners, earplugs and quiet moments is a less stressful place for me, whether or not I'm officially autistic. I'm happy in the liminal space of being a BAP, just another tender pillow of human dough.

Sam Elkin is a writer, community lawyer and author of *Detachable Penis: A Queer Legal Saga*. He co-hosts the Triple R radio show *Queer View Mirror* and is the 2024 City of Melbourne Boyd Garret writer in residence.

NON-FICTION

When adults are at risk

What should modern safeguarding entail?

John Chesterman

ELEVEN YEARS AGO I visited Washington state on a fellowship to better understand its adult protection system. I took with me some real-life scenarios and was interested to find out how services there would respond to similar situations. One of these scenarios involved a man I referred to as Andrew, who was in his fifties and had an intellectual disability. He was living alone following the death of his mother, who had been his carer. Andrew was living in a state of severe domestic mess and had a serious though treatable medical condition, but he was rejecting any offers of assistance at his front door.

After being ushered into the Adult Protective Services' secure offices in Washington, I asked their representatives how they would respond to Andrew's situation. What would they do? Nothing, I was told; it was his human right to reject services.

I was equally surprised by a similarly skewed, in my view, usage of human rights rhetoric at a mental-health forum in Melbourne some years ago. On that occasion a visiting mental-health advocate voiced the view shared by some that a person in acute psychosis who wished to end their life should essentially be free to do so.

Both arguments were couched in terms of respecting the human rights of the individual concerned, yet both struck me as profoundly inhumane. In their defence, both arguments recognise that intervening to 'protect' adults who ostensibly don't want protection will never be easy, neither philosophically nor practically, and will often fail. And both arguments stem at least in part from the terrible things that have been done historically to people in the name of their protection.

In my earlier life as an academic I researched the ways in which Indigenous Australians were denied the most basic rights under the guise of protection (for many years the governing state and territory legislation had the word 'protection' in its title). Similarly, people with disability suffered – and still suffer – violence, exploitation and neglect through impulses and structures that are essentially 'protective' in nature. Laws and practices here have been and are being reformed in at least partial compliance with the UN's Convention on the Rights of Persons with Disabilities, though reform continues to be somewhat uneasy amid vociferous debate about what constitutes full compliance. The Disability Royal Commission has now added its voice and made recommendations that, if adopted, would continue us on this reform pathway.

So what are the future implications of this trajectory?

IN 2022 I was in Mt Isa asking similar questions to those that I posed in Washington state. This time I was surrounded by a range of people with service and experiential expertise in the broadly defined adult-safeguarding system.

My colleagues, who support me in my role as Queensland public advocate, and I held eight of these in-person roundtables throughout Queensland, in places as diverse as Townsville, Southport, Mt Isa, Rockhampton, Caloundra, Toowoomba and Brisbane. We also held one in-person and three online forums with people with disability and with people with dementia and their supporters.

The roundtable discussions involved police and ambulance officers, Royal Flying Doctor staff, people with disability, disability and aged-care advocates, service providers, health professionals, community legal centre lawyers, local council staff, guardians, trustees, regulators and funding bodies (including the National Disability Insurance Agency).

To get discussion going I asked people to respond to a number of hypothetical scenarios drawn from real life and put together by my colleagues. They included:

Janet, an older woman whose adult son accompanies her to a bank where, not for the first time, they withdraw a large amount of money from her

account, prompting the branch manager to suspect that Janet is being financially abused;
Troy, a young man with a brain injury from a motorbike accident whose frustration with his support workers has prompted the service to stop working with him;
Leon, an older man reluctantly living with his adult son who has told Leon's support workers that they are no longer needed;
Samara, a mother with an acquired brain injury who lives in a remote area but whose service needs may not be able to be met there; and
Maureen, an older Indigenous woman whose family members pressure her to give them most of her aged pension.

I posed three simple questions: what currently happens to address scenarios like these? What ideally should happen? And how, if at all, could they be prevented?

This, I think it is fair to say, proved educative for all of us. These situations were easily stated but hard to work through. No one at the roundtables had all the answers, but there was manifest wisdom in the collective.

I was surprised by a couple of things. First, it seemed like this kind of group discussion of difficult social-care scenarios was relatively rare. And second, people at the roundtables were impressively willing to switch into a group problem-solving mindset. I had expected some degree of defensiveness or buck-passing.

At one roundtable, two service providers discovered that each was engaged in providing a few hours a week of support to the same person. As both participants observed, it would make sense for them to share with each other any concerns they might have about the wellbeing of that person; however, privacy concerns – both real and imagined – discourage this kind of activity.

As we learnt, or remembered, at the roundtables the ability to 'case conference' particularly difficult scenarios has the potential to be extremely beneficial. One truism I was surprised to discover was that while advocates, service providers, emergency services and regulators come from very different theoretical positions and service experiences, they tend to agree – on hearing a range of possible intervention ideas – on preferred approaches in particular scenarios. The freedom and encouragement to case conference in difficult situations is important. One Gold Coast roundtable attendee wanted to take participants back to her office to help work through some other particularly complex scenarios.

But I didn't just want to work through ideal approaches to all the scenarios. I wanted to draw from those workings-through to identify and promote broader reforms. In spite of all the service and regulatory activity presently underway in Queensland, there are significant adult-safeguarding gaps that my roundtable hypotheticals were designed to highlight.

CURRENTLY OUR RESPONSES to situations where adults are experiencing harm, or are at risk of it, can involve generic services – police and ambulance. We also have some specific services for particular cohorts – elder-abuse services, community legal centres, advocacy for people with disability or older people.

We even have some innovative service-delivery models. One example of this is the health-justice partnership; this sees a lawyer, for instance, placed in a hospital or a health centre or other setting to speak with people who might not ordinarily seek out a lawyer, maybe because they don't feel safe to do so, or fear the expense, or simply don't conceptualise their situation as potentially benefitting from legal assistance.

In addition to specific services, we have regulatory safeguarding agencies – such as the Aged Care Quality and Safety Commission and the NDIS Quality and Safeguards Commission – that are designed to ensure the adequacy of services to particular cohorts of people. And we have more coercive mechanisms by which at-risk adults are sought to be protected. Mental-health laws in every state and territory enable compulsory action (treatment and detention) to be taken to protect people with mental illness from harming either themselves or others. Every year thousands of people are treated compulsorily in Australia as inpatients of mental-health facilities, while thousands are treated compulsorily as outpatients (and required to take medication in the community).

Adult guardianship laws in each state and territory also enable thousands of people to have their financial decision-making taken over by an administrator or financial manager, and their personal decision-making – such as where they live or what medical treatment or other services they receive – determined by a guardian. In Queensland the criteria for the appointment of a guardian or administrator (financial manager) require that 'the adult has impaired capacity for the matter' and there is either simply a 'need' for an appointment or the likelihood that the person will do something that jeopardises their health or property. Enduring powers of attorney and similar instruments enable people to choose who plays these decision-making roles.

The Disability Royal Commission has made recommendations that would see a term such as 'guardian' replaced by 'representative' and that would promote alternatives to guardianship – including supported decision-making. Reforms would also require decisions to accord, wherever possible, with what the person themselves wants or would have wanted, although the protective architecture would remain.

The more coercive safeguarding mechanisms, such as compulsory mental-health treatment and adult guardianship, require specific criteria to be met and are very blunt last-resort strategies that should be used a lot less than they are. But other, less intrusive options are currently insufficient. Advocacy services are stretched thin and need innovative models to reach people. Emergency services are only designed to respond to situations involving likely criminality or immediate medical need.

Meanwhile the service-specific safeguarding agencies – principally the Aged Care Quality and Safety Commission and the NDIS Quality and Safeguards Commission – largely rely on complaints being made to them before addressing individual instances of inadequate service support, and even then they focus more on the quality of the service than the general wellbeing of the service recipient. Many of the most at-risk recipients of services have limited ability to complain – and have few, if any, supporters who could do this on their behalf. Indeed, that is partly what puts their wellbeing at risk.

THESE SAFEGUARDING GAPS manifest themselves in the hypothetical scenarios discussed at the roundtables I convened throughout Queensland. They depict circumstances in which people are clearly suffering, but it's not clear how they might best be helped. In some instances a person with an entitlement to service support is not getting it because they are unaware of their entitlement, or they are unable to navigate their way through the administrative tasks needed to have their eligibility assessed and services identified and engaged. Or they are unable to get support because they live in a rural or remote region, or because of the particular nature of their support need.

Or they are rejecting services, or service providers are refusing to work with them. Or they have service needs that have been inadequately assessed.

One significant subset of our modern adult-safeguarding environment is elder abuse, which we know is a significant and under-reported problem. In 2021 the Australian Institute of Family Studies released the results from the first-ever broad survey of elder-abuse prevalence in Australia. This showed that 14.8 per cent of adults aged sixty-five and over had suffered abuse in the previous twelve months. Importantly, only a little more than one third of people who experienced abuse sought help.

These predicaments can see adults suffering unnecessarily. What should they do? Who should they contact? A regulator such as the NDIS Quality and Safeguards Commission may be the right place to take a complaint about a particular service provider. But what if you don't know whether the problem is a particular service provider's actions, or the person's eligibility, or the absence of appropriate alternative services?

The changing service setting has led to greater emphasis being placed on 'consumer choice' and the development of a market of service providers from whom eligible 'consumers' are able to choose. This is the case in the aged-care sector and in the disability arena following the introduction of the NDIS. This works well when consumers are knowledgeable about the possibilities and are authorised to have their needs met. But sometimes this isn't the case: when the market has few or no services in a particular field or in a particular location (or both); when the consumer is unaware of options that might exist; or, in the case of someone with a significant cognitive disability, when the consumer is inexperienced in making such decisions, and inadequately supported to do so.

The Queensland Productivity Commission released a report in 2021 on the NDIS that made many of these observations and called for the National Disability Insurance Agency to consider buying supports for participants in certain circumstances, effectively bypassing the consumer-choice market model. The recent NDIS review has echoed this view.

The changing trend in care-service delivery is also seeing fewer services provided in institutional settings and more provided in-home, although the aged-care sector lags decades behind the disability sector in this regard. Of course the provision of more in-home care is, on the whole, positive. But it can lead to people being isolated if they live on their own and are only ever visited by service providers. The shocking death of Ann Marie Smith in Adelaide in 2020 is an example of the risks this can entail; Ann Marie received disability services from a single provider and died essentially of malnutrition and neglect.

Other broad societal trends are also effectively dismantling some of our traditional safeguards, resulting in more people being at risk in the general community. For a start, we have an ageing population, with a trend for smaller family sizes, meaning less engaged family contact. There is also a hard-to-measure but noticeable 'don't get involved' trend that sees bystanders reluctant to help people in need. The providence of this trend is complex: a mixture, arguably, of a 'busy-ness' default mindset, society's promotion of the autonomous unencumbered individual, and the professionalisation of caring ('it's their job, not mine').

This was crystallised in one anecdote from an emergency services worker at one of my roundtables. The worker had been contacted by a member of the public in relation to someone who had been acting in an unusual manner. The worker responded, 'Have you asked the person how they are?'

'No,' was the response.

The uncertainty about where to take adult-safeguarding concerns only serves to exacerbate this trend. People are naturally reluctant to ask questions if they don't know what to do with the answers.

SO HOW SHOULD we change?

Back in 2017, the Australian Law Reform Commission in its report *Elder Abuse – A National Legal Response* sought reforms to adult-safeguarding legislation and practices in every state and territory, and called on each jurisdiction to identify an adult-safeguarding agency that had broad powers to investigate the situation of any 'at-risk adult'. The subsequent 'National Plan to Respond to the Abuse of Older Australians [Elder Abuse]' required all jurisdictions to review their adult-safeguarding laws.

The Disability Royal Commission has also entered this debate, recommending that 'independent statutory bodies' in each state and territory perform 'adult safeguarding functions'.

So far only New South Wales and South Australia have acted. In July 2019 an independent office of the Ageing and Disability Commissioner was established in NSW with broad investigative powers. Soon after, an Adult

Safeguarding Unit was established in South Australia, within a government department, again with broad investigative powers. The other jurisdictions are yet to meaningfully respond. This needs to change.

I learnt a lot from holding the roundtables throughout Queensland, just as I have from discussions over the past ten years about how best to promote the human rights of people whose freedom will inevitably be jeopardised by protective actions taken on their behalf.

I have put these lessons into a two-volume report, *Adult Safeguarding in Queensland*, that attempts to do two things. The first, obviously, is to improve our responses to situations in which people are experiencing harm, in a way that is as least intrusive for the person concerned as possible and geared towards addressing the actual harm the person is facing. The second aim is to energise people to be concerned about the wellbeing of their fellow citizens by giving them somewhere to take concerns.

In my report I have called for the appointment in Queensland of an adult-safeguarding commissioner who would have power to receive information from anyone about adults who are at risk, for whatever reason, in our community, and who would be able to investigate and organise 'supportive interventions' in response, such as the provision of aged-care or disability services. But the commissioner would generally require the person's consent to take action on their behalf. Only extreme circumstances would provide an exception: for instance, if the person couldn't be contacted, or if they were currently suffering 'a serious case of abuse, exploitation, or neglect'. Even then, the commissioner's coercive powers would extend only to investigating what was occurring and making appropriate referrals (to police, for example).

I have also sought the establishment of adult-safeguarding networks throughout Queensland, which would largely be geographically based but could also be developed for specific cohorts, such as First Nations people and members of culturally and linguistically diverse communities. These networks would have two primary functions. First, they would provide a place where local service providers, emergency services, advocates and others would be able to consider the circumstances of particular individuals in that local community who may require greater support. And second, they would build knowledge among network members about what they can do in complex social-care situations. In a sense, the networks would be similar to a permanent local adult-safeguarding roundtable, a recommendation that

I made after witnessing the considerable collective wisdom on display at the roundtables I convened throughout Queensland.

ADULT SAFEGUARDING IS a complex area; like all complex areas, it is not given to simple solutions (as HL Mencken famously observed).

With enough goodwill – and I have seen plenty in my travels throughout Queensland – we are capable of addressing the many and complex challenges faced by people at the margins of our society. And those people, of course, could one day be us, or our family members or friends. So the question of 'What should we do here?' might instead simply be rendered: 'What would I want to happen if this were me?'

John Chesterman is the Queensland public advocate. The two-volume report *Adult Safeguarding in Queensland* is available at justice.qld.gov.au/public-advocate.

FICTION

The Juansons

Alex Cothren

WHEN THE LAST passenger disembarks, the minibus pulls back onto the highway, leaving behind a thick finger of dust that gradually shifts north in the hot air. They also walk north, away from the highway, through mangy scrubland that has forgotten even the concept of rain. The sweat on their exposed skin glistens like pool water as they move.

After fifteen minutes, they reach a small hill and begin to climb, slipping here or there in the loose topsoil, swearing under their breath. Some stop at the hill's apex to admire the strata of stone-washed mountains to the far west, but most just go on.

At the base of the hill, tucked out of view, is a small prefab construction trailer, a generator whirring by its side. The group lines up at the trailer's only door. Selena and Jaime are somewhere in the middle of the line. They hold hands. After a few minutes, a man in a Nike singlet pops his head out of the trailer door, whistles like one would to a dog, and those in line begin to enter. Every thirty seconds or so, there is a brilliant flash of light visible in the edges of the trailer's single, curtained window and in the cracks of its doorframe. No one comes out.

AT HALF PAST six, the Johnsons' boy, Eric, knocks on Norma's front door. She takes him inside and pours him a glass of iced tea, and then calls his parents' mobile numbers three times. Sally and Jerry Johnson are friends of hers. Sally's phone rings out each time, but Jerry eventually picks up.

Hello?

Jerry, it's Norma. Where are you? Eric says you guys haven't come home from work.

What? No, no. I'm not Jerry. I found this phone on the sidewalk.

Norma calls the police.

THE TWO POLICE officers arrive minutes after her call. They cordially accept Norma's offer of coffee, and they talk to Eric in soothing tones. For as long as they are talking, she feels at ease. The worries return when they leave: car accident, mass shooting, terrorism? She focuses on the boy, the boy's needs. She feeds him a grilled cheese sandwich and then they cross the road to the Johnsons' house, a tidy white-and-navy bungalow, where Eric retrieves a key from the underside compartment of a fake stone. He changes into a T-shirt and pyjama bottoms, turns on the television to the Cartoon Network and curls up on the sofa like a cat. Norma sits next to him. It has been a while since she has watched a cartoon, and this variant leaves her dizzy and perplexed, but also enthralled. She doesn't even realise that Eric has fallen asleep until the knock at the door.

ONCE THE POLICE have taken him away, she crosses the road back to her own house. As empty as a tomb. She lies in bed for an hour and then gives up and goes downstairs. The sandwich press is still out on the counter, so she makes a grilled cheese for herself. As she eats, she remembers a winter lunch, what feels like a thousand years ago, when she had made sandwiches and tomato soup for her and her own boy in this same kitchen. He had tipped the bowl over and spilled the thick red soup all down his front. She had scolded him, far too harshly. The memory of his pouting lip a barb in her heart.

IN THE MORNING, she walks over to the Johnsons' place and knocks on the door. Nothing. She calls the police, but once the officer on the phone understands that Norma is not the boy's kin, he brushes her off. She makes coffee and goes into the living room and turns on CNN. A banner across the top of the screen reads: INSTANT E-DEPORTATIONS ACROSS US.

After ten minutes, she turns it off again and she goes to the bay window and looks out on the grey morning, and at the Johnsons' quiet house opposite.

You old and useless idiot, she says.

THEY HAD BEEN neighbours for close to a decade. She still remembers the day the two of them, this was before Eric, had arrived and unloaded their few boxes from the back of a mustard-yellow station wagon. She and Al had watched them from that same bay window. Norma was struck immediately by Sally's doll-like beauty, her long and corn-blonde hair. They went over later to introduce themselves, Norma holding Cody's hand, Al holding a welcome basket of fruit. When he handed the basket to Sally, Sally began to cry.

IT IS ALL anyone talks about at the Pattersons' dinner party that night.

Can you believe it, says Dan Stoltz. All this time, and we may actually have been living next to the *Juan*sons.

The way I heard it, says Julia Stoltz, the government's been building the satellites to pull this off ever since he got elected. There's some irregularity in their DNA or something it can pick up.

Ashley Woodland laughs. And to think I used to be jealous of that woman's hair.

Incredibly, the Stoltz's little girl actually saw it happen. One minute she was waving to Sally at Safeway and the next minute Sally was gone, her clothes slumping into a little heap. They all shake their heads at this.

Your poor girl, says Mary Patterson. What a thing to witness.

My boy played over there all the time, says Kaitlin DeBree. He slept over.

Norma feigns a stomach bug and leaves early. At home she turns on CNN, but it is all the same. She switches to Fox and watches the red faces gloat for an hour straight. Her blood boils. She goes back to the Pattersons'. They are eating dessert and the table quietens when they see her standing there in the dining room arch.

Shame on you, she says. These were our friends.

Well hang on, says Dan.

She turns and leaves. Although a fierce wind is blowing, and she has only a thin cardigan on, she walks the ten blocks to the corner of Collins and Lincoln. The bouquet that she taped to the stop sign only five days ago is already ragged. Grief hits her in a way it has not for years, and she sits down right there on the cold sidewalk. A passing car honks at her but does not stop. After a while, she gets up and goes home. She brews a pot of coffee, turns on her computer and begins a letter to her senator.

THAT DAY, SHE had come home early from work to pack. They were going to the country for the weekend, up to a lake house that they time-shared with the Stoltzes and Pattersons. She filled the cooler with food and soft drink and put Cody's clothes and a few favourite toys into a small suitcase, being careful to include Senor Burro, the stuffed donkey Cody could not sleep without. When she was finished, there was still fifteen minutes before Al would be home with Cody from kindergarten. She made an espresso and sat down on the couch with a collection of Chekhov short stories, and she had been reading for half an hour when the knock came. Two police officers stood with hats in hand on the front porch. The teal paint on the porch boards was faded and sun flaked. Al had promised he would touch it up in the summer.

SHE WAKES WITH a shock in a ragged armchair. The TV is back on CNN: DELETED? WHEREABOUTS OF E-DEPORTED 'PIRATE' IMMIGRANTS STILL UNKNOWN. She turns it off, heart sick. It is not yet dawn, an anaemic light just visible outside. Through the bay window, she sees a blur of movement on the Johnsons' side of the street.

She hurries out the front door and down her porch steps. Bone-cold mist in the air.

Eric, she hisses.

He freezes. The fake rock is in his hand. He is wearing a black hoodie, from which his breath emerges and pools above him like a thought bubble.

It's okay, she says, when she crosses over to him. I know.

THE JOHNSONS HAD brought an ice-blue bouquet of African lilies to the funeral. Seven months later, Norma crossed the street with a stuffed bear of the same colour. As she climbed the steps to their porch, she heard the baby wailing inside. She bent down to leave the bear and card on the welcome mat, but as she straightened the door clicked open. Sally stood there with Eric writhing in the crutch of her arm. Her eyes like empty wells.

Norma, she said. Help.

In the Johnsons' plushily carpeted living room, Norma gingerly took the child and laid him face down along her arm, putting pressure on his little belly. He immediately quieted.

Oh my god, whispered Sally. I'll pay you a thousand dollars an hour.

Norma sent her for a shower and sat down on the couch with Eric. His eyes were the same blue. Same wild thatch of hair, too – the colour of wet sand. She leant in and took in the aroma of milk and no time seemed to pass before Sally sat in the chair opposite, smiling at the two of them. She was in a towel and sandals, and Norma noticed for the first time a small tattoo just beneath the protrusion of her ankle. Ornate, cursive lettering. A name: Jaime.

Old boyfriend, said Sally.

THEY HAD FOSTERED Eric with a family twenty miles away. As soon as everyone was asleep, he stole his foster mother's phone and used the GPS to walk home.

She helps him take his Air Jordans off in the kitchen. Socks dripping with blood. She puts antiseptic and bandaids on his raw blisters and prepares him a bowl of Cheerios and a cup of hot cocoa.

I am so sorry I let them take you, she says, sitting across from him with a coffee. They told me they'd located your relatives.

He shakes his head.

We don't have anyone over here.

Well, you have me.

He crunches for a while, eyeing her shyly.

Did my parents tell you?

No, honey. I guess I figured it out.

Are you mad? Lots of people are mad.

Oh, I'm plenty mad, Norma says, reaching over and patting his hand. But not at them.

EVERYONE HAD JUST assumed that she would move. How could she stay there, ghosts greeting her in every room? She put the house on the market. Her neighbours told her how sorry they were to see her go, but she could see something like relief in their eyes too. No one wants to be constantly reminded of how brittle the ice is; she didn't resent them for that. It was only the Johnsons who seemed to be genuinely distraught. When she told Sally that she was going to accept a bid, there were tears, and then a demand that she go with them for dinner that night. The restaurant was a cosy Korean-fusion place tucked into an alleyway in the city. The manager knew the Johnsons. He bought chillies through the small food-distribution company they owned. The dishes arrived in unrelenting waves, as did the watermelon margaritas with gochujang chilli sauce, and before long Norma was shimmeringly drunk, the words and laughter rolling from her like the past year was a prank.

The next morning she took a black coffee in the backyard, letting the sun rise over the top of the willow tree to kiss her forehead. Then she went inside and called her real estate agent and told him she wanted more time.

I guess someone hasn't checked the news yet, he said. The bubble's burst. Big time.

ERIC SLAPS HIS hand to his forehead when he sees her ancient computer.

Does this thing even have Presence on it?

She shrugs and leaves him to figure it out. With the foster mother's phone in her hand, she goes out to the garden shed and takes the hammer from Al's meticulously organised tool wall and puts the phone on the brick patio step that Cody once chipped a tooth on, then reduces it to smithereens. The Stoltzes' tabby is perched on the back fence eyeing her coolly.

One word and you're next, she says.

After she has swept up the glass and plastic and dumped it all into the trash, she goes back inside and finds Eric chatting to the hovering hologram of an elderly woman. This woman jumps when she sees Norma lurking in the backlit arch of the kitchen doorway.

Estas bien, says Eric. This is her.

The woman laughs and puts her hand to her chest. She has a beautiful smile and soft brown eyes, above which are meticulously painted eyebrows the deep purple of blackberry juice.

Hi, says Norma, aware that her own untended eyebrows look more like a blackberry bush. It's nice to meet you.

Gracias por cuidar nuestro nieto, says the woman. *Familia es lo todo.*

WHEN THE ECONOMY went belly up, so too did the Johnsons' distribution company. Norma was worried they would lose their house and move away. She had already paid off her own mortgage with the sizable accident settlement from the trucking company, but others were not so lucky. Even on their beautiful, tree lined street, foreclosed properties had started showing up like dead teeth in a smile. The Johnsons, however, adapted quickly to the new reality, and within weeks both were working multiple low-wage jobs that provided just enough to make ends meet. But this meant long hours, sometimes arriving home well after Eric was asleep. Norma can't remember whether they had asked, or she had offered first. Whichever way, she began picking the boy up from school, always taking the long way to avoid Lincoln. She would make him an after-school snack and leave him to play in his room or watch TV until dinner, while she read a book on the Johnsons' couch. As he got older, she helped him with his homework, his heart beating on her arm as he leant in to watch how she multiplied and punctuated.

Eventually, he got old enough to catch the bus and stay home by himself. Then Sally managed to find an office job that allowed her to be home at a reasonable hour. And yet, it was still rare for Norma to eat dinner alone. She had quietly, without any fuss, become a member of the family. Birthdays, school plays, soccer games, she was there for all of them without question, but also for the quiet moments too. Many a night, Eric would fall asleep on her arm while the family watched *The Late Show*.

So, she was there, cradled in her corner of the Johnsons' increasingly frayed couch, on election night. It had been, even by the usual standards, a terrible election, the open wound of the economy bringing out the worst in everyone. The harmless deceptions that most people happily overlooked when it was convenient had been recast as the cancer poisoning the whole bloodstream. Just another churn of the endless cycle. So, Norma had been disgusted but not surprised when that horrible man, as if the country hadn't had its fair share of them, strode out to declare victory. What did shock her, however, was the violent burst of first Sally's and then Jerry's tears, and then the raw fear on Eric's usually jovial face.

THEY ARE WATCHING the wailing faces on Telemundo when the slam of car doors outside jolts them both. A black van is parked out in front of the Johnsons, the word ICE emblazoned across its side.

Upstairs, she says. Under the bed.

She rushes into the kitchen to stack his dishes in the dishwasher and then puts the kettle to boil and looks out over the sink at the lightly swaying willow and tries her best to empty her mind. The kettle is not yet steaming by the time they cross over and knock on her door. She makes her way through the kitchen, already feigning a look of surprise and worry, and only then does she notice the thin constellation of blood that trails across the linoleum and down the hallway carpet to the laundry room. She stops dead. Another knock, louder. Eric's socks are soaking in a bowl of reddening water atop the washing machine. The doorknob jiggles. Her car is in the driveway, the blaring TV clearly visible through the bay window. She bends down and tries to wipe at some of the blood with the inside of her sweater sleeve, but it is half-congealed and sticky, and refuses to come away. She rushes back to the kitchen bench, the door pounding now, and she slides a knife out of its wooden slot. For a brief moment, she just stands there, talking to her husband and child, cherishing them, and then she plunges the thing into her palm.

This story is one of four winners of the 2023 Griffith Review Emerging Voices competition, supported by the Copyright Agency Cultural Fund.

Alex Cothren is a lecturer in creative writing at Flinders University. He is a winner of the Carmel Bird, William van Dyke and Peter Carey awards for short fiction. His writing has been published in *Meanjin*, *Island*, *Overland* and *Australian Book Review*, among others.

Ella Jeffery

Habitat

It was early. I recognised
my fate in the bathroom mirror.
Behind which he slept deep
into the morning while below cars
fossicked through new roads. I agreed
with the gleaming premise
of their momentum. I sensed
I was at last at the beginning
of something: the suburb like a sheet
laid down but not yet
turned back. Nobody had stood before
in my apartment or knew
this view. At the day's prologue
I waited for a sign but received
no instruction. In such silence
I understood I would speak
only to myself. Later I walked
along the concrete paths
as was my new custom. I read plaques
relating to the drained wetlands,
wildlife arranged elsewhere.
I could hear my own voice saying
now I also inhabit a place
designed for my own kind.

Ella Jeffery's debut collection, *Dead Bolt*, won the Puncher & Wattmann First Book of Poetry Prize, was shortlisted for the Dame Mary Gilmore Award and won the Anne Elder Award. Her poetry has appeared extensively, including in *Best Australian Poems*, *HEAT*, *Meanjin* and *Island*. She is the recipient of a Queensland Writers Fellowship, the Mick Dark Fellowship for Environmental Writing and the Queensland Premier's Young Publishers and Writers Award.

NON-FICTION

Uninsurable nation

Counting the cost of extreme weather

Jarni Blakkarly

AS I DRIVE into the small Victorian riverside town of Rochester, a banner tied to a metal fence greets me on the main road. The banner is white and the text is written in heavy black lettering, like a desperate plea for help: *Can't do this again – Mitigate.* It's a warm November morning and the sky is a picturesque blue without a cloud in sight. It's hard to imagine what happened here over a year ago, the 'this' the sign refers to. But for the locals, it's hard to forget.

Karen Galliker is a calm woman who greets me with a smile when I pull up to the caravan park she now calls home. There are around twelve caravans and campers sprawled across the grounds up to the riverbank; the sites fill up with travelling Melbournians during the school holidays but are usually vacant this time of year. Everyone staying here at the moment is like Karen and her husband: locals displaced by the floods.

Karen, who is now retired, grew up on her parents' farm nearby and has been living in Rochester almost her whole life. 'I worked in Melbourne for a bit, but then Otto and I got married and came back here and had three daughters. We come and go, but this is our home,' she says. Built alongside the Campaspe River, the area is no stranger to floods; parts were hit hard in 2011. Karen's family home avoided the floods in 2011, but the flooding in October 2022 was different.

'We knew there was rain, we knew there was a chance of it flooding, but we were all told that at worst it would be 100 millilitres. We were away, but we got back home on Thursday, started packing and putting things up as high as we could, and got a knock on the door at about 5 pm telling us we had to evacuate by Friday morning, so we were just madly trying to put up stuff,' she says.

'We had some sandbags, but they were useless – didn't do a thing. By the morning we had already hooked the caravan up ready to go out to Lockington [the neighbouring town] because we knew we could get out there and it was flat and the water hadn't gotten there.'

Karen says when she woke up about 7 am she went out to the road and saw the water was rising quickly. She and Otto left immediately.

'Otto went back in two or three days later to see if there was anything to get out; I didn't go back. The water went pretty quickly, but it just decimated everything. We had it up to about a metre in the house. Some people had two metres in their houses. It came from a different way this time; it came from the south and the west. It was like a tsunami.'

FOURTEEN MONTHS ON from the floods, Karen's composed manner as she tells her story can't hide her frustration at how the insurers have handled the process, particularly the never-ending rebuild of her home.

Many in the town received payouts quickly for damaged goods in their houses – but Karen was told by her insurer, Suncorp, that she had to go through her damaged property and itemise everything that was lost or destroyed.

'Can you imagine?' she says. 'A four-bedroom, two-bathroom, two lounge-room house and you have to go itemise everything you have lost? It just broke me. My daughter came up from Geelong and she sat there for two days on her computer itemising every single item I could possibly think of. We had to have a photo of everything and send it through to the insurer. It was just hideous. Then other people with different companies got paid out straight away.'

Months afterwards she met with a Suncorp representative who said that itemising a list of all damaged goods wasn't necessary and organised for Karen to be paid out an estimate then and there.

Although Karen felt the estimate was fair, the slow pace of reconstruction is the reason she and Otto are still living in their caravan. She says the builders contracted to repair her house have subcontracted most of it out to 'cowboys' who have come up from Melbourne – their work has little or no craftsmanship and often has to be redone by the insurers' builders, which continues to cause significant delays.

'Here we are, nearly fourteen months on and still having major issues with the house, still having major issues with the builders and the tradies,' she says. 'They keep saying, *It will be all ready by mid-December; you'll be in by Christmas*. We know that it's not going to happen and they are just trying to smooth things over.'

After the 2022 floods, which were the worst in living memory, Karen says many people in the town have been selling their water-damaged houses and moving away. Many are afraid the town will flood again and can't face going through the process of rebuilding just to lose everything once more. She says the mental and emotional toll this experience puts on families and relationships is just too much.

'Otto would have left if it were up to him,' she says. 'He said we can't go through this again – and I said the same. Never again. We have lost a lot of people out of the town. The community has been amazing, but it takes its toll. It was the community that motivated me to stay; it's home. It's my home. [Otto] probably wishes now that we had taken a cash settlement for the house and sold up and gone. But I thought, I can't do it just yet.'

KAREN'S EXPERIENCE IS far from unique. The 2022 floods were the worst on record for many parts of the east coast of Australia according to the Climate Council, who warn we are heading into an 'era of climate disasters' that we are not prepared for. How do we, as a nation, respond to the increasing frequency of extreme weather events as climate change threatens the Australian dream of home ownership that remains so deeply ingrained in the country's psyche? Are there parts of the country where it simply isn't safe to live anymore? And if we don't make tough decisions about where and how we live now, what consequences lie in store down the track?

These questions are becoming increasingly pertinent – and so far, the insurance industry isn't offering much in the way of answers.

Damian Stock, the CEO of local Victorian community legal centre ARC Justice, says the feedback they have received from Rochester and elsewhere in the region is that insurance companies have let people down following the extreme weather of 2022.

'It's fourteen months on and what we know is that some 30 per cent or more of those claims are yet to be accepted, and payments still haven't been made,' Stock says.

'The problem is we have a private market here with interests that are focused on trying to reduce the amount of claims that are paid out. So, we see lots of either offers of part payment of the claim or refusal of a claim based on allegations of pre-existing issues or even landscaping or tree-placement issues, or allegations that buildings don't meet current codes.'

The Australian Financial Complaints Authority reported a record number of complaints last year, with delays in insurance claim-handling the most complained-about issue. In 2022–23 there were over 10,000 complaints to the body about delayed claims, up from 2,700 just four years earlier.

Stock adds that people's experiences are wildly different based on their insurer and that they have heard of many cases where insurers were offering 'low ball' cash settlements to flood victims to settle their claims, which were being accepted because people didn't have the will or energy to fight for the money they should rightfully be paid.

As the number of extreme weather events increase, so too do the premiums all Australians pay to insure their homes, regardless of where they live. Research from consumer group CHOICE in 2023 found that 87 per cent of home and contents insurance policyholders had seen their premiums rise at their last renewal. Julia Davis, senior policy and communications officer at the New South Wales-based Financial Rights Legal Centre, says in some parts of the country those rises in insurance premiums have been so severe that homes are now essentially 'uninsurable' even if the industry won't use the term.

'The Insurance Council of Australia [ICA] loves going around saying that there's no part of Australia that's "uninsurable". But we would argue that offering insurance for $20,000 a year is basically equivalent to not offering insurance. It's completely unaffordable,' she says. 'The industry doesn't want to say that there's complete market failure, but there's a large protection gap and it's only going to keep growing.'

Davis says studies have classified unaffordable insurance as annual premiums that are more than four weeks of gross annual income, and that in 2022 10 per cent of households fit that category. That figure rose to 12 per cent in 2023. A 2023 report by the Actuaries Institute found affordability pressures were disproportionately felt by households struggling financially in the most exposed areas of the country, predominantly flood-prone parts of southern Queensland and Northern Rivers, NSW.

'The cost of rising premiums is only going to lead to more people being uninsured or underinsured. Right now, when a disaster happens and people are uninsured, then it is a huge cost for government and for everyone,' Davis says.

She points to the need to increase government investment in areas such as climate mitigation and resilience, but adds there are also measures the insurance industry could be implementing to help with the problem.

'There's not going to be a silver bullet – there's not even going to be a dozen different silver bullets – but we need to look at all these things that may help,' Davis says.

The CHOICE survey found that 44 per cent of policyholders would consider investing in improvements to their home to make it more disaster resilient if this led to lower home-insurance premiums. However, many insurance companies often don't recognise or consider individual disaster-mitigation efforts – such as fireproofing or raising houses on stumps – in their pricing structures.

The Insurance Council of Australia say anecdotally they have been seeing worsening levels of underinsurance.

'During 2022 alone there were more than 302,000 disaster-related claims lodged from four declared insurance events, totalling $7.26 billion. These events are still having an impact on the price of insurance for every Australian insurance customer,' the ICA says.

'In addition to the impact of extreme weather events, insurance-premium increases are being driven by inflation, particularly in the building industry, and the growing cost of reinsurance, which is insurance that insurers buy.'

Tim Nelson from the Climate Council says there is a huge imbalance in the amount of data that insurance companies can access to forecast the likelihood of extreme weather events and the information they give consumers when they are making decisions about their homes. Nelson says insurers don't pass on long-term weather risk forecasting to their consumers and don't make their policies and the climate risks involved easy to understand so that their customers can make informed decisions.

'We need a central hazard-risk register,' he says. 'It needs to be accessible. It needs to be really easily digestible for the average home owner and for communities to understand what the risks look like to their properties.'

He says along with greater efforts to tackle climate change and reduce emissions, governments need to make some tough calls about funding buybacks and relocations from areas that are simply becoming unliveable.

Davis adds that the banking sector and the role home-loan providers play in peoples' ability to buy and sell houses is a 'ticking time bomb' in this discussion.

'People's entire home values are going to be wiped out,' she says. 'If you have banks that pull out of servicing areas because they can't be insured, then nobody can buy the home and the home has no value. It's a real thing on the horizon that I think most people just don't appreciate.

'That's not happening now, but when you buy a house it's a long-term decision, it's a thirty-year mortgage. It is totally foreseeable that this will happen within the lifetime of that purchase.'

Since the 2022 floods in Victoria, NSW, Queensland and parts of Tasmania, there has been a federal government inquiry held into the insurance industry's response. The inquiry is due to hand down its findings in September 2024, and while some changes may emerge from this, it's unlikely the myriad of problems facing home owners and the insurance industry will be addressed.

FAR NORTH QUEENSLAND during Christmas in 2023 was lashed by a cyclone and flash flooding that wiped out whole communities north of Cairns. In the early days of 2024, heavy rain and flooding returned to Rochester. Evacuation orders were given for the town once again – a town that was still reeling from the floods less than eighteen months earlier.

In February, I call Karen once more. 'The floods in January weren't that bad this time,' she says. The water got up to the hotel in the middle of town and not much further. 'But for the town psychologically these floods were terribly frightening, because people still haven't gotten over it – it was like, "Here we go again."'

She thanks me for my call and says she is busy in the backyard of her property – the home she's yet to move back into – overseeing some repairs. She and Otto are still living at the caravan park – the promise of being 'in by Christmas' long gone.

Jarni Blakkarly is an investigative journalist for CHOICE and a freelance writer based in Naarm (Melbourne).

NON-FICTION

The inspirations of radical nostalgia

On history, ecology and inheriting God

David Ritter

ON A WARM Monday morning in late February 1988, I tentatively entered a sandstone lecture theatre and climbed the wide stairs to one of the near-to-the-back rows. I was accompanied by two of my closest friends from high school, and we should have been well practised, having arrived to classrooms together literally thousands of times. Yet this was different. The teaching space was so much bigger, able to seat hundreds of pupils, and we were the little kids again, 'freshers' in our very first class at the oldest and largest university in our state, impressive to our young provincial eyes. That Beethoven's Ninth was playing over the loudspeaker added decidedly to the weight of the moment and my ambient sense of impostorism. The lecturer waiting behind the lectern was a middle-aged man with unruly dark hair and glasses. As the class began and the teacher introduced himself I wrote his name – *Professor Richard Bosworth* – in blue pen on a piece of paper that I still have in storage somewhere.

The unit was Late Modern European History 102 – an easy choice for my friends and me, as we'd all liked and done well at history in our leaving year. We soon found out, though, that this was no simple narrative account of events of the kind to which we were accustomed, but a different country altogether. The course was a steep introduction to 'history' as fundamentally unstable: a multivalenced, complicatedly ironic and endlessly nuanced dialogue between past and present. The feeling was unsettling; a departure from comforting certainties of neatly ordered understanding into a far more complex milieu of infinitely greater strangeness and richness, with still evolving tendrils that reached disconcertingly into the now.

The pedagogic intent of LME, as it was known, was accomplished through the examination of the work of select historians as well as an eclectic array of other interpreters of Europe's many histories, including film directors, novelists, comedians and diarists. Though the temporal span of the course began with the French Revolution of 1789, there was particular focus on studying explanations of the 'long' Second World War, and how, why and when these interpretations had changed and evolved over time. I was enthralled by the epic nature of the subject matter and charmed by the ample charisma and engaged humanity of the teacher. Perhaps above all, though, it was the ethical, political and intellectual offering of the course that I found gripping: the invitation to participate in serious inquiry into the moral crisis of Europe's age of mass violence through historiographical engagement as a civically important and challenging obligation. To be trusted with this was an intoxicating initiatory promise to a callow sixteen-year-old in search of meaning.

In hindsight, both the intensity and scale of the course seem astounding. LME was a whole-year unit with more than thirty weeks of teaching. The class outline had a scrapbook aesthetic and was dense with readings, roughly cut-out pictures and excerpts of text – an assemblage that had been hard-earnt in those days before the instant results of internet searches. Two in-person lectures per week were supplemented by fortnightly tutorials delivered by Richard Bosworth or one of the other tenured historians from what was then a whole history department within an intact Faculty of Arts. There was also an optional but well-subscribed weekly film program. Marking was careful and personalised, done line by line in handwriting on paper copies of assessments. The grading of every assignment was followed by a substantive discussion with the teacher who had assessed the piece. Tutorial groups were no more than ten or twelve, typically held in the academic's personal office, beginning with the offer of tea or coffee. There were, from memory, at least seven pieces of graded 'take home' written work and an end-of-year exam, as well as a minimum of six verbal presentations to be made in tutorial groups. That the course was meant to be demanding was a point of pride, meant as a statement of trust in our commitment and intelligence as students.

To some extent, the scepticism and interrogative habits of LME only made sense so long as certain long-established precepts of university life continued to pertain. In those days there was still genuine confidence within the halls of the academy. Universities themselves, of course, are neither static nor uniform, and the function of higher education has no doubt always been contested, but as the twentieth century deepened, certain assumptions – for example, that faculty members needed space and long-term security to be able to research and think, and that students had similar requirements to participate in campus life and to learn – were commonplace. Despite or perhaps enhanced by the upheavals of the 1960s, both academics and the forms of knowledge they produced seemed to still retain a greater prestige and authority than now.

But 'higher education reform' was on the way, even while we first years progressed, as oblivious to the fate of the sector as animals deep in a forest scheduled for logging. The Hawke Labor government marked the 200th anniversary of the revolution of liberté, égalité, fraternité by initiating student fees in the form of the Higher Education Contribution Scheme, abolishing the era of free education that had been introduced by Gough Whitlam.

The subsequent *trente années misérables*-plus of 'higher education reform' – the systematic degradation of Australia's university sector in the name of neoliberal economic orthodoxy – has been particularly harsh on the arts and humanities, including the teaching of history. According to historians Martin Crotty, Frank Bongiorno and Paul Sendziuk, in 1989 there were about 450 full-time equivalent paid positions in history in Australian universities, a number that had been reduced to 319 full-time equivalent positions by 2023. That number is set to be further reduced by the cutting of thirty-two full-time humanities posts at the Australian Catholic University, with the disciplines of history and philosophy to be the worst affected.

In context it seems onomatopoeically apt that the word 'reform', particularly when repeated, can sound a little like the starting of a chainsaw. Since 1989, fees have been repeatedly raised; management has come before vocation; universities have been marketised, digitised and commodified; and many staff have been casualised and driven to precarity. In what Raimond Gaita once described as managerial newspeak, students are recast as consumers or service users, and academics as content providers whose work is assessed through an asinine and perverting focus on outputs and rankings. Richard Bosworth once mocked neoliberal politicians and administrators for holding that 'real estate studies should be the centre of the modern university'. Thirty years later, obeisance to the market and managerial ideology has become the central organising principle of higher education in Australia.

On top of the broader trends, an especially pernicious attack was launched under the federal government of Scott Morrison. Having first singled out Australian public universities for punishment by excluding the sector from JobKeeper during the Covid pandemic, the Morrison government then introduced 'reforms' in 2021 known as the 'Job-ready Graduates Package' that rendered humanities subjects more than 113 per cent more expensive. As Raewyn Connell noted, Morrison's government disliked 'humanities and social sciences, basically because they encourage critical thinking', so purposefully set about making these courses more difficult to access and burdening those who persisted regardless with much heavier debt. If the study of history within the university has constituted one of the primary means of the making of public memory in the modern nation state, then this was a policy designed to drive an agenda of collective amnesia. Reforms not to foster learning but to drive forgetting. Reform, reform, reform...until the trees crack and fall.

LIKE THE OVERWHELMING majority of university history students, I did not end up becoming an academic historian. I've no doubt, though, that the habits of humane critical inquiry acquired in LME and then reinforced across later units informed my vocational choices, first to work as an Indigenous rights lawyer, then to serve the cause of Greenpeace. In career terms and notwithstanding all the inherent ironies and complications, working particularly in the field of native title acting for traditional owners in the wake of the Mabo decision, among many other motivations, felt like an appropriate moral response to the hideous excesses of nationalism that we'd studied in LME.

Later, I would find clear parallels between the practice of history that I'd learnt as an undergraduate and the work of being an environmental campaigner. Environmentalism, like history, is a civic discourse that critically engages with change in the world, contemplates the nature of limits and challenges ahistorical self-absorption. Like all good historians, environmentalists create recognition that the structures and conditions of today are not natural, inevitable or preordained but thoroughly contingent. The study of history and ecologically motivated advocacy also both demand reasoned scepticism towards the ideological claims of the powerful. And in contemporary Australia it is inevitable that both academic history and ecological consciousness involve a reckoning with paradigms of diminishment and decline; the dwindling of the humanities in our universities echoes a greater and more irrevocable story of diminuation, that of appalling systemic ecological loss on our continent.

While there are isolated stories of resurgence and recovery, the broader picture of Australia's biodiversity is a tableau of massive-scale rapid depletion and deterioration. Just over a year after the 'Job-ready Graduates Package' was unveiled by the Morrison government, the national five-yearly assessment of the state of the environment was provided by the relevant statutory authority to minister Sussan Ley. The government declined to release the report prior to the election, with the consequence that it was only published by the incoming portfolio holder, Labor's Tanya Plibersek, a year later. Headline findings included: the diversity of wild animals and plants in Australia is declining, and the number of threatened species is increasing; at least nineteen Australian ecosystems are showing signs of collapse or near collapse; more mammal species have been driven to extinction in Australia than any other continent; and Australia has one of the highest rates of species decline in the developed world. The report also archly noted that 'biodiversity overall is monitored very poorly in Australia, and we cannot assess the state and trend of most species with any confidence'.

While the scientific surveying might be patchy, you don't have to go far to hear stories of waning and vanishing. For example, one of my relatives told me recently that the herring run he'd reliably fished off the Perth coast for at least five decades had no longer been present on the last few trips out. In another instance, a former colleague, an Indigenous man of high standing within his language group in the Pilbara, lamented the drastic drop in wildlife, with game animals such as kangaroo and emu decreasing in number as mining developments and their associated infrastructure continue to carve up the traditional lands of the Marlpa nations of that country. On the day I wrote this paragraph an old woman I know well who is a keen twitcher remarked to me that 'these days' the only bird she sees in her yard with any frequency is the invasive common myna. And of course any Australian of a certain age will tell you that a drive in the country at dusk used to mean a windscreen covered in hapless, splattered insect bodies. Not anymore.

Given my role I often hear stories of this kind, told almost as if in confessional mode, of living things, once prolific, disappearing. Gone. Last year I visited the Northern Rivers twelve months after two massive floods had inundated the region in quick succession. There was no agenda but witnessing: informing my campaign advocacy through seeing and listening to people's experiences of extreme climate damage. In the heat and humidity, so different to the unstopping rains of twelve months before, I heard survivors describe what they had been through, both in the crazy disruption of the days and nights of disaster and in the drying, dreary, wearying aftermath. In one backyard, a young man I'll call Abe recounted his experience of near drowning and escape, and the destruction and hardship that had followed in the wake of the vandalistic waters. Even heavy furniture had been washed away. Abe and his pregnant partner had done their best to clean the place up and waterproof a couple of rooms, but the house remained structurally stuffed and they couldn't afford to move, so life continued as cheerfully as possible.

Abe and others who survived the unnatural tempest conveyed a bleak sense of time interrupted – not dissimilar, in a way, to the brutal breaking of life's assumed pattern and shape by the catastrophic events of Europe's violent twentieth century, as evoked in so many of the sources that I'd studied back in LME. Severe changes in nature were part of the harm. The once prolific frogs especially loved by Abe, for instance, had completely vanished from his yard in the wake of the stormwaters. According to the Lismore City Council Flood Response, the 'prolonged and intense rainfall in the upper catchment, and the resultant major flooding…had very significant environmental impacts across the entire local government area'. For example, a vast fish-kill had occurred in the Richmond River, brought about by deoxygenation in the water caused by rotting vegetation washed in from the floodplains by the unprecedented rains – unleashed by climate change driven primarily by the mining and burning of gas, coal and oil.

MOST OF THE time, when we gaze out on the world, we see what is there, not what is gone. Social scientists call this phenomenon 'survivorship bias' – we are more likely to notice people and things that are still with us, rather than those that have vanished. There's nothing inherently sinister about this – after all, we can only see what is there to be seen – but in context, the consequences are profound and troubling. As time passes, the recollection of the conditions that prevailed before each cataclysm will become dimmer and, inevitably, held by ever-decreasing numbers of people.

Callum Roberts' *The Unnatural History of the Sea* (a book that I have admiringly referred to in a previous *Griffith Review* essay) straddles the boundaries of history and ecology, using historical sources to track the extent and trajectory of the decline of wildlife in the oceans. The point Roberts makes is that in the consequence of a trend of sharp ecological impoverishment, each generation assuming what it finds to be 'normal' necessarily becomes an exercise in mass erasure. Significantly, as Roberts observes:

> [t]he idea of shifting baselines is familiar to us all and does not relate only to the natural environment. It helps explain why people tolerate the slow crawl of urban sprawl and loss of green space, why they fail to notice increasing noise pollution, and why they put up with longer and longer commutes to work. Changes creep up on us, unnoticed by younger generations who have never known anything different. The young write off old people who rue the losses they have witnessed as either backward or dewy-eyed romantics.

So just as young moderns may doubt the tales of prolific wildlife populations narrated by their elders or written down by previous generations, contemporary university students may perhaps regard stories of what higher education used to be like with a similar sense of dubiousness or outright disbelief. Yet the likes of LME did exist as part of the ordinary reality of undergraduate life, and the oceans once heaved with shoals of enormous fish – as unimaginable as each may now be in the bleak light of a world that is being churned and burned in the name of corporate greed and market ideology.

Looking backwards and recognising that some stuff was just unquestionably superior at various points in the past may feel counterintuitive to Australian 'progressives', for whom contemporary historical consciousness is rightly (and tightly) bound up with attempts to reckon with the nation's legacy of colonisation, racism, sexism, intolerance and so on. The very designation *progressive* optimistically conjoins forward motion with social, political and economic change leading to greater equality, justice and sustainability. Yet casual disavowal of the past can amount to the replacement of one form of simplistic narrative with another, providing a conveniently blank canvas to every CEO, techno lord or free marketeer who insists that there is no alternative. An LME-style interrogation would invite an impatience with simplistic declamations or narratives of any sort, but itself relies on the affordance of a level of institutional continuity as a given that no longer pertains. In each and every case, ironic detachment is of limited use for a planet on fire.

History is too important to simply be ceded to either the tyranny of relentless presentism or the oppressive purposes of reactionary atavism. We can simultaneously reject the tyrannies and cruelties of the past and be energised and inspired by that which was kinder and more nurturing of humanity and nature. Acknowledging that 'some things were better' is in no way to offer apologia for all that was very much worse. The situation in relation to greenhouse gas concentrations, for example, can be rendered straightforwardly. The year I studied LME, 1988, was the first year carbon in the atmosphere passed 350 parts per million; today the world is at more than 420 ppm. The trajectory in relation to biodiversity loss, plastic pollution and a host of other environmental indicators is similarly clear. A form of nostalgia for when the world was in much better shape in environmental terms – a time before the climate and ecological crisis became so manifest – is not schmaltz, but actively subversive of the status quo in which too many political and business decision-makers continue to usher humanity and biodiversity towards a fate of ecological oblivion.

There is nothing natural or inevitable about the 'decline' of history and the broader arts and humanities, any more than there is the destruction of nature. Neither are passive or natural processes; both occur as a consequence of deliberate decision-making made in accordance with ideological preferences, usually supporting the material objectives of the vested interests that systematically corrupt our democracy and society.

Redeeming universities and other public institutions requires sustained political effort. The decline of academic history can be reversed through ending the ideological sway of neoliberal managerialism in universities, the allocation of reasonable levels of resourcing, and the provision of job security and professional autonomy to sufficient numbers of historians, plus time and space to learn for their students. Loss of historical consciousness, unlike extinction, need not be forever. With air returned to their lungs once more, the disciplines preoccupied with human purpose and meaning, fostering habits of critical thinking, are amenable to full resuscitation.

TOWARDS THE END of 1988, Bosworth concluded LME with a final expansive lecture. 'History,' he said emphatically, 'is a real course, a course that matters' for great moral reasons. The conception of events as the unfolding of divine will had, in the aftermath of the Enlightenment and the onset of modernity in Europe, been largely substituted with the idea of human agency as the engine of historical change. In that multiply ironic sense, Richard told us that, as students of history, we had 'inherited the past; inherited god'.

His declaration was, I am certain, intended to instil humility rather than hubris, because none can presume to know 'the mind of god', even as a metaphor, in the form of the secular analogue of historical explanation. Thus, there was a characteristic impishness to the message: history has no final answer, but is instead, in a phrase coined by Dutch historian Pieter Geyl, an 'argument without end', not in the sense of discounting the relative probity of evidence, but because of the fluctuating contexts, methodologies, politics and valencies of competing interpretations. Historical consciousness, then, might nourish the humanity of our sensibilities and encourage resistance towards the over-simplification of life that invariably provides the preconditions to oppression. Engaging with history could also help foster multiple perspectives, enabling deeper and more pluralistic democracy as a perpetual means of holding the powerful to account.

In the context of climate and ecological emergency, the suggestion that history has in some way succeeded the mantle of the divine takes on an altogether different implication. As David Attenborough said bluntly in 2019, 'the garden of Eden is no more'; but as work like that of Callum Roberts shows, history enables us not only to evoke the riches of paradise before the fall but by implication to glimpse what might yet grow again. Knowing what has been lost frees us to imagine what could flourish in the future and should inspire our collective will to act in the hope of life resurgent. This idea of resurrection is derived not from any religious text but a forensic awareness of the shifts in society and environment that have been caused by human hands, and so can conceivably be redirected towards regeneration through active agency. Roberts is one of many scientists who, along with organisations such as Greenpeace, have long advocated for the creation of vast high-seas marine sanctuaries, to enable the oceans to recover – a possibility that was enabled for the first time under international governance with the United Nations' passing of the Global Oceans Treaty in 2023. So it is that the profane instruments of transnational governance can offer the prospect of sublime renewal.

That the ecology of the world can be changed drastically by humanity has been amply demonstrated, but this means that transformation in the opposite direction, towards restabilising the climate, remediating pollution and regenerating the magnificent diversity of life on Earth, is also possible to a partial but nonetheless wonderful extent. We cannot reanimate the extinct from the abyss of forever or altogether make whole what has been smashed, but nature, given the chance, will always resurge. History not only enables lamentation and reckoning, but the bright light of what is realisable based on an apprehension of the world we once knew.

David Ritter is the chief executive officer of Greenpeace Australia Pacific.

NON-FICTION

Radioactive fallout

Negotiating Japan's fraught relationship with nuclear power

Haruko Koga

ON 9 JUNE 2021, my teenage son and I were at the theatre of HOTA, Home of the Arts, on the Gold Coast with a couple of hundred new Aussies. Mayor Tom Tate was onstage and congratulated us in his distinct husky voice. He asked, 'Who is from the UK?' 'Who is from South Africa?' 'Who is from China?' The attendees reacted in subtly unique ways. The Brits replied in low, steady murmurs; the Koreans and Taiwanese were quiet; the Chinese were jaunty; and the Brazilians' cheers were the loudest and most musical.

'Who is from Japan?'

My son and I were shy. We couldn't respond verbally, so we raised the Australian flags we'd received at the reception and shook them.

In contrast to the well-lit stage, the audience seats were dim. I looked at my new citizenship certificate for the third time. On sleek, off-white paper sat the crest depicting the kangaroo and emu holding the shield with a background of wattle flowers, and the golden letters, 'Australian Citizenship'.

Ten years and ninety days. It had been an arduous journey.

THE TOHOKU EARTHQUAKE occurred at 2.46 pm, 11 March 2011. The magnitude was 9.0. The epicentre was below the North Pacific Ocean, 130 kilometres east of Sendai, the largest city in the Tohoku region. When it hit, I was at my office in Tokyo, 370 kilometres from the epicentre.

Up until then, I wasn't particularly scared of earthquakes. Because there are so many, we Japanese are used to them. Seismologists predict that a possible catastrophic earthquake will occur within thirty years or so, warning that the casualties might exceed 100,000. But you can't live in constant fear. We just hope it won't come yet. Pushing aside any anxiety, we get on with our lives.

But that day, during the most powerful and longest shake I'd ever experienced, ducking under the desk and unable to move or even let out a cry, I thought I might die. I thought my loved ones might die.

The quake lasted six minutes – the office floor jolted convulsively; metal shelves rattled, files fell with a cacophony of thuds, and the structure of the building seemed to be squeaking. And then it stopped. My office building hadn't collapsed. Neither had our apartment; my husband and son weren't hurt.

But it wasn't the end. The Fukushima Daiichi Nuclear Power Plant had lost power, which was required to cool both the reactors and spent fuel rods. The government was braced for the worst: massive explosions or core meltdowns. A nuclear emergency was declared at 7.03 pm. My husband and I learnt little about what was going on, but we took a leap and evacuated from Tokyo in the middle of the night.

Sometimes, the mind plays tricks on you. What was hanging over us was terrifying, but I carry a cinematic, striking image of that night: Shinjuku-Dori Avenue in Yotsuya gridlocked with thousands of cars, streams of amber headlights and crimson tail lamps held captive in mesmerising parallel lines. The lustrous lights suffused the indigo sky with an ethereal otherworldliness. The tranquil, stray moments amid the once-in-a-lifetime crisis – they haunt and console me still.

MY DREAD OF nuclear weapons and nuclear fuels informed our choice to flee.

I was a child in the 1970s, when World War II wasn't all that long ago. My father had been eleven when the war ended. His family had come back from North Korea, and the exodus had been an ordeal. The memories of it were vividly etched in his mind, and he told me about it over and over again.

'We were in Kilju in North Hamgyong that summer. When we heard the rumour that Japan was losing in early August, we hid in the mountains. When the Soviet army crossed the border, Kilju was air raided, but we weren't in the town and were okay. In early September, we walked to Songjin. It took about three days. Then in late September, we left for Munchon in a freight train. We stayed there for about a month. Then we moved to Wonsan. Our acquaintance was a doctor there, and he let us stay in his house. This saved our lives. Many of those who slept at schools or temples died of epidemic typhus. We were always hungry. There was no rice or wheat.'

My father never got tired of telling those stories. His childhood in North Korea and the exodus shaped him.

To prevent the mistake of fighting a war again, teachers were instructed to carry out peace education catered towards primary and junior-high school students. Peace education had two faces: bright and dark. The bright side was Japan's 'peace constitution' that came into effect in 1947. We were taught that ours is the only constitution in the world that pledges renunciation of war. Article 9 declares:

> Aspiring sincerely to an international peace based on justice and order, the Japanese people forever renounce war as a sovereign right of the nation and the threat or use of force as means of settling international disputes.
>
> In order to accomplish the aim of the preceding paragraph, land, sea, and air forces, as well as other war potential, will never be maintained. The right of belligerency of the state will not be recognized.

Controversy has surrounded Article 9 since day one. Some people say it's idiotic and idealistic, that it disregards the reality of international politics. If Japan doesn't have military forces at all, how can it maintain its sovereignty and protect its people? However, we have the Japan Self-Defence Force – essentially land, sea and air forces. Insisting they are not a military is a misrepresentation. The right-wing criticises this contradiction and wants to delete the second clause of Article 9. But mainstream opinion seems to support the current state, maintaining that it's good for Japan to have 'self-defence forces' so that we can protect our country in case we are attacked, so long as we never send them overseas or get involved in other countries' wars. As a reminder of this, keeping Article 9 is meaningful. However, it's noteworthy that for the Allies, implementing the peace constitution had nothing to do with idealism. It was a means to disarm fascist Japan. But in the 1970s, to my pure child's mind, it didn't matter. The utopian resolution had an unadulterated appeal, and I was proud of it.

The dark side of peace education was to have students know how brutally and pointlessly people had been killed during the war.

The Bombing of Tokyo on the night of 9–10 March 1945 killed more than 100,000 civilians. In the Battle of Okinawa approximately 200,000 people died – 94,000 civilians, 94,000 Japanese soldiers and 12,500 American soldiers. Those are staggering numbers, but the focus of peace education was the atomic bombings of Hiroshima and Nagasaki. In Hiroshima about 140,000 out of the city's 350,000 inhabitants died, while in Nagasaki around 74,000 of 240,000 people lost their lives by the end of 1945.

Japan is the only country in history where atomic bombs have been dropped in wartime. It became a part of our national identity: *We experienced the devastating inhumanity of atomic bombs firsthand. As witnesses, we have a moral obligation to advocate for a better world without nuclear weapons.*

Japan wasn't a victim, though, but an aggressor. Many more people were killed in Asia-Pacific countries, including Australians. It's impossible to count the number of casualties precisely, but it's said that up to twenty million people died in China. It's beyond comprehension; my imagination falters there. Up to 500,000 died in Korea under Japan's control; between 500,000 and one million were killed in the Philippines; approximately 100,000 died in Malaya; and the list goes on. But we students were taught about the loss of our nationals' lives, not the deaths caused by Japanese. The fact that our grandfathers or great-uncles robbed, raped, shot, slashed or impaled innocent civilians is hard to accept, I know, but not teaching it to younger generations was moral weakness.

WHEN I WAS in Year 6, we went to Nagasaki for a school trip. We saw the Peace Statue and the Fountain of Peace in Peace Park. The guide explained that, struck by the 3,000-degree Celsius blast, the victims were burnt all over and died in agonising thirst. The Fountain of Peace was built to console their souls so that they could drink water as they pleased. But it was difficult for me to take their torment to heart. It was a sunny, pleasant day, and Peace Park was neat and clean, with paved paths and deep green trees. Everything looked normal and peaceful, the tragedy in the past perfectly concealed.

We also visited the Immaculate Conception Cathedral, more commonly known as the Urakami Cathedral. Christianity was banned in Japan for nearly 300 years, and many missionaries and Christians were executed – impaled by lances on crosses, burnt or decapitated. But the brethren in Nagasaki went underground and handed down their faith from generation to generation. When the proscription was finally lifted in 1873, the congregation of

Urakami decided to build a church. After forty years, the construction was completed in 1914. It was a brick Neo-Romanesque cathedral, the largest Christian structure in the Asia-Pacific.

At 11.02 am on 9 August 1945, a few dozen Christians were at the Urakami Cathedral for a sacrament of penance and reconciliation when the nuclear bomb Fat Man exploded above Matsuyama-machi. The hypocentre was 500 metres from the Urakami Cathedral. The blast and heat ray completely destroyed the cathedral. The people inside, including the priest, Saburo Nishida, and the curate, Fusayoshi Tamaya, were killed instantly.

The cathedral was rebuilt in 1959 but it wasn't restored to its original appearance until 1980. When we visited, it was not fancy and didn't impress me, but a comment I read years later (I'm not sure now who said it) made the Urakami Cathedral important to me: *If they knew Christians were among the dead, they might understand the victims were also humans, and feel sorry.*

To truly grasp this sentiment, I have to delve into the argument of whether it was justified to drop the atomic bombs.

The official account in the US is that the decision was made as a measure to end the war quickly and to save American soldiers' and Japanese people's lives. More would've died if the US had had to invade Japan. But some historians disagree. They claim that the bombs were dropped to intimidate the USSR and to test these revolutionary weapons on humans. That's why the US dropped two bombs, not one; they were different kinds. Little Boy was a uranium gun-type bomb and Fat Man was a plutonium implosion bomb. Presumably the US wanted to know which worked better.

Also, there is a suspicion that racism played a part. The Black American poet Langston Hughes voiced this in an article in the *Chicago Defender*, 'Here to Yonder: Simple and the Atom Bomb', in 18 August 1945, only nine days after Nagasaki. 'And how come we did not try them out on Germany?' Hughes had his 'Simple Minded Friend' say. 'They just did not want to use them on white folks.' Hughes could've been speculating; the development of atomic bombs hadn't been completed when Germany surrendered in May. But the Hyde Park Aide-Mémoire, a short agreement between Roosevelt and Churchill made in September 1944, seems to validate Hughes' hunch. It stated, 'When a "bomb" is finally available, it might perhaps, after mature consideration, be used against the Japanese.' The Allies were still fighting against Germany, but Roosevelt and Churchill had already decided that atomic weapons should be dropped on Japan.

It might not have been racism. Considering the magnitude of the atrocities the Japanese had committed, it's no wonder that hatred of the Japanese had grown sharply among the American people. Yet a part of me can't dismiss the suspicion.

This isn't the notion the majority of Japanese people hold. They accept the orthodox take, that the Japanese were too desperate and incapable of surrendering – that they asked for atomic bombs. Sort of. But the person who expressed the symbolic importance of the Urakami Cathedral might've had this suspicion. I hear their inexhaustible sorrow. *We aren't experimental animals. We're Christians. We're humans. The same as you.*

Having said that, we Japanese don't bear any grudge against the US. That applies to me, too. What resonates in that phrase is just sadness and grief, not resentment. Partly because we cheered for peace. Most Japanese people were sick of the war, sick of dying or losing loved ones, sick of hunger and sick of the oppressive, inhumane government. They welcomed Americans as liberators. And Japanese people seemed to see the atomic bombings almost like natural disasters. It wasn't that Truman or anybody had made a call – it just happened.

TWO YEARS AFTER our school trip to Nagasaki, we went to Hiroshima.

The exhibits at the Peace Memorial Museum were nauseating. There was a photo of a charred body, its limbs stiff and shrunk. It looked like a charcoal log. I couldn't tell whether it was an adult or a child, male or female. A sketch showed a boy who was catching his eyeball falling from his eye socket with his hand. I saw portraits of twelve- or thirteen-year-old boys and girls, taken when they were fit and healthy, who perished that morning. They were so young and innocent. They'd been assigned to fill the workforce shortages, since most of the men had been drafted and were away. They were demolishing houses to make firebreaks as a defence against air raids when Little Boy detonated. About 6,000 of them were killed.

In other photos, we saw heavily injured people at makeshift first-aid stations. Their skin was peeling, showing seared, oozing flesh. They'd been alive when the photos were taken but must've died afterwards. Their pain is unimaginable. If I were them, I would've screamed and begged for death.

Those images stuck with me.

Not all schools chose Hiroshima or Nagasaki as their travel destinations. It happened to be both for me. Looking back, they feel like defining moments in my life. If I hadn't gone, I might not be living in Australia now, because it was after the trip to Hiroshima that I started to pay attention to news and articles about nuclear weapons.

In 1980, the USSR had around 30,000 nuclear warheads. The US had 24,000, the UK 500, France 250, China 200 and Israel thirty, approximately, though Israel has neither acknowledged nor denied its possession to date. Together, they possessed more than enough to wipe out humanity dozens of times. I was dumbstruck. It was sheer insanity. I watched a documentary on the Cuban missile crisis. It gave me the impression that the world had been saved by Kennedy and Khrushchev. But a similar crisis could happen again. What if somebody reckless or less clever was running the country then? I was astonished at people's optimism, or indifference.

Forty years later, I'm barely scared. Maybe because nothing happened after all. I've lost the young, fervent sensitivity I once had. While it's true there are fewer warheads now, many of them are more powerful, and there are still more than enough to destroy the world. And more countries have nuclear weapons, with India, Pakistan and North Korea in the mix. My lack of concern is not logical.

While my trepidation about nuclear war has dulled, my worries over radiation exposure have remained.

ON THE NIGHT of 11 March 2011, the residents of Tokyo didn't seem concerned about the impending disaster. Strong and frequent aftershocks left us on edge, and we were frightened that another powerful quake could cause already damaged buildings to collapse. Trains and subways had halted, and roads were congested and buses and taxis scarce, stranding many people far from home. The tsunamis dominated the news, leaving little space for the evolving threat of nuclear disaster.

I was an outlier. Walking home via Shinjuku-Dori Avenue, I was obsessed with the idea that the reactors might be melting down at that very moment, deadly radiation already approaching. The news hadn't said as much, but official announcements are always late. In my head swirled images: deformed babies in Iraq, affected by depleted uranium bombs; sick children in Chernobyl; and two workers from the Tokaimura nuclear accident in 1999 – they looked not too bad right after the incident, but their DNA was destroyed and their bodies were unable to produce new cells. They suffered multiple organ failure, skin loss and unimaginable pain for eighty-three and 211 days respectively before their hearts ceased beating. The photos of their skinless, disintegrating faces and bodies are the most horrific things I've ever seen.

Around midnight, we left Tokyo in our car, packing passports, bank cards, photo albums and SD cards in the boot. It took us over two hours to get out of the traffic. Then we drove throughout the night to the south.

Tokyo is 220 kilometres away from Fukushima, while the evacuation zone the government set at the time was a three-kilometre radius from the plant. Fleeing from Tokyo might've been seen as hysteric, but being a mother makes you desperate, neurotic. Our son was three years old. I couldn't stand the thought that he could be hurt.

The next day, at 3.36 pm on 12 March, the reactor one building exploded. At 11.01 am two days later, so did reactor three. At around 6.14 am on 15 March, the suppression chamber of reactor two broke, and the reactor four building had a hydrogen explosion.

Those first five days were like a vivid dream. What was unfolding was so intense that it felt like my brain's neural circuits switched to a power-save mode. All I can recollect are constant nervousness, pain in my chest, shallow sleep and the foggy chunks of time when I took care of my son between watching TV or browsing the internet for information. There was also the weight of explaining my absence from work, as my office operated as usual from Monday 14 March.

After the last explosions on 15 March, there were no further dramatic incidents. The worst seemed to have passed. I should have been happy – and I was, but it was also the beginning of a fresh battle. When the situation at Fukushima was dire, nobody explicitly blamed or ridiculed us for evacuating from Tokyo. My boss, colleagues and parents were understanding to a certain point. But as the media coverage of the accident started to decrease, people were quick to get back to their normal routines and dismiss the danger. Leaving our child with my husband in Fukuoka, the largest city on the southern island of Kyushu, I flew in and out for work. But I only attended a third or quarter of my workdays, which made me feel guilty, despite my boss being extremely tolerant.

While everybody continued as if nothing had happened, I was petrified and couldn't bring myself to return permanently to Tokyo. I felt like a black sheep. In a society where conformity is the foremost virtue, believing in and sticking to my gut feeling was a trying and lonely act.

Several things had disturbed my equilibrium. One was that the majority of Tokyo residents went to work and school during the week immediately after the accident, when it looked catastrophic. I couldn't understand why they weren't terrified. Another was the backlash a popular weekly magazine called *AERA* copped. The edition published on 19 March featured a photo of a man in protective gear and a gas mask, with the words 'Radiation is coming' on its cover. It reported that a core meltdown could still happen and that it could be worse than Chernobyl. The publisher was bombarded with complaints that they were inciting fear with 'fake news', and he was forced to apologise. It later turned out the magazine's warnings were accurate. Nuclear cores did melt down and the accident was deemed as severe as Chernobyl. Back then, I didn't know whether it was fake news or not, but it debilitated me to see the relentless criticism. Also, from around April, TV and the media started to promote food from Fukushima and the Tohoku region with the slogan 'eat and support'. They said that the businesses and people there were suffering from 'reputational damage' and insisted that local produce was safe. According to them, those who avoided it were selfish and lacked compassion.

Voluntary evacuees like us were marginalised. Ostracised. The media even made up a word to jeer at us. *Houshano* – radiation paranoiacs.

For the first several months after the earthquake and the accident, we didn't think of going overseas. We had good jobs and had recently purchased a cosy apartment in Tokyo. We weren't fluent in English. What life would we be able to build in a foreign country? It didn't seem viable.

I quit my job. We sold our apartment and relocated to Fukuoka. Thus, we burnt bridges and started drifting. Concerns over raising our son on possibly contaminated land and having him eat risky food became driving forces, but ultimately, the sense of isolation and not belonging was what propelled us out of Japan.

Where should we go?

Buried in a sea of information on the internet, we looked for our promised land – a place where there are few earthquakes and no nuclear power plants. When we considered Australia, the small nuclear power plant for research and industrial use in Lucas Heights in New South Wales was only a minor drawback. But obtaining visas posed a huge hurdle. Even now, I can't believe we succeeded. We put in a lot of effort, but we were lucky. Many people tried as hard but didn't make it.

I don't know if it was necessary to move away from Japan. Some celebrities and several of my acquaintances in Tokyo got sick with cancer, and it felt like there were too many cases in young people. But the government denies any link between the accident and the diseases – except for thyroid cancer in Fukushima. If you believe the authorities, the dead were meant to die anyway; it had nothing to do with radiation.

Even if we'd stayed in Tokyo, we might've been fine. But my fear was impossible to suppress. I would've been trapped in the never-ending aftermath if I'd stayed. Any trivial ailment of my family's would've driven me into a panic. For me, it was necessary to leave to get my life back.

'THAT'S HOW THE disaster happened. That's why that place is poisoned. And that's it. When we heard the story, we all felt no good inside.'

One year after the accident, I came across a short video clip on Twitter. There, Mirarr woman Yvonne Margarula voiced her suspicion that uranium sourced from Ranger Uranium Mine on her traditional land had fuelled Fukushima, which was later confirmed by the director-general of the Australian Safeguards and Non-Proliferation Office. She felt responsible for the Fukushima disaster, even though she'd never supported the mining. But it's the other way around. Because we wanted electricity and convenient lives, their sacred land had been dug up and contaminated. We are responsible.

Our lives are intertwined in a perverted way, regardless of man-drawn borders.

Five months prior to the citizenship ceremony, I'd heard that the uranium mine at Ranger had closed after four decades of operation. It was a historic achievement for the Mirarr people, testament to the unyielding efforts led by Yvonne and other traditional owners. In that video recorded after Fukushima, she looked tired and distraught. Is she relieved now? I hope so.

When we left the HOTA building after the ceremony, the sun was dazzling and the winter sky was crystal clear. Over us, over the Mirarr people, over Fukushima and over Tokyo, the vivacious metropolitan city I once deeply loved, was the opalescent blue sky, oblivious of human hubris or suffering.

Haruko Koga is an emerging writer currently working on her first novel. Born and raised in Japan, she worked as a writer specialising in TV drama novelisations and as an English-to-Japanese translator before immigrating to Australia.

FICTION

Lifedorm

Greg Foyster

THE MANUAL WAS the most useful thing our parents left us. Without it we wouldn't have known how to operate the generators or grow food in the greenhouse, or anything. We wouldn't have known our own bodies. Hunter had started asking questions, saying the manual was out of date and we couldn't trust it, but I thought the opposite. What if the manual contained the secret to crossing the mountains? But yeah, I got where Hunter was coming from. He was bored. We were all so fucking bored. After a while, boredom takes over everything.

The first decade on our own was kind of exciting. We kept expecting someone to come in and say, *Don't touch that! Put that down! Go to bed. It's late!* The second decade we were all like, *Okay, this is our place now.* We decorated the corridors with torn pages from old picture books, painted the inside of the glass dome in bright colours, tried to read as much of the manual as we could. Then boredom started settling in, so we made our first attempts at travelling, but the surrounding mountains were too rocky and steep, no matter which path we took. By the third decade I wondered why our parents hadn't left us a vehicle. Sometimes the lake froze over, but we had no skates and the ice was too thin for a sled. The fourth, fifth, sixth and seventh decades filled me with bitterness. I felt like the big oak tree in the centre of our play garden, stuck in the same place forever. Except even the oak tree's life was more interesting because when it was small Parent 3 had told us to be careful not to step on it, and now it was this huge thing with ugly tree wrinkles and scars in the trunk from the branches we cut off to build a raft one summer, but I'd hardly grown at all. I guess I wasn't a lot of fun to be around when I had these thoughts.

Halfway through our eighth decade everything changed because I sort of maybe began to fall in love with Hunter.

I must have been feeling it for while, but only noticed when we took a shower together. Hunter had decided to make a small change to the manual, just a test, in the part about the temperature of the water. He crossed out *41 degrees* with a pencil and wrote *38* above it. Standing beside him, it was like words zapped between us without speaking: *What now?*

We stood there in our underwear, water cascading down our limbs, weird feelings churning inside me. So awkward.

'It's warm,' I said.

'Less or more than before?'

I shrugged as water splashed off my shoulders.

He shrugged too, then used a thermometer to check the water temperature near the shower nozzle. It varied between 38 and 41 degrees, and one time it even got down to 37, but another time it went up to 42, so we were both like, *Nah* – that proves nothing.

Then Hunter rubbed out the pencil marks so no one else would know.

The thing between us, it wasn't like *love* love. The manual said we weren't really capable of getting obsessed with someone and that was a good thing. How could we live in the mountains for ages and ages with each other if we got all crazy and jealous like our parents used to? *Crush* was the word for it. I saw his eyes looking all focused on something, like maybe he was fixing the sprinkler in the greenhouse or adding another handhold to the climbing wall he built, and I got all melty-tingly. It was super weird. I mean, I'd known Hunter forever, and he hadn't changed much, aside from getting a little taller. So what was new? Why Hunter? Why now? The manual didn't explain these things, despite its ten different volumes. Totally useless. Why didn't our parents leave us something that could speak and answer questions, like a computer, not these stupid old books? I guess they thought technology doesn't last but paper does. But still, sometimes I agreed with Hunter and wanted to blame the manual too. Then I would get goosepimples on my neck and was glad I didn't say anything out loud.

AT DINNER THAT night Jade was being super annoying. She said, 'This summer I'm going swimming in the lake again.'

'You're totally not,' said Bear.

'Am!' said Jade.

'You always say that and never do,' said Skyler.

'In summer,' said Jade. 'Just wait and see.'

Summer was ages away, but we knew she wouldn't do it because the lake was fed by snow melt and always freezing. Super deep and really cold – the manual said cold water could rise up from the bottom and freeze you instantly. Years ago, Jade tried to swim across in search of a path out of the mountains on the other side. She was probably just frustrated because it was her idea to build the oak-tree raft, but it fell apart and sank to the bottom. She got really cold and nearly died and Bear had to rescue her. Bear is twice my size with huge muscles, even though he is lazy and doesn't do any exercise. The manual says he's made that way.

After dinner the others went to bed but Hunter and I sat in the lounge room looking up through the clear glass dome at the sparkly stars.

'What do you think Jade is *for*?' he said, stressing the word *for*.

I was like, 'What do you mean?'

And he said, 'The manual explains how to use all the technology our parents left us, and everything has a purpose, right?'

'Right.'

'But then there's this whole section on us and our bodies and how to stay healthy but it doesn't say what *we* are for.'

He really stressed the word *we*. I didn't say anything.

'So, what is Jade for?'

'Being annoying.'

He laughed but his eyes were still focused on the stars, and it was like the joke was water rolling down his back. Not important. 'What about you, Ash? What are you *for*? What am I *for*? What is our *purpose*?' he said.

The stars were brighter than ever as this feeling of *wowness* washed over me. Like there's this huge world just beyond my reach, but with Hunter's help maybe I could get there. I watched him staring out into the dark with his reflective cat eyes, remembering his body next to mine in the shower. Blushing, I quickly turned away, because the manual said he could see in the dark.

I SPENT THE next few days watching Jade because she wasn't being herself. She was usually loud, always wanting attention and saying stupid things to make people laugh, but now she barely spoke and one time while we were turning the compost I caught her staring out across the lake at the mountains with a strange look on her face.

Late that night when everyone else was in bed, I asked Hunter, 'What's up with Jade?'

He smirked and pulled a stubby pencil out of his pocket.

'You didn't!'

He smirked even wider and I punched him on the arm.

'Show me!'

So we went to the special cupboard where the manual is kept and he took down Volume IV, *Inhabitants*, and flicked through to the section for Jade. And yeah, I was right. He'd made a change. At the top, next to her name, an asterisk. Then at the bottom of the page he had written in pencil: **Jade is for working out what Jade is for.*

'Fuck!'

I don't usually swear but this was like a special occasion.

Hunter grinned, looking proud. 'Yeah.'

'Rub it out, rub it out!'

'Why?'

'Something bad will happen!'

'Like what?'

I didn't say anything because I didn't know.

We sat on the couch. Hunter seemed so excited, like he'd just discovered an amazing magic trick or something and then this feeling travelled across to me too – *zap!* – and so I said, 'You could write anything in the manual! You could write that we have a new bedroom! Or a dog!'

And he was like, 'Nah, I don't think it works that way. We can't create totally new things, just make revisions to things already there.'

Revisions.

Not a word Hunter would normally say out loud. And why was he so confident about how the manual worked? 'You totally changed your own section to make yourself smarter! I know you did!'

He laughed. 'Did not!'

'Show me!'

He got up, holding the book beyond my reach. 'I'm going to keep this and you have to guess the changes.' He wiggled his pencil in the air.

So annoying – I wanted to keep reading, looking for clues how to escape to the mountains, but it was only one volume so I stuck out my tongue and said, 'Okay, you're on.'

THE ONLY WAY to keep track of everyone to see whether they had changed was to make notes. I snuck into the office room and took four sheets of clean paper, which we were supposed to save, but Skyler had drawn on everything else, so what choice did I have? Parent 3 used to call me 'my little scientist' and that's what I was going to be. Make observations and work things out.

Parent 3 looked like me, with light brown skin and dark frizzy hair, but she was really old and the first to say goodbye. When she was gone I cried and cried until the leaves on the oak tree grew back green again, even though the manual said we aren't supposed to be able to cry like that.

On the paper I wrote:

Bear – quiet as usual. Pimples on neck. Yuck.

Skyler – smiling. Happy mood. Wearing one of Bear's old T-shirts. Size B9?

Jade – frowning at breakfast. Not eating much. Flicking hair. Looking across at Hunter.

Hunter – cheeky. Smiling and winking at me.

Which was probably just Hunter being Hunter, not a change due to a *revision*, but I wrote it down anyway because that's what scientists do. Record everything. I didn't wink back because you're not supposed to react during observation. Parent 3 taught me that too. I don't remember all her lessons, but that one stuck. We used to talk about our parents all the time and what they had told us. You could win an argument by saying 'Parent 1 told me to do it this way' or 'Parent 4 said that wasn't allowed'. But after the last parent left, we got into arguments about what they had *really* said because we all remembered something different. From then on we used the manual to decide everything, because words written down wouldn't change. Questioning the manual was like questioning a parent – and that felt wrong because it reminded us they were gone.

Parent 5 had been the last to leave. He had dark skin, exactly the same as Hunter's, but with many wrinkles like the bark on the oak tree. One day he told me to meet him in the equipment room where he was packing his winter gear. He knelt down so his face was level with mine and whispered, 'Watch my boy. If he turns too soon, you're the only one who can stop him.'

I didn't tell Hunter about it at the time, but yeah, from that point on I did watch him more closely.

That night as we ate together, I kept taking notes. Afterwards Hunter and Jade stayed behind to do the dishes. Hunter accidentally splashed Jade and then she said 'Hey!' and bumped him with her hip, totally deliberate. He returned the bump, then she giggled and stood behind him, hands on his waist, and my mind hissed *pair bonding ritual*, which sounded like words from the manual. The strangest feeling kicked in, like a full-on fever. It started in my neck and my face went red – hot hot cheeks – and suddenly I was out of the chair, reaching forward to slap Jade hard across the face.

Hunter froze. Jade stepped back, shocked. I stared at my hand and the fever switched from extreme hot to extreme cold so fast my body shook. I ran to my room, still holding the paper and pen, and slammed the door shut. Thoughts spinning around and around. New feelings so strong and so sudden. Why did I care so much about Hunter? I'd started to like him before he stole the manual, but what if he'd made a revision to make me think that? Or he could have written, *Jade begins to like Hunter too*, and that would explain her behaviour?

As if my thoughts were calling him, I heard a knock on the door and Hunter's voice saying, 'Ash? Ash? Can I come in?'

'Go away!'

The knocking stopped.

I couldn't sleep that night. When dawn came, I decided to get up and go to the lounge room. The hallway was dim and Skyler's drawings on the walls looked creepy, all these purple vines climbing to the ceiling.

At the doorway I stopped because Skyler and Bear were sitting on the couch kissing. Like, really kissing. She is small and he is much, much bigger and she was on top of him. Strange because we were still kids – that's what the manual said. We weren't supposed to have these desires.

I turned around and went back to my bedroom just as the tears started up again, and my mind whispered another strange word: *hormones*.

I DOZED ALL day and woke up in darkness, my mind all fizzy and excited. The pen and paper sat beside my bed. I wrote across the blank page: *NEW Operations Manual for Lifedorm 48 and Its Inhabitants*

Which is just what it says on the proper manual except I added the word NEW.

After that I wasn't sure what to write but it felt like a really good start, and I was much calmer. Then I had another idea and wrote underneath: *This revised manual overrides the old manual*

Yes! *Overrides* being the word in my head when I woke up. Not a word I would say out loud, but this was the language of the manual and must be what gave it power. Pleased, I sat in bed for a long time with my pen hovering over the page. When more words came to me I added them: *but Hunter doesn't know and can't find out. Everything in the old manual applies EXCEPT when this new manual says it doesn't and the owner of the new manual (ie, Ash) is unaffected by any revisions to the old manual made by Hunter.*

Ever since Hunter took the *Inhabitants* volume of the original manual and could make changes without the rest of us knowing, I had started to think that it's this *knowing* that has power. I mean, if you know something everyone else doesn't then you are above them. You can *override* them. So I took out the pen and started writing in the NEW manual *Ash knows everything* but then I had crazy goosebumps. Because knowing everything would be way too much! Your brain would explode! My pen was still touching the paper so there was still time to save myself. I quickly added: *Ash knows everything in the old manual.*

But even that was too much and I blacked out, flopping onto my bed.

HERE'S THE THING about the manual. I'd tried to read it thousands of times, but there were always parts I couldn't understand.

The manual wasn't written the same way start to finish. Each section was a huge mountain that got steeper and steeper until you couldn't hold on to the words anymore. The section about me, Ash, started really simple: *Ash is a girl. She has black hair and brown eyes. Ash likes to play with her friends. Ash is clever and thinks a lot about things.*

These were the easy parts to understand. After those I was able to work out some more difficult parts later on: *Ash is a pre-pubescent female with a human equivalent age of eleven.*

Every person's section was like this, and so were the sections on technology. So the part about the showers started out saying, *The red tap is for hot water*, and then later on had words like *geothermal reservoir*, which we didn't understand until we had been taking hot showers for years and years.

Over the decades I could read pretty far into my own section and learn more about myself. I could sort of understand some words like *body stasis*, which means not changing, and that was in a paragraph with the word *dormant*, which must mean pretty much the same thing, and later on there was a heading *Cocooning Phase*, which I knew from a section on butterflies in Volume VII, *Nature*. But after that part, the manual was full-on difficult with headings like *genome enhancements* and *mTor longevity pathway*, and although I could guess what this meant – that me and the others were different from our parents, who had made us this way so we would live a really long time – I still couldn't read the complex diagrams and equations underneath.

As I woke up that day, everything started to make sense. It was like flicking the power switch in the big storage shed where we get new clothes every five years – row after row of lights turning on, helping me to see further and further into the darkness. The information had been inside me all along, reinforced every time I scanned my eyes down the pages of the manual, memorising words but not understanding their meaning yet. Now I could, and a voice in my head started speaking these words aloud. *Scaffolded pedagogy. Retention through osmosis.* So confusing! *Affective-state revelations.* It was difficult to hear myself think.

I sat up, fully awake, looking at the pages of my NEW manual scattered around the bed. What an idiot I was! A child, a silly girl. I picked up the pen, found a blank page, and wrote down my speech to tell the others. I had to use words they would know, which made it really hard: *The manual is not a God that makes things happen. Revising the manual will not change the world around us or ourselves.*

The manual is a teacher that helps us know and understand. Soon all of the manual will be available to us.

The manual is a ladder to help us climb out of this place and start new lives as adults.

I knew that last word would get everyone's attention for sure.

OUT IN THE corridor everything looked different. I walked past the same old walls thinking *silicon aerogel insulation with thermal rating of R-30* and under the same old ceiling vent thinking *air purifier to remove toxic particulate matter.*

Jade was in the lounge room and my new super-smart mind said *pubescent female with extraversion-dominant traits* and I knew what she was for.

Jade said, 'Hey.'

I said, 'Hey.'

Jade said, 'So as you know, Hunter's gone whack.'

I said, 'Whack?'

Jade said, 'Yeah.'

I said, 'Damn.' But what I was really thinking was *Crisis Scenario 87: Inhabitant experiences sudden and acute mental distress from overly rapid uptake of contextual information.*

Jade said, 'He went out to the lake carrying this massive backpack.'

I turned and ran for the door.

IT WAS LIKE I was seeing the mountains and the sky for the very first time. So beautiful, and that made me so fucking mad at our parents. I mean, what were they thinking? That we'd be grateful? Oh, thanks for saving us! Thanks for keeping us stuck here and bored out of our minds for ages and ages because you totally trashed the planet! At least we had some pretty mountains to look at!

The heat welled up inside me and this time I could name it as *rage*. I squatted, pounding my fists into the snow, counting down from ten. Breathing deeply.

Once calmer, I continued to the lake. Just past the big boulder, I turned around and saw the others coming behind me, rugged up in bright puffer jackets, orange dots against white snow. Did they know what I knew? Their bodies were changing too, and my mind said *onset of post-dormancy phase*. It was super weird having new words pop into my head like that. Words that had been there all along, only hidden. I was developing ahead of the others – that had to be the reason. Hunter was too, only he'd figured out just enough to put himself in danger.

I spotted him way out on the frozen lake, wearing a hiking backpack. It made him look super tall, and also kind of hunched over. I waved and yelled, 'Hunter, stop!'

He turned, thin body swaying under the heavy pack. I reached the shoreline and started running across the ice, then realised the danger and slowed to a walk. My mind screamed *treacherous, treacherous, treacherous*. Don't freak out, I thought. Hunter needs you.

'Come back!' But he was still too far off to hear me.

When I finally caught up we both stood in the middle of the frozen lake with the mountains all around, and I saw them for what they were – the walls of our playpen. Deliberately steep. Designed that way.

'It's not time!' I yelled across at him. He was about ten steps ahead, still staring at me. Just then we heard the ice start to crack. Hunter looked down at his feet in shock. 'But it's meant to be frozen,' he said. 'The manual says…'

'You're right. But not this year. It's still too warm.'

His eyes popped wide. 'Y-y-you know?'

'Yes.'

'But how? I've got the manual.' He jerked his head, indicating his overstuffed backpack, and I thought, *Oh you stupid boy. You took the whole heavy thing?*

Then we heard another loud crack and everything happened so fast. One moment Hunter was standing there and the next he was in the water, his arms waving about, and I was yelling his name like crazy, getting down on my knees to pull him out, but I remembered Parent 5 had said you couldn't rescue someone that way, it was too risky, and you needed an *assistance device*.

My jacket? Hold one sleeve, pass the other to him? I started to unzip, then felt a hand on my shoulder. I looked up – it was Bear. Yes! Yes! Bear would help. That was his role in the group, why he was made so strong. To protect us.

Bear calmly removed a rope from his own pack and flung one end into the water. I watched Hunter's shaking hands tie the rope around his body, and then Bear started pulling. Once Hunter's torso was out, Bear lay down on the ice with his arm outstretched to grab Hunter by the collar of his jacket and drag him back to safety.

'The m-m-manual…' said Hunter, teeth chattering. 'It's gone.'

I looked at the hole in the ice, where his backpack had sunk. 'It's okay,' I said. 'We don't need it anymore.'

Bear carried Hunter across the ice, walking as fast as he could while taking really gentle steps to prevent more cracking. We soon reached thicker ice and the others joined us to carry Hunter to the shoreline. I held his hand, which was scary cold, but he managed to squeeze my fingers. We all worked together to strip off Hunter's wet clothes. His body was shivering like crazy and new words popped into my head. *Hypothermic shock*. I started to strip too, right there in front of everyone, leaving only my thermals and boots, and then I hugged Hunter tight. 'Wrap us in blankets,' I said to the others.

Poor Hunter. I held him close and let the warmth from my body flow into his. Cold is the worst and we'd all have to get used to colder seasons now. Every winter the lake would freeze a little bit more until one day we could walk all the way across. The mountains on the other side would have a pass that wasn't too steep to climb, I was sure of it. But we could only reach them once the climate chilled enough for the lake to freeze properly. Our parents designed it that way. They wanted to make sure the world had repaired before we were let out.

Somewhere beyond the mountains lay other Lifedorms. People would escape from those too, one after another. *Sequential repopulation of temperate latitudes*. Hunter probably hadn't gotten far enough to understand the science of it, the equations for how long CH_4 and CO_2 stay in the atmosphere, and the temperature triggers in our bodies. It's not like there was a section at the back labelled *Appendix: Secrets for Inhabitants Like Ash and Hunter Who Have Matured Early*. I had to work it out by fitting all the parts together myself.

Now I knew what I was *for*. Thinking and remembering and working things out. That was my job in the group.

Hunter looked into my eyes and – *zap!* – we were connected again. He was back! He was alive! 'We'll have to write a new manual now,' I said.

Hunter grinned.

Greg Foyster is a writer and illustrator living on Wadawurrung country, Geelong. His short stories have been published in *Meanjin, Overland, Aurealis, The Big Issue Fiction Edition* and science journal *Nature*. In 2023 he won the Peter Carey Short Story Award. He can be found at www.gregfoyster.com